Expectations: Theory and Evidence

Expectations: Theory and Evidence

K. Holden, D. A. Peel
and J. L. Thompson

ST. MARTIN'S PRESS   New York

All rights reserved. For information, write:
St. Martin's Press, Inc., 175 Fifth Avenue, New York, NY 10010
Printed in Hong Kong
Published in the United Kingdom by Macmillan Publishers Ltd.
First published in the United States of America in 1985

ISBN 0–312–27599–4

Library of Congress Cataloging in Publication Data
Holden, K.
Expectations: theory and evidence.
Bibliography: p.
Includes index.
1. Rational expectations (Economic theory)
I. Peel, D.   II. Thompson, John L.   III. Title.
HB172.5.H65   1985   339'.0724   84-24762
ISBN 0–312–27599–4

To our parents

Contents

Preface

The explanation of how economic agents form their expectations about the future is currently a matter of controversy in macroeconomics. This book is intended as an introduction both to theories of expectation formation and to the empirical evidence concerning those theories. It is intended for advanced undergraduates and postgraduates taking courses in macroeconomics and monetary economics. Some prior knowledge of intermediate economics is assumed, as is a familiarity with algebra and introductory statistics. Much of the material should be accessible to students with little quantitative background; for others, detailed derivations and explanations are included in the appendices to chapter 2.

A list of references is included at the end of the text. Equations are numbered sequentially in each chapter. We acknowledge financial assistance from the Economic and Social Research Council (Grant HR6305) in the preliminary stages of preparing the manuscript. Our thanks are also due to Vivienne Oakes for her accurate and efficient typing of several drafts of the text. As always, any errors and omissions are the responsibility of the authors.

K. Holden
D. A. Peel
J. L. Thompson

1

Introduction to Expectations

1.1 Introduction

This book is concerned with expectations in economics – that is, with anticipations or views about the future. Since 1930, when Irving Fisher introduced the 'anticipated rate of inflation' as the difference between the nominal and real interest rates, expectations have played an important role in economic theory. This is because economics is generally concerned with the implications of current actions for the *future*. The importance of expectations in money markets, stock markets and foreign exchange markets is quite obvious. Views about the future dominate the actions of traders. In mainstream macro-economic theory, the consumption function (via permanent income), the investment function (via expected demand), and the Phillips curve all require expectations to perform an important role. The development over the past thirty years of macroeconometric models has forced economists to recognise that expectations are not something to be treated as exogenous – which can be ignored at will – but instead are central to our understanding of how the economy works. Attention has switched from more or less mechanical forms of expectations generation which are essentially *ad hoc* to the theoretically attractive approach of the 'rational expectations' hypothesis. This states that agents use economic theory to form their expectations, and should not make systematic errors in their forecasts of the future.

This chapter provides an introduction to concepts which are developed in the rest of the book. Historically, there have been two distinct methods of dealing with expectations in economic analysis – one is to conduct a survey to discover expectations, the other is to provide a simple model of expectations formation. In 1.2, below, the problems of surveys are discussed; some of the more well-known ones are described in 1.3. Various simple models of expectations formation are presented in 1.4. The concept of rational expectations is introduced in simple terms in 1.5, and the chapter ends with an introduction to time-series modelling, which serves as a preliminary to chapter 2 where the rational expectations hypothesis is presented in detail.

Ways of solving rational expectations models under various assumptions involve the use of some algebra, which is tedious rather than difficult. Much of this has been relegated to the appendices to chapter 2. The policy implications of rational expectations and criticisms are also presented.

Chapter 3 reviews the evidence from surveys on how expectations are formed with respect to consumer and business prices, wages, interest rates and money supply, and the next two chapters consider the role of expectations in single-equation studies. In chapter 4 the efficient markets hypothesis is presented, and evidence from the money market and foreign exchange markets is assessed. The consumption function, wage equation and capital gains are discussed in chapter 5. Simultaneous-equation studies involving expectations are reviewed in chapter 6, where both large econometric models and smaller theoretical models are considered. In chapter 7 various explanations are presented of how aggregate expectations are formed; ways of combining forecasts are discussed, and a way of implementing rational expectations is suggested. The conclusions are summarised in chapter 8.

1.2 Surveys of expectations

The most obvious approach to the understanding of what agents' expectations are, and how they are determined, is to conduct some sort of *survey*. This raises several questions: Who should be asked? What should the questions cover? Which time horizon is relevant? What information is available to the agent? Taking each of these in turn, it is clear that the questions should be addressed to the appropriate agent for the market being considered. For example, consumers' expectations of inflation might be surveyed by interviewing members of the public, whereas producers' expectations of inflation might be obtained from a sample of firms in manufacturing industry. In many cases, it is the views of 'experts' that are wanted, and the sample might then be selected from, say, financial journalists or industrial and business economists professionally involved in forecasting.

The second point concerns what the questions should cover. A common confusion occurs between expectations about the price level and expectations about the rate of inflation. These are, of course, directly related but logically distinct. At a time of high inflation, it will be more appropriate to focus on the inflation rate than on the price level. Problems also arise when comparisons with past values are requested. Since few individuals keep detailed personal accounts, questions like 'How do prices compare with those twelve months ago?' are likely to be answered with errors because of lapses of memory. This also introduces the need for a decision on the choice of *time horizon*. The annual rate of inflation may, for example, be defined as the percentage rate of change of the price level over a twelve-month period, or twice the rate of change over six months, or four times the rate of change over three months, or twelve times the rate of change over one month. Measured over the past, different numerical values are likely to arise for each of these different time periods. When expectations of the future are considered, similar difficulties in interpretation will occur.

The information available to the agent at the time the expectations are formed – known as the *information set* – is of crucial importance. In many cases it is not clear what this information set includes – for most economic variables, the current values are unknown. A consumer price index, for example, might be published monthly, so that the current price level is not yet available but last month's figure may be known. Profits figures may similarly be known only six weeks after the end of the quarter to which they refer. In contrast, interest rates, stock market prices and exchange rates are (in principle) observable almost instantaneously, with possibly only a few minutes' delay. This means that the information set the agent has access to is likely to include some current values of variables, and many lagged values. When surveys of expectations are made, differences between agents may be the result of either different information sets or different evaluations of a common information set. One way of avoiding the former is for questionnaires to include details of the most recently available data on the economy. The problem of different data sets is likely to be more serious when surveys are conducted continuously rather than at particular times of the year (the implications of an incomplete current information set will be considered more fully in chapter 2).

Before looking at some individual surveys of expectations, we must consider next the ways in which responses are recorded. Broadly, these will be *qualitative* or *quantitative*. An example of the former is the reply to the question: Do you think that in six months' time prices will be lower than/the same as/higher than they are now? Responses come into the three categories lower/same/higher, and so do not give a numerical value of the expected rate of price change. Various attempts have been made at converting such data into numerical form, in order to allow survey results both to be compared with outcomes (see chapter 3) and to be used in econometric studies (see chapter 4). Theil (1965) has suggested a 'balance' statistic

$$B = \frac{H - L}{L + S + H} \tag{1.1}$$

where H = percentage replying 'higher'
         S = percentage replying 'the same'
         L = percentage replying 'lower'

So if $H = 60$ per cent, $S = 30$ per cent, $L = 10$ per cent

         $B = 0.5$

It can be seen that B will lie between -1 and $+1$, and a value of 0 occurs when $H = L$. Notice that any 'don't know' responses are ignored in this analysis.

A slightly different approach is used in the EEC Consumer Survey. The respondent is asked about price trends over the next twelve months, and whether he or she expects a more rapid increase ($+3$), some increase ($+2$), a slower increase ($+1$), stability (0), a slight fall (-1) or don't know (0). The percentages of respondents giving each answer are combined by using the weights in brackets to give an overall index of *consumer perceptions* of inflation.

A third and perhaps more widely used method of dealing with qualitative data is to assume that the frequency distribution of

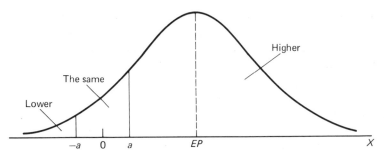

Fig. 1.1

responses has the shape of a particular probability distribution. This is the method used by Knöbl (1974) and Carlson and Parkin (1975).

For simplicity we will assume that X – the random variable representing the expected rate of inflation – has a normal distribution with mean EP and variance σ^2. The problem is that given H, S and L, can EP and σ^2 be determined? If so, the qualitative responses can be represented by the mean and variance of the distribution. The probability distribution is given in Figure 1.1, where it is assumed for expositional purposes that $EP > 0$. Since the probability that $X = 0$ is 0 for a continuous random variable, we assume that there is a fixed small area around $X = 0$ for which the response will be 'the same', and the limits of this – known as the *difference limen* – are denoted $-a$ and $+a$. The normal distribution can be standardised to have a mean of 0 and a variance of 1 by putting

$$Z = \frac{X - EP}{\sigma}$$

letting the standardised values of $-a$ and $+a$ be respectively b and c, we have

$$p(X < -a) = L = p(Z < b)$$
$$p(-a < X < +a) = S = p(b < Z < c)$$
$$p(+a < X) = H = p(c < Z)$$

Given H, S and L, then b and c can be found from tables of the normal distribution

If $\quad$ $H = 60$ per cent, $S = 30$ per cent, $L = 10$ per cent

$\quad p(Z < -1.282) = 0.10$, so $b = -1.282$

$\quad p(-0.253 < Z) = 0.60$, so $c = -0.253$

From standardising

$$b = \frac{-a - EP}{\sigma} = -1.282$$

$$c = \frac{a - EP}{\sigma} = -0.253$$

and solving for EP and σ gives

$$EP = 1.49a$$

$$\sigma = 1.94a$$

The only problem remaining is the choice of value of a, where $2a$ gives the range over which the response is 'the same'. Knöbl (1974) assumes $a = 2$; Carlson and Parkin (1975) choose a such that the mean value of EP over the data period is the same as the mean actual rate of inflation. However, Batchelor (1982), using a rather different approach, estimates the value of a to be 2.3 for France and 3.74 for Italy. If we take $a = 2$, then $EP = 2.98$, and $\sigma = 3.88$ for our example, which compares with the balance statistic of $B = 0.5$.

Calculations such as these require a number of assumptions about the distribution of expectations and so the resulting numbers are, to some extent, subjective. However, Agenor (1982) finds that the differences between assuming a normal distribution, a Cauchy distribution (which is similar in shape to a normal distribution, but has a higher peak) and an asymmetric log-normal distribution are small. Furthermore, Danes (1975) and Defris and Williams (1979b) compare series derived using the balance statistic and the Carlson and Parkin technique from the same responses, and find that they are close together; a detailed criticism of the Carlson and Parkin approach is provided by Pesaran (1984).

When *quantitative* data are collected, many of these problems are avoided, but there still remains the difficulty of how to summarise the individuals' expectations. Usually the arithmetic mean is presented, and occasionally the variance. These in effect give equal weight to each observation, but do not give any indication of the pattern of variability or skewness of the data. An interesting example of the dispersion of expectations is given by Hall and King (1976), who report a survey of executives in New Zealand which asked for a numerical estimate of the expected rate of inflation. The percentages of the sample responding 9, 10, 11 and 12 per cent inflation were respectively 6, 13, 4 and 25 per cent, implying either a multi-modal distribution or an inability of respondents to distinguish differences of 1 per cent.

1.3 Literature on expectations surveys

We must now consider the various surveys of expectations reported in the literature. First we will discuss surveys of consumers' expectations, then those of businessmen, and finally those of 'experts'. Our discussion here is limited to the characteristics of the surveys; in chapter 3, we will examine the properties of the resulting series.

One important survey of consumers' expectations is the Carlson and Parkin (1975) series obtained from a qualitative question in the UK Gallup Poll. The series is derived, using the methods outlined in 1.2 above, from the responses of a stratified quota sample of about 1 000 people each month to the question of whether prices will go up, go down or stay the same over the next six months. Foster and Gregory (1977) are among several authors who have questioned the Carlson and Parkin approach. Among the points raised are the use of a normal distribution (requiring symmetry), the setting of the mean of expected inflation to equal the mean of the actual rate of inflation, and the assumption of a constant difference limen (a, in 1.2 above).

Similar surveys and derived series are available for other countries. The Survey of Consumer Finances carried out by the Survey Research Center, University of Michigan was conducted annually from 1946–59, and quarterly since then. Before 1966, only qualitative data were collected but since then a range of intervals for price increases (1–2 per cent, 3–4 per cent, 5 per cent, 10 per cent or more) has been provided. The survey covers a representative sample of about 3 000 US households. De Menil and Bhalla (1975) and Gramlich (1983) give details of the methodology. For Australia, a quarterly sample of 2 000 consumers has been interviewed by the Institute of Applied Economic and Social Research (IAESR), University of Melbourne, to give both qualitative and quantitative measures of the expected price change over the next twelve months.

Defris and Williams (1979a) give details of the assumptions used to derive price expectations series. Finally, as mentioned previously, the Commission of the EEC conducts surveys of consumer opinion. Since 1973, these four-monthly surveys have included questions on price trends over the last twelve months, and over the next twelve months in the member countries of the EEC. Details are published regularly in *European Economy Supplement C*. As well as the indices for each of the member countries, an overall index for the EEC is reported. Ward and Pickering (1981) discuss how responses to different questions can be combined.

Turning now to surveys of businessmen, the most far-ranging is the EEC survey reported in *European Economy Supplement B*. This again covers each of the member states of the community, and questions the heads of business enterprises on a range of industrial matters, including expectations of future selling prices and production levels. The responses are usually in the three categories of up/the same/ down, and Theil's balance statistics (see 1.2 above) are reported. Among the users of these surveys are Knöbl (1974) and Batchelor (1982), who in fact use the raw data on up/the same/down to derive the quantitative measures of expectations described above.

The Bureau of Economic Analysis conducts an annual survey of around 5 000 US businessmen in which quantitative expectations of changes in the prices of (a) capital goods purchased and (b) goods and services sold, are collected; the results are published in the January issues of the *Survey of Current Business*. De Leeuw and McKelvey (1981) discuss the survey, and analyse the results.

For Australia, there are two main surveys of businessmen. These are the Australian Chamber of Manufacturers/Bank of New South Wales Survey of Industrial Trends (ACM), and the Department of Industry and Commerce Survey of Manufacturing Activity (SOMA). The ACM survey covers manufacturing industry, and asks whether average selling prices over the next three months will go up/stay the same/go down. Danes (1975) uses the Carlson and Parkin technique to obtain a quarterly quantitative series from these answers. The SOMA questionnaire also covers manufacturing industry, but requests numerical data on the expected rate of change of prices over the next six months. Details of the survey are given by Saunders (1980).

In New Zealand, the Institute of Economic Research's Quarterly Survey of Business Opinion covers three sectors of the economy – the distribution sector, the service sector and the manufacturers and builders sector. The questions are similar to the Australian ACM survey and Hall and King (1976) use a slight variation on the Carlson and Parkin method to derive series of expected inflation. They also present the balance statistic for the same data.

Smith (1978) derives producers expectations for the UK from Confederation of British Industry (CBI) surveys using the Carlson and Parkin method. The questions concern expected future costs and expected selling prices over the next four months. The price expectations series are considered by Holden and Peel (1977). An alternative analysis of this survey is reported by Pesaran (1984). Also in the UK, the *Financial Times* Survey of Business Opinion is a monthly survey of employers' wage expectations. Hudson (1978) provides the details.

The weekly journal *Mondo Economico* organises a twice-yearly survey of Italian businessmen, asking for a quantitative indication of the expected price change over the next six months. Five categories of answer are recorded – up by 5 per cent or more, up by 2–4 per cent, a change between $+1$ and -1 per cent, down by 2–4 per cent, down by 5 per cent or more. Visco (1979) describes the survey, and analyses the responses.

A rather different type of survey of businessmen is that conducted annually by F. Endicott of Northwestern University, USA which asks employers to forecast 'end of recruiting season' average monthly starting wages of inexperienced college graduates by field of speciality. Details of the survey are given by Leonard (1982).

There are a large number of other surveys of business opinion, and the interested reader is referred to *OECD Main Economic Indicators: Sources and Methods, no. 37*, 1983, and to Strigel (1980) and Laumer and Ziegler (1982) for details and further references. As the bias of these surveys is towards investment intentions, we shall not pursue them here.

The final group of surveys of expectations that we must consider are those covering 'experts'. The most celebrated of these is the Livingston series. Joseph Livingston is a financial journalist with the *Philadelphia Bulletin* in the USA who twice yearly since 1946 has conducted a survey of professional economists in business, government and academic posts requesting numerical forecasts of consumer and wholesale price indices for six-, twelve- and eighteen-month time horizons. The respondents were selected because of their likely influence on business decisions; Gibson (1972) provides a list of the respondents in 1947 and 1970. One problem with this series is that the forecasts are of the *price index* level, and so an assumption about its current value is required before a forecast of the rate of inflation can be derived. Another problem is that Livingston made his own judgemental adjustment to responses before publishing them, since his survey takes place a month prior to publication. Details of the series are given by Carlson (1977a).

Another survey of experts in the USA is the American Statistical Association–National Bureau of Economic Research Survey of Forecasts by Economic Statisticians. This is a quarterly survey, and is limited to those regularly engaged in preparing quarterly forecasts of economic variables. The first survey was in December 1968 and is described by Zarnowitz (1969). Wachtel (1977) reports the results for 1968–74 and Zarnowitz (1984) lists sources where more recent results can be found. Kane and Malkiel (1976) also conducted three surveys of US institutional investors in 1969–72. Participants – who were all active in the securities markets – were asked about their expectations of the rate of inflation over various time horizons.

Money Market Services Inc. of San Francisco has conducted surveys of 50–60 money-market traders and economists to get their predictions of the change in money supply (M1 or M1B) announced on the Friday of each week. From September 1977–February 1980, the surveys were conducted on both Tuesdays and Thursdays; since this period, only the Tuesday survey has continued. Roley (1983) and Grossman (1981) analyse the median of the forecasts.

Experts' forecasts of interest rates are given by a quarterly survey conducted by Goldsmith–Nagan Inc. who publish a bi-weekly newsletter in the USA. A selected panel of well-known 'market professionals' employed by major financial institutions are asked to predict various rates of interest at the ends of the next two quarters. The published series consists of the means of the individual responses. Prell (1973) presents charts of the forecasts and outcomes.

We have now seen the range and variety of surveys of expectations. Whilst they have made important contributions to our understanding of expectations-generation processes, analysis and use of them has occurred in parallel with both empirically attractive arbitrary methods and significant theoretical developments. It is to these we turn in the remainder of this chapter.

1.4 Adaptive expectations mechanisms

In modelling expectations of future price changes, the simplest assumption is that the expected rate of change of prices over the next time period will be the same as the change which has occurred over the previous period, so that

$$E_t P_{t+1} = P_t \tag{1.2}$$

where $E_t P_{t+1}$ = expected rate of change of prices from period t to $t+1$

P_t = actual rate of change of prices from $t-1$ to t

This was used by, among others, Turnovsky (1972). A slightly more general model is that provided by the *regressive* or *extrapolative* expectations hypothesis

$$E_t P_{t+1} = P_t + \theta(P_t - P_{t-1}) \tag{1.3}$$

where θ = a parameter

If θ is 0, equation (1.2) is obtained, and if it is -1, then

$$E_t P_{t+1} = P_{t-1} \tag{1.4}$$

so that the expected rate of change of prices from t to $t+1$ is the same as the actual change from $t-2$ to $t-1$.

One justification for this (in preference to equation (1.2)) is that the current aggregate price level (and hence the current rate of inflation) may not be observed until the end of period t. The most interesting cases of equation (1.3) are where θ is neither 0 nor -1. If θ is positive, past changes in inflation are extrapolated and are assumed to continue, while if θ is negative, past trends are expected to be reversed. Equation (1.3) can also be re-arranged to give

$$E_t P_{t+1} = (1+\theta)P_t - \theta P_{t-1} \tag{1.5}$$

where the expectation is a weighted average of the two most recent actual values used.

This can be regarded as a particular case of

$$E_t P_{t+1} = \beta_0 P_t + \beta_1 P_{t-1} + \beta_2 P_{t-2} + \ldots \tag{1.6}$$

where the expectation is determined by the current and all past actual values. This specification is not useful in empirical work unless some restrictions are placed on the β_i values. A common restriction is

$$\sum \beta_i = 1 \tag{1.7}$$

which requires that when all the actual rates of inflation are equal, then expectations are realised. Thus there is no systematic error of prediction in the steady state. Further restrictions on the β_i are still needed for empirical work, and the ones suggested have taken a variety of forms. Vanderkamp (1972) assumes a linear rate decline so that

$$\beta_i = \frac{2(n-i)}{n(n+1)} \qquad \text{for } i = 0, 1, \ldots n-1$$

$$\beta_i = 0 \qquad \text{for } i \geqslant n$$

If $\quad n = 4,$

$$\beta_0 = 0.4, \ \beta_1 = 0.3, \ \beta_2 = 0.2 \text{ and } \beta_3 = 0.1$$

An alternative, which has theoretical attractions, is to assume

$$\beta_i = (1 - \lambda)\lambda^i \qquad 0 \leqslant \lambda < 1 \tag{1.8}$$

which gives the geometric distributed lag or the Koyck lag. In this case $\beta_i > \beta_{i+1}$, so that the largest β_i is β_0 and all past values of P_t affect expectations. The term $(1 - \lambda)$ is included in equation (1.8) to satisfy equation (1.7). Substitution of equation (1.8) into equation (1.6) gives

$$E_t P_{t+1} = (1 - \lambda)P_t + (1 - \lambda)\lambda P_{t-1}$$
$$+ (1 - \lambda)\lambda^2 P_{t-2} + \ldots \tag{1.9}$$

which was used by Cagan (1956), who evaluates the right-hand side for different values of λ. A more convenient form, however, arises from a simple transformation by lagging equation (1.9) one period, so that

$$E_{t-1} P_t = (1 - \lambda)P_{t-1} + (1 - \lambda)P_{t-2}$$
$$+ (1 - \lambda)\lambda^2 P_{t-3} + \ldots \tag{1.10}$$

and then subtracting $\lambda \times$ equation (1.10) from equation (1.9), to give

$$E_t P_{t+1} - \lambda E_{t-1} P_t = (1 - \lambda)P_t$$

or

$$E_t P_{t+1} = \lambda E_{t-1} P_t + (1 - \lambda)P_t \tag{1.11}$$

or

$$E_t P_{t+1} - E_{t-1} P_t = (1 - \lambda)(P_t - E_{t-1} P_t) \qquad (1.12)$$

Thus in equation (1.11), the current expectation is a weighted average of the previous expectation and the current actual rate of inflation. Alternatively, equation (1.12) – which is the version commonly known as the *adaptive expectations* model or the *error-learning* model – expresses the change in the expectation as an *adjustment* depending on the error between the actual rate of inflation from $t-1$ to t and the expectation for that period. If λ is 0 then equation (1.2) results, while if λ is close to unity there is only a small change in the expectation even for a large error. Since $0 \leqslant \lambda < 1$, only a fraction of the error is corrected in any one period. In times of accelerating inflation, expectations will consequently consistently *under-predict* the future actual rate of inflation, and the error will continue to increase until the acceleration ceases. In times of reducing inflation, conversely, the expectation will persistently *over-predict* the rate of inflation, again with an increasing error. It is only, in fact, in the situation where the variable concerned has no trend that adaptive expectations will be unbiased or correct 'on the average'.

Several variations of the adaptive expectations model have been suggested. Carlson and Parkin (1975), for example, found some empirical support for the inclusion of a second error term

$$E_t P_{t+1} - E_{t-1} P_t = (1 - \lambda_0)(P_t - E_{t-1} P_t)$$
$$+ (1 - \lambda_1)(P_{t-1} - E_{t-2} P_{t-1}) \qquad (1.13)$$

This can be generalised to the inclusion of all past errors in expectations, so that

$$E_t P_{t+1} - E_{t-1} P_t = \sum \beta_i (P_{t-i} - E_{t-i-1} P_{t-i})$$

for $i = 0, 1, \ldots$

and if a geometric rate of decline of the β_i is assumed, so that

$$\beta_i = \beta \gamma^i \qquad 0 \leqslant \gamma < 1$$

then performing the Koyck transformation (as for equation (1.9) above) gives

$$E_t P_{t+1} - E_{t-1} P_t = \beta(P_t - E_{t-1} P_t)$$
$$+ \gamma(E_{t-1} P_t - E_{t-2} P_{t-1}) \qquad (1.14)$$

In this case, the revision to the expectation is related to the previous error and also to the previous correction.

A further example is provided by Frenkel (1975), who suggests a model which combines both regressive and adaptive components. It is based on the idea that if there is a sudden acceleration of prices, expectations are such that it is believed that the process will reverse itself – this type of hypothesis was suggested by Keynes (1923, p. 40–1). Frenkel differentiates between long-term and short-term expectations. Long-term expectations (EP^L) are related to actual inflation by the adaptive model in equation (1.12)

$$E_t P_{t+1}^L - E_{t-1} P_t^L = (1 - \lambda)(P_t - E_{t-1} P_t^L) \tag{1.15}$$

with $0 \leqslant \lambda < 1$. Short-term expectations are determined by two elements – first, the difference between the expected long-term rate and the actual rate, second, the difference between the expected short-term rate and the actual rate. This can be written

$$E_t P_{t+1} - E_{t-1} P_t = \alpha_0 (E_{t-1} P_t^L - P_t) + \alpha_1 (E_{t-1} P_t - P_t)$$

$$\alpha_0 > 0, \; \alpha_1 < 0. \tag{1.16}$$

The short-term and long-term expectations can be combined by re-writing equation (1.16) as

$$E_{t-1} P_t^L = E_t P_{t+1} - E_{t-1} P_t + \alpha_0 P_t - \alpha_1 (E_{t-1} P_t - P_t)$$

and substituting into equation (1.15). After simplifying

$$E_t P_{t+1} - E_{t-1} P_t = (\lambda + \alpha_1)(E_{t-1} P_t - E_{t-2} P_{t-1})$$

$$- \alpha_1 (1 - \lambda)(P_{t-1} - E_{t-2} P_{t-1})$$

$$- (\alpha_1 + \alpha_0)(P_t - P_{t-1}) \tag{1.17}$$

and this can be interpreted as the revision to expectations depending on both the revision and error in the previous period, plus an adjustment for the change in the *actual* rate of inflation.

Our discussion of the different ways in which expectations of future price changes have been modelled in terms of past price changes has revealed several problems with such an approach. The form of distributed lag assumed is generally linear or Koyck, resulting in strong restrictions on the possible weights attached to past inflation. One way of avoiding this is to follow Almon (1965), and introduce flexible polynomial distributed lag functions over a limited number of past values. Suppose that in equation (1.6) $\beta_i = 0$ for all $i > 5$, so that

$$E_t P_{t+1} = \beta_0 P_t + \beta_1 P_{t-1} + \beta_2 P_{t-2} + \beta_3 P_{t-3} + \beta_4 P_{t-4}$$
$$\tag{1.18}$$

Here there are five unknown β values, and it is assumed that the relationship between β_i and i is a smooth curve. A simple example might be a quadratic function

$$\beta_i = \lambda_0 + \lambda_1 i + \lambda_2 i^2 \qquad \text{for } i < 5 \tag{1.19}$$

Thus

$$\beta_0 = \lambda_0$$
$$\beta_1 = \lambda_0 + \lambda_1 + \lambda_2$$
$$\beta_2 = \lambda_0 + 2\lambda_1 + 4\lambda_2$$
$$\beta_3 = \lambda_0 + 3\lambda_1 + 9\lambda_2$$
$$\beta_4 = \lambda_0 + 4\lambda_1 + 16\lambda_2$$

and substitution into equation (1.18) gives

$$\begin{aligned} E_t P_{t+1} &= \lambda_0 (P_t + P_{t-1} + P_{t-2} + P_{t-3} + P_{t-4}) \\ &\quad + \lambda_1 (P_{t-1} + 2P_{t-2} + 3P_{t-3} + 4P_{t-4}) \\ &\quad + \lambda_2 (P_{t-1} + 4P_{t-2} + 9P_{t-3} + 16P_{t-4}) \\ &= \lambda_0 Z_{0t} + \lambda_1 Z_{1t} + \lambda_2 Z_{2t} \end{aligned} \tag{1.20}$$

where the Z_{it} can be determined from the data.

Notice that there are now three unknowns – $(\lambda_0, \lambda_1, \lambda_2)$ – while in equation (1.18) there are five. A further reduction in the number of unknowns can be achieved if restrictions are imposed on other values of β. Thus implicitly equation (1.18) requires $\beta_5 = 0$. From equation (1.19), this gives

$$\beta_5 = 0 = \lambda_0 + 5\lambda_1 + 25\lambda_2$$

or

$$\lambda_0 = -5\lambda_1 - 25\lambda_2 \tag{1.21}$$

which can be substituted in equation (1.20) to remove λ_0. Similarly setting $\beta_{-1} = 0$ gives (in equation (1.19))

$$\beta_{-1} = 0 = \lambda_0 - \lambda_1 + \lambda_2$$

or

$$\lambda_1 = \lambda_0 + \lambda_2 = -4\lambda_2 \tag{1.22}$$

using equation (1.21). By substituting equations (1.21) and (1.22) into equation (1.20), both λ_0 and λ_1 can be eliminated leaving λ_2 as the remaining unknown. This is perhaps an atypical use of a polynomial distributed lag, since in general equation (1.18) would include more terms and equation (1.19) might be replaced by a cubic or quartic specification. The validity of end-point restrictions (such as on β_5 and β_{-1} above) is also questioned by Dhrymes (1971) and others. The important advantage of the polynomial distributed lag is its flexible shape, which is determined by the data – in contrast to the linear and Koyck schemes where the shape is determined *a priori*.

Another generalisation is the time-series modelling approach of Box and Jenkins (1970). Feige and Pearce (1976) suggest fitting an ARIMA (autoregressive integrated moving-average) model to observations of inflation, and using the forecasts from this as expectations (an introduction to the principles of time-series modelling is provided in 1.6 below). For the present, the emphasis is on the time-series approach being a more general version of the distributed lag models outlined above. The formulations in equations (1.2)–(1.6) and (1.12)–(1.14) can be interpreted as special cases of

$$E_t P_{t+1} = \alpha_1 E_{t-1} P_t + \alpha_2 E_{t-2} P_{t-1} + \ldots$$
$$+ \beta_0 P_t + \beta_1 P_{t-1} + \ldots \tag{1.23}$$

so that, for example, equation (1.6) sets all $\alpha_i = 0$. This relationship is deterministic, and an obvious generalisation is to add a random term u_{t+1}. One justification for this is that the behaviour of agents is represented by equation (1.23) 'on average', and there are innumerable factors other than past expectations and past inflation which affect current expectations. Each of these factors is unimportant individually, but taken together they have some effect. Rearranging equation (1.23), and including a disturbance term u_{t+1} gives

$$E_t P_{t+1} - \alpha_1 E_{t-1} P_t - \alpha_2 E_{t-1} P_{t-1} \ldots$$
$$= \beta_0 P_t + \beta_1 P_{t-1} + \ldots + u_{t+1} \tag{1.24}$$

Next the lag operator, L, is introduced which is defined in general terms by

$$LX_t = X_{t-1}$$
$$L^m X_t = X_{t-m}$$

so that equation (1.24) can be written

$$(1 - \alpha_1 L - \alpha_2 L^2 - \ldots)E_t P_{t+1}$$
$$= (\beta_0 + \beta_1 L + \beta_2 L^2 + \ldots)P_t + u_{t+1}$$

or

$$\alpha(L)E_t P_{t+1} = \beta(L)P_t + u_{t+1} \qquad (1.25)$$

or

$$E_t P_{t+1} = \frac{\beta(L)P_t}{\alpha(L)} + \frac{u_{t+1}}{\alpha(L)} \qquad (1.26)$$

where $\alpha(L)$ and $\beta(L) = $ polynomials in the lag operator

Feige and Pearce replace $E_t P_{t+1}$ by its realisation P_{t+1}, which on substitution in equation (1.26) and rearranging gives

$$\phi(L)P_{t+1} = \theta(L)u_{t+1} \qquad (1.27)$$

where $\phi(L)$ and $\theta(L) = $ polynomials in L

This is an ARMA (autoregressive moving-average) model and, given a series of observations on P the methods of Box and Jenkins (1970) can be used to estimate $\phi(L)$ and $\theta(L)$. These are discussed in 1.6 below.

The advantages of the time-series modelling approach are first the flexibility of the functional relationship (in contrast to the limited possibilities with linear, Koyck and Almon forms), and second the explicit treatment of *stochastic* factors (the latter point compares with the typical approach of adding a disturbance term to equation (1.12) and assuming it is truly random). However, it is well known that if a white noise error (i.e. with zero mean, constant variance and no autocorrelation) – say, ε_t – is added to equation (1.9), then the transformation to equation (1.12) introduces $\varepsilon_t - \lambda\varepsilon_{t-1}$, which is a moving-average error. This does not have the classical properties, and an allowance for this fact ought to be made in the empirical estimation procedure.

The above variations of the adaptive expectations mechanism all require the appropriate adjustment coefficients to be *constants*. Several methods of relaxing this assumption have been suggested. One alternative is to use a continuous updating procedure (see Khan, 1983), whereby empirically λ is re-estimated in each time period and so gradual changes in λ will be detected. A variation on this is the Kalman filter approach (see Chow, 1975), in which the emphasis is on the parameters being stochastic rather than fixed. This method gives the current expectation as the previous expectation adjusted by the previous error, but now with a variable weight in place of the fixed weight of equation (1.12). Similar results are obtained using a Bayesian approach (see Turnovsky, 1969; and Cyert and De Groot, 1974).

A criticism which applies to these models, however, as well as to the simpler models outlined previously, is that information other than past actual inflation and past expectations is ignored. A monetarist would expect recent changes in the money supply to affect future prices, whilst a Keynesian might expect future fiscal policy to have some effect. A much wider information set than simply past inflation and expectations will thus be relevant in determining current expectations.

1.5 Concept of rational expectations

The concept of rational expectations was proposed by Muth (1961), who suggested that agents form their expectations in the same way as they undertake other activities – that is, they use economic theory to predict the value of the variable and this is their 'rational' expectation. Rational expectations are thus simply predictions from economic theory, using the information available at the time the predictions are made. Walters (1971) prefers the name 'consistent' to 'rational', since the expectations are consistent with the relevant economic theory (it is assumed agents use information efficiently so that the aggregate of all agents' expectations will not be systematically wrong). In our previous notation, the result is that, for a one-period horizon

$$E_t P_{t+1} = P_{t+1} + \varepsilon_{t+1} \qquad\qquad (1.28)$$

where $E_t P_{t+1}$ = expected rate of change of prices from t to $t+1$
P_{t+1} = actual rate of change of prices from t to $t+1$
ε_{t+1} = random error term

The rational expectations hypothesis requires that ε should have a mean of 0 and be serially uncorrelated. It is important to realise that ε is not always 0; under the rational expectations hypothesis expectations can thus be wrong, but they cannot be systematically wrong. Errors are random, and hence unpredictable. Once an error is observed it does not affect future expectations since as it is known to be random it contains no new information. This contrasts with the adaptive expectations model in equation (1.12), where past errors modify *current* expectations.

The behavioural motivation behind the rational expectations hypothesis is that agents use the information available to them in an efficient manner, and consequently the *ex post* forecast error will be uncorrelated with any element in the information set. A true model of the market is assumed to exist, and to be known to the agents. They use the model to process the relevant information, and hence form their expectations. Any errors in these expectations are the results of *unanticipated* shocks. The information set includes all past data on the market, and also the rules controlling government policy behaviour.

There are three main differences between the rational expectations approach and the adaptive expectations type of mechanism described previously. First, the emphasis is on expectations being forward-looking, rather than simply being extrapolations of past trends; second, agents are acting in an optimising manner by processing all the relevant information, which includes past data, current and future announced policy changes, etc.; third, the rational expectations approach provides a central role for economic theory in determining expectations.

Section 1.6 outlines the time-series approach to modelling expectations. It will, however, be useful at this stage to try to draw together some conclusions on the various ways of representing expectations discussed in this chapter. Simply asking agents what their expectations are has its attractions, and the result of this process will be considered in detail in chapter 3. But we have seen that there are problems in surveying expectations and interpreting the results, and so perhaps the most useful aspect of such surveys is in providing guidance of the appropriateness of theoretical models of expectations formation. These theoretical models – with the exception of rational expectations – are essentially backward-looking, in that the past is extrapolated in some way to predict the future. With rational expectations the emphasis switches to taking economic theory and making efficient use of the available information to predict the future.

Adaptive expectations might be characterised as 'using a rule of thumb', while strict rational expectations requires the specification and estimation of a full macroeconomic model. These might be viewed as the two polar cases, and intuitively one might expect the truth to lie somewhere between. This question has yet to be decided, and it provides the motivation for the remainder of this book after the exposition of the rational expectations hypothesis in chapter 2.

1.6   Time-series modelling

In this section we provide an introduction to time-series methods. After a preliminary discussion of stochastic processes we turn to autoregressive and moving-average models, and consider the problems of specification and estimation. We limit consideration to univariate models (that is, single series in isolation) which are linear. More complex multiple time-series models are analysed by, for example, Granger and Newbold (1977).

The starting point in modelling a time series is the assumption that the series of past values of a variable – say, $y_1, y_2, \ldots y_n$ – has been generated by a *stochastic* process. That is, the observed series is one realisation of a drawing from the joint probability distribution of $y_1 y_2 \ldots y_n$. A different realisation would give a different series of values. If the process generating the series can be assumed to be invariant with respect to time, then the series is said to be *stationary* and has constant mean, variance and covariances. Thus

$$E(y_t) = \mu \qquad \text{for all } t$$

$$\text{Var}(y_t) = E(y_t - \mu)^2 = \sigma^2 \qquad \text{for all } t$$

$$\text{Cov}(y_t y_{t-s}) = E\{(y_t - \mu)(y_{t-s} - \mu)\} = \gamma_s \qquad \text{for all } t$$

Notice in particular that γ_s depends only on s, the lag between y_t and y_{t-s}. The effect of the assumption of stationarity is that we can interpret $y_1 \ldots y_n$ as being a sample of observations on the variable y_t, and so can estimate μ, σ^2 and γ_s.

Examples of non-stationary series are any series with trends in the mean, variance or covariances. We will see below that in some cases non-stationary series can be transformed into stationary series.

In 1.4 above, the idea of a white noise error ε_t was introduced. This is generated by a stationary process as it has a constant mean of 0, a constant variance and all covariances are 0. The best prediction of ε_{t+1} is therefore 0. Very few time series are white noise processes; however, Wold's decomposition theorem (see Wold, 1954, theorem 7) states that any stationary process can be uniquely represented as the linear sum of white noise errors and a deterministic component. If we ignore the deterministic component, which can be removed by subtraction, we can write

$$y_t = \sum_{i=0}^{\infty} \theta_i \varepsilon_{t-i}$$

$$= \varepsilon_t + \theta_1 \varepsilon_{t-1} + \theta_2 \varepsilon_{t-2} + \theta_3 \varepsilon_{t-3} \dots$$

$$= (1 + \theta_1 L + \theta_2 L^2 + \theta_3 L^3 + \dots) \varepsilon_t$$

$$= \theta(L) \varepsilon_t \qquad (1.29)$$

where $L =$ the lag operator

which is defined by

$$L\varepsilon_t = \varepsilon_{t-1}$$

$$L^m \varepsilon_t = \varepsilon_{t-m}$$

and

$$\theta(L) = \sum_{i=0}^{\infty} \theta_i L^i \qquad \text{with} \quad \theta_0 = 1 \qquad (1.30)$$

A representation such as equation (1.29) is known as a *moving average*, and y_t is determined as a weighted sum of random shocks. An alternative representation of a stationary process has been proposed by Whittle (1963, p. 21), in which

$$y_t = \phi_1 y_{t-1} + \phi_2 y_{t-2} + \phi_3 y_{t-3} + \dots + \varepsilon_t \qquad (1.31)$$

so that the series is expressed in terms of its own past values and a white noise error. This is known as an autoregressive process. Using the lag operator, equation (1.31) can be written

$$\varepsilon_t = (1 - \phi_1 L - \phi_2 L^2 - \phi_3 L^3 \dots) y_t$$

$$= \phi(L) y_t \qquad (1.32)$$

where $\phi(L) = \sum_{i=0}^{\infty} -\phi_i L^i \qquad \text{with} \quad \phi_0 = -1$

The representations of y_t in both equation (1.29) and equation (1.31) involve a possibly infinite number of parameters, and so are likely to require strong assumptions before the parameters (θ_i, ϕ_i) can be estimated. An alternative representation has been suggested by Box and Jenkins (1970) which combines autoregressive (AR) and moving-average (MA) models into autoregressive moving-average (ARMA) models. Thus

$$\phi(L) y_t = \theta(L) \varepsilon_t \qquad (1.33)$$

where
$$\phi(L) = 1 - \phi_1 L - \phi_2 L^2 \ldots - \phi_p L^p \qquad (1.34)$$

$$\theta(L) = 1 + \theta_1 L + \theta_2 L^2 + \ldots + \theta_q L^q \qquad (1.35)$$

so that $\phi(L)$ is of order p and $\theta(L)$ is of order q. In this case, equation (1.33) is referred to as an ARMA (p, q) model, and there are $p + q$ unknown parameters. For the model in equation (1.33) to be stationary, there are certain restrictions on the possible values of the parameters. A *necessary* condition for stationarity is that

$$\phi_1 + \phi_2 + \ldots + \phi_p < 1 \qquad (1.36)$$

while a *necessary and sufficient* condition for stationarity is that the roots of

$$\phi(L) = 0 \qquad (1.37)$$

which is the characteristic equation, lie outside the unit circle. Thus the solutions $L_1 L_2 \ldots L_p$ of equation (1.37) must all be absolutely greater than 1. Box and Jenkins (1970) give the proof of this.

Many series which occur in economics are non-stationary and have linear (or non-linear) trends in the mean or variance. They can frequently be transformed to become stationary so that, for example, if the monthly money supply level m has a non-linear trend, $y = \Delta^d m$ may be stationary. Thus, while y has an ARMA (p, q) representation, m has what is known as an autoregressive integrated moving-average or ARIMA (p, d, q) representation. Other examples of transformations which might achieve stationarity are

$$y_t = \Delta m_t = m_t - m_{t-1} = (1 - L) m_t$$

$$y_t = \Delta^2 m_t = \Delta m_t - \Delta m_{t-1} = (1 - L)^2 m_t$$

$$y_t = \log (m/m_{-12})$$

where L = the lag operator

The choice between these transformations, and others, is to some extent subjective. The researcher has to decide whether the original series appears to be stationary and, if not, how it can be made so.

This is in fact the first step in fitting a time-series model to a set of data. In practice, checking for stationarity involves graphing the data, checking whether the mean is changing (by comparing the means of, say, the first third and last third of the data) and also whether the variance and covariances are constant. If there is evidence of non-stationarity, the series is transformed to remove it.

Next, the properties of the stationary series are examined to see if an appropriate ARMA model can be identified. An excellent introduction to how this might be done is given by Pindyck and Rubinfeld (1981). Once the model is selected, the next step is the estimation of parameters. For example, in the case of an ARMA $(1,1)$ model

$$y_t = \phi_1 y_{t-1} + \varepsilon_t - \theta_1 \varepsilon_{t-1} \tag{1.38}$$

the parameters are ϕ_1 and θ_1. The presence of the moving-average error means that ordinary least squares cannot be used for estimation. Instead an iterative process is used, whereby equation (1.38) is written

$$\varepsilon_t = y_t - \phi_1 y_{t-1} + \theta_1 \varepsilon_{t-1} \tag{1.39}$$

and, by setting $\varepsilon_0 = 0$ and taking initial guesses for ϕ_1 and θ_1, a series of ε values can be obtained. The guesses for ϕ_1 and θ_1 are then modified until the minimum $\sum \varepsilon_t^2$ is found.

Finally, the fitted ARMA model has to be checked for goodness of fit. If the model is correct, the residuals will be purely random and so should be free from autocorrelation. The estimated parameters will also be statistically significant.

2

The Theory of Rational Expectations

2.1 Introduction

In the previous chapter the concept of rational expectations was briefly introduced. The purpose of this chapter is to consider in detail some of the issues raised by this modelling technique. There has been an immense amount of research over the past decade investigating the implications of the rational expectations hypothesis for economic behaviour, and so our choice of topics for discussion will be somewhat less than comprehensive and will be introductory in nature. The reader requiring a more detailed consideration of these issues is strongly recommended to consult the specialist books by Begg (1982), Lucas and Sargent (1981), or Minford and Peel (1983).

The plan of the chapter is as follows. In this section we define more precisely the concept of rational expectations, and outline some of the properties of this method of forming expectations. Then in 2.2 and 2.3 we show how a linear model embodying rational expectations can be formally solved under a variety of different information assumptions, and illustrate some of the theoretical problems that arise in the solution. In 2.4 we consider the implications for the design of government macroeconomic stabilisation policy of assuming that agents possess rational expectations. We show the effects of rational expectations on the evaluation of alternative government policies by macroeconomic builders in 2.5; this is based on the Lucas critique of policy evaluation. In 2.6 we consider some of the criticisms of the rational expectations hypothesis, and the salient conclusions of this chapter are briefly summarised in 2.7.

The methods outlined in this chapter require the use of algebra. As a compromise between including every step (which might hide the wood from the trees), and omitting it all (which might leave the conscientious reader confused), much of the algebra is relegated to the appendices to this chapter.

The essential idea of the Muth (1961) concept of rational expectations is that agents make use of all available relevant information by deriving their expectations of the future values of variables from the underlying true economic model that (theoretically, at least) generates the variable to be forecast. It follows that agents' subjective probability distributions about future outcomes will be the same as the actual probability distributions, conditional on the information available to them. In principle, the rational expectations hypothesis is thus concerned with all moments of a distribution. However, as a practical matter, considerations of analytic tractability will limit our concern usually to the mean (and sometimes the variance) of a distribution.

Notation

The mean of a distribution, or its expected value, will be denoted by Ey (mathematically, the expected value of y). Under the rational expectations hypothesis we will identify the rational expectation of y as the mathematically-expected value of y. On reflection, it is clear that there are three different dimensions to be defined when considering the expectation of the future value of an economic variable – these are the future dates for which the variable is to be forecast, the date at which the expectation is formed, and the information set available to the agent at this time. We will denote

$$E_{t-k}(y_{t+i}/\theta_{t-k})$$

as the expectation of y for time period $t+i$, formed in time period $t-k$ on an information set θ available in time period $t-k$. Both i and k can be positive or negative. It is clear that the dating of components of the information set which agents possess is the crucial feature of expectations formation, rather than the calendar date at which expectations are formed. One could consequently define all expectations as $E(y_{t+i}/\theta_{t-k})$, and simply spell out the precise information in

θ. However, this is a little unwieldy, so we will denote expectations of a variable as $E_{t-k}y_{t+i}$, which will mean the expectation of y for time period $t+i$ formed on the available information set dated at time $t-k$. $E_{t-6}y_{t+7}$, for example, is the expectation of y in time period $t+7$ formed on the information set dated six periods ago. The expectation formed *today* of a variable, if all information is available with a two-period delay, is consequently given in our notation by $E_{t-2}y_t$.

Before considering in detail the properties of rational expectations, we must restate the result that, in a stochastic *linear* economic system, a variable can always be written as an infinite moving-average process in a white noise or random error. This is Wold's decomposition theorem (see 1.6 above), which will be widely used in the rest of this chapter. We can thus write a variable y_t as

$$y_t = \bar{y} + \sum_{i=0}^{\infty} \pi_i \varepsilon_{t-i} \tag{2.1}$$

or

$$y_t = \bar{y} + \pi_0 \varepsilon_t + \pi_1 \varepsilon_{t-1} + \pi_2 \varepsilon_{t-2} + \dots \tag{2.2}$$

where　　$\bar{y}$ = the mean of the series

　　　　π_i = constant parameters, and

　　　　ε = a normally-distributed error with a mean of 0, constant variance, σ_ε^2 and 0 covariances

An illustration of this is given in appendix 1 of this chapter (2.8 below). If there are more random shocks in the model, we can represent our variable as

$$y_t = \bar{y} + \sum_{i=0}^{\infty} \pi_i \varepsilon_{t-i} + \sum_{i=0}^{\infty} \gamma_i u_{t-i} + \dots \tag{2.3}$$

where we simply add extra infinite summations in the different errors.

The expectations operator

Using the Wold decomposition theorem, we now show how to derive the expectation of y_{t+1} formed on different information sets. For simplicity, we assume there is one random shock, so that

$$y_{t+1} = \bar{y} + \pi_0 \varepsilon_{t+1} + \pi_1 \varepsilon_t + \pi_2 \varepsilon_{t-1} + \pi_3 \varepsilon_{t-2} + \dots \tag{2.4}$$

Taking mathematical expectations at time t

$$E_t y_{t+1} = E(\bar{y}) + \pi_0 E(\varepsilon_{t+1}) + \pi_1 E(\varepsilon_t) + \pi_2 E(\varepsilon_{t-1})$$
$$+ \pi_3 E(\varepsilon_{t-2}) + \dots \tag{2.5}$$

Now the information set at time t includes ε_t, ε_{t-1}, etc. Also the expected value of future errors, such as ε_{t+1} must be 0

$$\therefore E_t y_{t+1} = \bar{y} + \pi_1 \varepsilon_t + \pi_2 \varepsilon_{t-1} + \pi_3 \varepsilon_{t-2} + \dots \tag{2.6}$$

Similarly, on the information set in earlier periods

$$E_{t-1} y_{t+1} = \bar{y} + \pi_2 \varepsilon_{t-1} + \pi_3 \varepsilon_{t-2} + \pi_4 \varepsilon_{t-3} + \dots \tag{2.7}$$

$$E_{t-2} y_{t+1} = \bar{y} + \pi_3 \varepsilon_{t-2} + \pi_4 \varepsilon_{t-3} + \dots \tag{2.8}$$

Since a clear understanding of the expectations operator is essential, the reader should confirm the following

$$E_{t-1} y_t = \bar{y} + \pi_1 \varepsilon_{t-1} + \pi_2 \varepsilon_{t-2} + \pi_3 \varepsilon_{t-3} + \dots \tag{2.9}$$

$$E_{t-2} y_{t-1} = \bar{y} + \pi_1 \varepsilon_{t-2} + \pi_2 \varepsilon_{t-3} + \pi_3 \varepsilon_{t-4} + \dots \tag{2.10}$$

$$E_{t-2} y_{t+4} = \bar{y} + \pi_6 \varepsilon_{t-2} + \pi_7 \varepsilon_{t-3} + \pi_8 \varepsilon_{t-4} + \dots \tag{2.11}$$

Properties of rational expectations

We now consider the properties of rational expectations models. Our approach is to examine three aspects which are of interest (a) the mean or expected value of the one-period ahead forecast error, (b) the variance of the error, and (c) the relationship between forecasting errors over different time horizons. These will indicate general properties which will allow us to examine the empirical evidence for rational expectations in the rest of this book.

The one-period horizon forecast error is obtained by subtracting equation (2.6) from equation (2.4), to give

$$y_{t+1} - E_t y_{t+1} = \pi_0 \varepsilon_{t+1} \tag{2.12}$$

Since the mean (or expected value) of ε_{t+1} is 0, as ε is white noise, equation (2.12) indicates that the mean forecast error is 0 – that is, $E_t y_{t+1}$ is an *unbiased* predictor of y_{t+1}. In general, the rational expectation of a variable will have the property of unbiasedness (compare with equation (1.28)).

The rational expectation can also be defined as the *efficient* predictor of y_{t+1}. This means that the variance of the prediction error ($\pi_0^2 \sigma_\varepsilon^2$) is smaller than that of any other possible predictor. It follows because the error, ε_{t+1}, is random (and hence uncorrelated with any previous events), so that there is no information available at the time the expectations are formed which can help to predict ε_{t+1}.

Unbiasedness and efficiency are two of the key properties of rational expectations which are not generally possessed by more mechanical expectations formation mechanisms such as adaptive and regressive expectations. In particular circumstances, however, adaptive or regressive expectations can be rational (see Muth, 1961; Dornbusch, 1976). For an illustration of this see appendix 2 of this chapter (2.9, below).

We now turn to the third aspect of rational expectations – the relationships between forecasting errors over successive time periods. The *ex post* forecast error for the one-period forecast y_{t+1} when information is dated at time $t-1$ is given by the difference between equation (2.4) and equation (2.7), and is

$$y_{t+1} - E_{t-1} y_{t+1} = \pi_0 \varepsilon_{t+1} + \pi_1 \varepsilon_t \qquad (2.13)$$

If we consider the forecast error in the previous period, we have

$$y_t - E_{t-2} y_t = \pi_0 \varepsilon_t + \pi_1 \varepsilon_{t-1} \qquad (2.14)$$

The expected correlation between two successive errors is given by

$$E(\pi_0 \varepsilon_{t+1} + \pi_1 \varepsilon_t)(\pi_0 \varepsilon_t + \pi_1 \varepsilon_{t-1}) = \pi_1 \pi_0 \sigma_\varepsilon^2 \qquad (2.15)$$

since $E(\varepsilon_t \varepsilon_{t+j}) = 0$ for $j \neq 0$, from the assumptions about ε_t. That is, when there is a two-period forecast horizon (between information dated at $t-1$ and the forecast for $t+1$), successive forecast errors from rational expectations will be correlated. Frequently it is stated that 'rational expectations implies that forecast errors are serially uncorrelated'. This is true *only* in the case of one-period ahead forecasts; in our example, there will be first-order serial correlation. In general, forecast errors will be correlated up to the length of the forecast horizon -1. However, the forecast errors will not be correlated with any information known at the time the forecast is made. If this were not so, the information could be exploited to improve the forecast and the original forecast would not be efficient. It follows that if we take some subset θ' of the full information set θ used by agents in making the forecast, then the *ex post* forecast errors of a rational expectations scheme must be uncorrelated with any combination of elements in θ'. More formally

$$E[(y_{t+i} - E(y_{t+i}/\theta_{t-k})), \theta'_{t-k}] = 0 \qquad (2.16)$$

This property relates directly to the concept of 'efficiency' discussed above, and in many studies efficiency is defined by equation (2.16).

Our previous definition of efficiency was in terms of the smallest possible variance of the prediction error. If equation (2.16) is not satisfied, then information in θ' can be incorporated to reduce both the forecast error and its variance. Minimum variance of the prediction error therefore implies full – or efficient – utilisation of the available information. To test for the efficiency of a forecast scheme we can take the *ex post* forecast errors and correlate them with elements of the information set presumed to be known to agents at the time of expectation formation. The resulting correlations should be 0 if the forecasts are rational. We also notice that the correlation which emerges in equation (2.15) due to the forecast horizon of two periods does not violate the assumption that the forecasts are unbiased. The expectation of equation (2.13) based on information dated at $t-1$ is 0. Thus

$$E_{t-1}(y_{t+1} - E_{t-1}y_{t+1}) = 0 \tag{2.17}$$

given that $E_{t-1}\varepsilon_{t+1}$ and $E_{t-1}\varepsilon_t$ are both 0.

There are two further properties of rational expectations which we must set out before discussing the formal solution of models. The first concerns the way expectations in the future will be revised, and states

$$E_{t-j}(E_t y_{t+i}) = E_{t-j} y_{t+i} \tag{2.18}$$

or, more precisely

$$E[E(y_{t+i}/\theta_t)/\theta_{t-j}] = E(y_{t+i}/\theta_{t-j}) \quad \text{for } j > 0 \tag{2.19}$$

The right-hand side of equation (2.18) or equation (2.19) is the expectation of y for period $t+i$, based on an information set dated at $t-j$. The left-hand side is the expectation at $t-j$ of what the expectation of y_{t+i} will be j periods in the future. Quite obviously, if the left- and right-hand sides of equation (2.18) or equation (2.19) were unequal, this would suggests that agents now know how expectations will be revised as future information accrues, which implies incomplete exploitation of the information set dated at $t-j$. Two examples of the proposition written more briefly are

$$E_{t-2}(E_{t-1}y_{t+3}) = E_{t-2}y_{t+3} \tag{2.20}$$

$$E_t(E_{t+4}y_{t+8}) = E_t y_{t+8} \tag{2.21}$$

The final property of rational expectations occurs only in *linear* models and is not unique to rational expectations. It is that they satisfy the *chain rule of forecasting*, which is a method of obtaining expressions for future values of a variable in terms of information known at the time the forecast is made (see Wold, 1963). A simple example will illustrate this. Suppose that a variable can be written

$$y_t = ay_{t-1} + \varepsilon_t \tag{2.22}$$

where $|a| < 1$

Consider now the expectations of current and future values of y formed on the information set dated at $t-1$. Thus

$$E_{-1}y_t = ay_{t-1} \tag{2.23}$$

$$E_{-1}y_{t+1} = E_{-1}(ay_t + \varepsilon_{t+1}) = aE_{-1}y_t = a^2 y_{t-1} \tag{2.24}$$

$$E_{-1}y_{t+2} = E_{-1}(ay_{t+1} + \varepsilon_{t+2}) = aE_{-1}(y_{t+1})$$
$$= a^2 E_{-1}y_t = a^3 y_{t-1} \tag{2.25}$$

and, in general

$$E_{-1}y_{t+i} = a^{i+1}y_{t-1} \tag{2.26}$$

In each case, repeated use of equation (2.22) provides the 'chain' which allows future values of y to be expressed in terms of y_{t-1}, which is already known at time $t-1$, thus demonstrating the chain rule of forecasting.

We now turn to methods of solution of rational expectations models.

2.2 Solution of rational expectations models

The starting point of the rational expectations hypothesis is that agents use the underlying true model of the economy to derive their expectations. We now consider how this is done. Throughout this section we shall use variants of a simple Keynesian multiplier/accelerator model with a fixed price level to demonstrate methods of solution of rational expectations models. The Keynesian model has been selected for two reasons. First, the reader should be familiar with the underlying rationale and behaviour of the model. Second, it demonstrates that applications of the rational expectations hypothesis are not confined to monetarist models. The structure of the basic model is given by equations (2.27)–(2.30)

$$y_t = C_t + I_t + G_t \tag{2.27}$$

$$C_t = cy_t + \varepsilon_t \qquad (0 < c < 1) \tag{2.28}$$

$$I_t = d(E_{t-1}y_t - y_{t-1}) \tag{2.29}$$

$$G_t = \bar{G} \tag{2.30}$$

where y_t, C_t, I_t and G_t = respectively real income, real consumption, real investment and real government expenditure

c, d and $\bar{G}$ = constants

$E_{t-1}y_t$ = the expectation of y_t formed on the basis of the information set dated in the previous period (which we know from our previous discussion is the crucial factor), and

ε_t = a normally-distributed error with a mean of 0 and constant variance

Equation (2.28) is the usual Keynesian consumption function, with a random error, and equation (2.29) defines the accelerator relationship with investment depending on the expected change in output, with information timed at $t - 1$. There is thus a one-period time horizon, and the expectation is for the current period, t.

We now consider three different methods for finding the rational expectations solution for output (and hence other variables) in this model.

Taking expectations of the reduced form

This method involves three stages. First, the reduced form equations are obtained, treating the expectational variables as exogenous. Second, these equations are solved for the expectational variables. Finally, these solutions for the expectational variables are substituted back into the reduced-form equations to obtain the solutions for the endogenous variables.

Using this methodology, we first obtain the reduced-form equations by substituting equations (2.28), (2.29) and (2.30) into equation (2.27), to obtain

$$y_t = cy_t + d(E_{t-1}y_t - y_{t-1}) + \bar{G} + \varepsilon_t \tag{2.31}$$

and hence

$$y_t = e(E_{t-1} y_t - y_{t-1}) + \frac{\bar{G}}{1-c} + \frac{\varepsilon_t}{1-c} \qquad (2.32)$$

where $e = d/1 - c$

This is a type of reduced form for output in this model, in that it relates output to past values of output, expectations of output and the exogenous variable ($\bar{G}$).

Moving on to the second stage, we take the expectation of equation (2.32) – timed at $t-1$ – to give

$$E_{t-1} y_t = E_{t-1}(e(E_{t-1} y_t - y_{t-1}))$$

$$+ E_{t-1} \frac{\bar{G}}{1-c} + E_{t-1} \frac{\varepsilon_t}{1-c} \qquad (2.33)$$

Noting that $E_{t-1}\varepsilon_t$ is 0 as ε_t is white noise, and that $\bar{G}$ is a constant

$$E_{t-1} y_t = e(E_{t-1} y_t - y_{t-1}) + \frac{\bar{G}}{1-c} \qquad (2.34)$$

Rearranging gives

$$E_{t-1} y_t = \frac{-e}{1-e} y_{t-1} + \frac{\bar{G}}{(1-c)(1-e)} \qquad (2.35)$$

This gives the solution for the expectational variable, and we now substitute from equation (2.35) into equation (2.32) to obtain the solution to the models (after some simplification)

$$y_t = \frac{-e}{1-e} y_{t-1} + \frac{\bar{G}}{(1-c)(1-e)} + \frac{\varepsilon_t}{1-c} \qquad (2.36)$$

Thus equation (2.36) is the rational expectations solution for output in this model. While this method works well in our example, it is not always convenient to take expectations of the reduced form, so other approaches are needed.

Muthian method of undetermined coefficients

The second method of solution – known as the Muthian method of undetermined coefficients – also starts from the reduced form of the model (i.e. equation (2.32)). We assume, from Wold's decomposition

theorem and our discussion of equation (2.1), that the general solution
can be written in the form of equation (2.4). Our solution to equation
(2.32) consequently is

$$y_t = \bar{y} + \sum_{i=0}^{\infty} \pi_i \varepsilon_{t-i} \tag{2.37}$$

The problem is to find the values of $\bar{y}$ and the π_i such that we have a
rational expectations solution to our model. The procedure is to
substitute the appropriate expression for y from equation (2.37) into
the reduced form of the model in equation (2.32). Doing this, we
obtain

$$\bar{y} + \sum_{i=0}^{\infty} \pi_i \varepsilon_{t-i} = e\left[\bar{y} + \sum_{i=1}^{\infty} \pi_i \varepsilon_{t-i} - \left(\bar{y} + \sum_{i=0}^{\infty} \pi_i \varepsilon_{t-i-1} \right) \right]$$
$$+ \frac{\bar{G}}{1-c} + \frac{\varepsilon_t}{1-c} \tag{2.38}$$

For equation (2.38) to hold, two conditions are essential. First the
only value that $\bar{y}$ can take is

$$\bar{y} = \frac{\bar{G}}{1-c} \tag{2.39}$$

because the constant terms on each side of equation (2.38) must be
equal. Second, since the ε can be any number, the only way which
equation (2.38) can hold is if the coefficients on ε_t, ε_{t-1}, etc. are all
equal to 0. Equating coefficients, we thus find

$$\pi_0 \varepsilon_t = \frac{\varepsilon_t}{1-c} \qquad \therefore \pi_0 = \frac{1}{1-c} \tag{2.40}$$

$$\pi_1 \varepsilon_{t-1} = e(\pi_1 - \pi_0)\varepsilon_{t-1} \qquad \therefore \pi_1 = \frac{-e}{1-e} \pi_0 \tag{2.41}$$

$$\pi_2 \varepsilon_{t-2} = e(\pi_2 - \pi_1)\varepsilon_{t-2} \qquad \therefore \pi_2 = \frac{-e}{1-e} \pi_1 \tag{2.42}$$

and in general

$$\pi_i = \frac{-e}{1-e} \pi_{i-1} \qquad \text{for } i \geqslant 1 \tag{2.43}$$

Consequently equations (2.37), (2.39), (2.40) and (2.43) define our solution. To illustrate that this is precisely the same as equation (2.36) – the solution obtained by the previous method – we notice that since

$$y_t = \bar{y} + \pi_0 \varepsilon_t + \pi_1 \varepsilon_{t-1} + \pi_2 \varepsilon_{t-2} + \pi_3 \varepsilon_{t-2} + \ldots \tag{2.44}$$

then

$$f y_{t-1} = f\bar{y} + f\pi_0 \varepsilon_{t-1} + f\pi_1 \varepsilon_{t-2} + f\pi_2 \varepsilon_{t-3} + \ldots \tag{2.45}$$

where $\quad f = -e/(1-e)$

If we subtract equation (2.45) from equation (2.44), we obtain

$$y_t - f y_{t-1} = \bar{y} - f\bar{y} + \pi_0 \varepsilon_t + (\pi_1 - f\pi_0)\varepsilon_{t-1}$$
$$+ (\pi_2 - f\pi_1)\varepsilon_{t-2} + \ldots \tag{2.46}$$

From conditions (2.39), (2.40) and (2.43), equation (2.46) collapses to give

$$y_t = \frac{-e}{1-e} y_{t-1} + \frac{\bar{G}}{(1-c)(1-e)} + \frac{\varepsilon_t}{1-c} \tag{2.47}$$

which is of course the same solution as equation (2.36).

Lucas solution method

The third basic method of solution we consider, which is related to the Muthian method of undetermined coefficients, requires a 'guess' of a solution for the endogenous variables of the model in terms of past values of endogenous variables, current and past values of exogenous variables, and current and past values of the error terms which appear in the structural equations. This approach was used by Lucas (1972), and is frequently employed in the literature (see McCallum, 1983a). Clearly the nature of the 'guess' solution depends on our experience with the models. For the model under consideration we propose a solution of the form

$$y_t = A y_{t-1} + \bar{y} + B\varepsilon_t \tag{2.48}$$

where $\quad A, B, \bar{y} = \text{constants to be determined}$

Taking expectations timed at $t-1$

$$E_{t-1} y_t = A y_{t-1} + \bar{y} \tag{2.49}$$

Substitution of equation (2.49) into the reduced-form equation (2.32) gives

$$y_t = e(A-1)y_{t-1} + e\bar{y} + \frac{\bar{G}}{1-c} + \frac{\varepsilon_t}{1-c} \tag{2.50}$$

If equations (2.48) and (2.50) are the solution to our model (and consequently equivalent), it follows that

$$A = e(A-1) \quad \text{or} \quad A = \frac{-e}{1-e} \tag{2.51}$$

$$\bar{y} = e\bar{y} + \frac{\bar{G}}{1-c} \quad \text{or} \quad \bar{y} = \frac{\bar{G}}{(1-c)(1-e)} \tag{2.52}$$

$$B = \frac{1}{1-c} \tag{2.53}$$

Substituting these in equation (2.48) therefore gives the solution

$$y_t = \frac{-e}{1-e} y_{t-1} + \frac{\bar{G}}{(1-c)(1-e)} + \frac{\varepsilon_t}{1-c} \tag{2.54}$$

The three basic methods of solution thus give the same result. If inappropriate variables were added in the solution in equation (2.48) – (for example, y_{t-2}) – they would be found to have 0 coefficients. Obviously the model chosen above for the solution was special in that there were no expectations of *future* values of variables (variables dated $t+1$ or further in the future).

Forward expectations

We must now consider some of the issues that arise if a model does contain forward expectations. The major complication is that the model no longer possesses a *unique* solution. In order to demonstrate this, we now modify equation (2.29) by replacing the expectational variable $E_{t-1} y_t$ by $E_{t-1} y_{t+1}$, so that the reduced form of the model incorporates future expectations

$$y_t = e(E_{t-1} y_{t+1} - y_t) + \bar{G} + \varepsilon_t \tag{2.55}$$

Suppose we take expectations of equation (2.55) dated at $t-1$, then

$$E_{t-1} y_t = eE_{t-1} y_{t+1} - E_{t-1} y_t) + \bar{G} \tag{2.56}$$

or

$$E_{t-1} y_t = \frac{e}{(1+e)} E_{t-1} y_{t+1} + \frac{\bar{G}}{(1+e)} \tag{2.57}$$

Unlike the previous example, we cannot substitute equation (2.57) into equation (2.55) to eliminate expectations, and obtain an expression purely in current and past values of y and the error (free of expectations terms). In fact, we notice from equation (2.55) that

$$y_{t+1} = e(E_t y_{t+2} - y_{t+1}) + \bar{G} + \varepsilon_{t+1} \tag{2.58}$$

and hence, rearranging and taking expectations at $t-1$

$$E_{t-1} y_{t+1} = \frac{e}{1+e} E_{t-1} y_{t+2} + \frac{\bar{G}}{1+e} \tag{2.59}$$

We thus see from equations (2.57) and (2.59) that when a model contains expectations of the future value of a variable, this expectation will be linked to the expectation of all future values of this variable. For this particular model, the general case from equations (2.57) and (2.59) is

$$E_{t-1} y_{t+i} = \frac{e}{1+e} E_{t-1} y_{t+i+1} + \frac{\bar{G}}{1+e} \qquad \text{for } i \geqslant 0 \tag{2.60}$$

Now equation (2.60) is a first-order difference equation in a variable which we can define as X_i, where

$$X_i = E_{t-1} y_{t+i+1} \tag{2.61}$$

Consequently, we can write equation (2.60) as

$$X_i = \frac{(1+e)}{e} X_{i-1} - \frac{\bar{G}}{e} \tag{2.62}$$

The solution to this equation (see, for example, Baumol, 1970) is given by

$$X_i = (X_0 - \bar{G}) \left(\frac{1+e}{e} \right)^i + \bar{G} \qquad \text{for } i \geqslant 0 \tag{2.63}$$

This solution is of some interest since it allows $X_0 = E_{t-1} y_{t+1}$ to be any value we choose. From equation (2.60), another way of saying this is that if we expect the future value of y_{t+i+1} to take a particular value, there will always be a value X_0, which will be consistent with it: any expectation can be self-justifying. Yet another way of stating this is that there is no unique solution to the model which generates the particular reduced form equation (2.55).

We now show how this problem presents itself if we use the Muthian method of solution on the reduced form given by equation (2.55). Assuming a solution of the form equation (2.37)

$$\bar{y} + \sum_{i=0}^{\infty} \pi_i \varepsilon_{t-i} = e\left[\bar{y} + \sum_{i=2}^{\infty} \pi_i \varepsilon_{t-i+1} - \left(\bar{y} + \sum_{i=0}^{\infty} \pi_i \varepsilon_{t-i} \right) \right]$$
$$+ \bar{G} + \varepsilon_t \qquad (2.64)$$

Equating the coefficients, we find

$$\bar{y} = \bar{G} \qquad (2.65)$$

$$\pi_0 = 1/1 + e$$

$$\pi_1(1 + e) = e\pi_2$$

and

$$\pi_i = \frac{(1+e)}{e} \pi_{i-1} \qquad \text{for } i \geqslant 1 \qquad (2.66)$$

We see from these equations that whilst π_0 has a unique value, there is nothing in the formal structure of the model to pin down π_1 and it can take any value. Once π_1 is determined, however, all the other π_i are given.

This problem of non-uniqueness of solution typically occurs in rational expectations models where there are future expectations. A number of ways of ensuring a unique solution have been proposed in the literature. One method, which is not general, is to suppose that agents would *a priori* rule out unstable roots on the empirical grounds that such 'explosive' behaviour is not observed in the real world which we are attempting to model. Consequently in the above model if the modulus of $(1 + e)/e$ is greater than or equal to unity, then we set π_1 equal to 0 and hence all the π_i for $i \geqslant 1$ are 0. Equivalently, in equation (2.63), we set

$$X_0 = E_{t-1} y_{t+1} = \bar{G}$$

which implies $X_i = \bar{G}$. This generates a rational expectations solution for the model of

$$y_t = \bar{G} + \frac{1}{1 + e} \varepsilon_t \qquad (2.67)$$

Whilst it may be regarded as reasonable to rule out unstable roots as being economically irrelevant (though see Burmeister, 1980, for an alternative view) this approach does not in general give a unique solution to all rational models. For instance, if the modulus of $(1 + e)/e$ was less than 1 in the above model, there is a non-unique but stable solution. This possibility was first stressed by Taylor (1977); he proposed that the solution be chosen which minimised the variance of the exogenous variable concerned, but his choice of criterion is arbitrary. Alternatively Minford *et al.* (1979) propose that a terminal condition should be imposed on a model whereby agents anticipate that the model will reach equilibrium at some finite point (N) in the future (equivalent to choosing $\pi_N = 0$ in equation (2.66)). We are left with the conclusion that the appropriate method of choosing a unique solution in rational expectations models is still an active research issue (see McCallum, 1983b).

For the remainder of this chapter we will utilise the Muthian and Lucas methods of solution of rational expectations models, since in our opinion they are the simplest generally applicable methods for small models. Another example of the use of these methods is given in appendix 3 of this chapter (2.10, below). For further analysis of solution methods, and other theoretical problems which occur, see Sargent (1979a) and Minford and Peel (1983).

2.3 Incomplete current information

So far we have considered the solution of rational expectations models when all the information available to an agent had the same dating (say, a one-quarter lag). In practice, of course, this is generally not the case. Agents have access to the current values of some variables (such as exchange rates, interest rates and local prices), but other variables are observed only with a lag (such as consumer prices, national income and money supply). However, it is possible in many cases to use the information currently observed to make inferences about the unobserved variables. For example, the currently-observed interest rate (R) is affected by the levels of the (unobserved) money supply and (unobserved) consumption expenditure. These unobserved variables can be predicted, except for a random component. If we ignore means, suppose

$$R_t = m_t + \varepsilon_t \tag{2.68}$$

where m = the random part of money supply
ε = the random part of consumption

we assume m and ε are uncorrelated

Only R is observed, but agents have some idea (from past data) as to the size of the variances of m and ε (σ_m^2 and σ_ε^2). Using signal extraction methods as proposed by Kalman (1960) and Graybill (1961), the optimal current expectations of m and ε, given the observation of R, are

$$E(m_t) = \frac{\sigma_m^2}{\sigma_m^2 + \sigma_\varepsilon^2} R_t \qquad (2.69)$$

$$E(\varepsilon_t) = \frac{\sigma_\varepsilon^2}{\sigma_m^2 + \sigma_\varepsilon^2} R_t \qquad (2.70)$$

Equations (2.69) and (2.70) thus give information about the current values of the unobserved variables.

The procedure for solving rational expectations models with incomplete current information uses signal extraction methods together with the Muthian approach described in the previous section. An example, showing the detailed steps in arriving at a solution, is given in appendix 4 to this chapter (2.11, below). Here we will consider briefly the two main implications. The first is that the particular assumptions made about the timing and availability of information can have important consequences for the solution of a model. The impact effect of a particular random shock can be quite different if these assumptions are changed (compare, for example, the result for the model in appendix 4 shown in equations (2.152), (2.153) and (2.154)). For further details of recent research see Barro (1980), Lucas (1973), Saidi (1980), and Minford and Peel (1983).

The second main implication is that incomplete current information will affect the properties of the *ex post* rational expectations forecast errors. We saw in 2.1 above (following equation (2.15)) that forecast errors will be correlated up to the length of the forecast horizon -1. If there is incomplete current information, the extent of the serial correlation will be increased by the lag on the current information. For a one-period forecast horizon, it is only when there is full current information (so that the variable to be forecast is actually observed) that the *ex post* forecast error will be serially uncorrelated. This has implications for testing the rationality of survey data, which is the subject-matter of chapter 3.

Following our review of the ways in which linear rational expectations models can be solved under different information assumptions, we now turn to the policy implications of the rational expectations hypothesis.

2.4 Rational expectations and stabilisation policy

The purpose in this section is to consider the implications that rational expectations may have for the design of government stabilisation policies. We will define 'stabilisation policies' as those policies intended to influence the behaviour of *real output* (or sometimes prices) in an economy. It is often stated that incorporation of the rational expectations hypothesis into the specification of a macroeconomic model leads inevitably to the proposition that stabilisation policy is ineffective. Intuitively, it may be thought that economic agents out-guess the government and anticipate policy changes. In fact, this proposition is a special result which depends on a restrictive specification of the behavioural equations of the model.

To illustrate this, we will use a simple macroeconomic model which is more monetarist in concept than the previous Keynesian multiplier/accelerator model. The structure is given by equations (2.71)–(2.75), and both current and future expectations are included

$$(1 - T)(y^d - \bar{y}) = -\alpha(R_t - (E_{t-1}P_{t+1} - E_{t-1}P_t)) \tag{2.71}$$

$$m_t^d = P_t + y_t - cR_t \tag{2.72}$$

$$y_t^s = \bar{y} + \beta(P_t - E_{t-1}P_t) \tag{2.73}$$

$$m_t^s = \bar{m} + \rho(y_{t-1} - \bar{y}) + \varepsilon_t \tag{2.74}$$

$$\begin{aligned} m_t^d = m_t^s = m_t \\ y_t^d = y_t^s = y_t \end{aligned} \tag{2.75}$$

where y = real output
R = the nominal interest rate
m = money supply or demand
P = the price level
E defines the expectation operator conditional on an appropriate information set, and
T = the constant tax parameter

all variables except R are in logarithms

Equation (2.71) is the *IS* curve. Aggregate demand (y^d) depends on the anticipated real interest rate (the nominal rate *less* expected inflation). Direct taxes (on consumption, etc.) are allowed for in the term $(1 - T)$. Equation (2.72) is the demand for money function. Equation (2.73) is the Sargent–Wallace (1975) supply curve. Output deviates around its normal level ($\bar{y}$) as the price level differs from its expected value. Note that we can rearrange equation (2.73) as

$$P_t - P_{t-1} = \frac{1}{\beta}(y_t^s - \bar{y}) + E_{t-1}P_t - P_{t-1} \tag{2.76}$$

which will be recognised as an augmented Phillips curve, though the interpretation in that case would be different from equation (2.73) – see Friedman (1968), Minford and Peel (1983).

Equation (2.74) is the government's money supply rule and ρ is the stabilisation parameter. The money supply is changed around its normal level ($\bar{m}$) as output deviates from its normal level. Only one random disturbance ε_t is included in the model, for simplicity. Notice that in this model the interest rate is assumed to convey no information about aggregate shocks, in contrast to the example in appendix 4 (2.11, below).

We now solve for the reduced form in prices by eliminating m, y, R and the expectations variables. Substitution of equation (2.71) into equation (2.72) for R_t yields

$$m_t = P_t + by_t - \frac{c}{\alpha}(1-T)\bar{y} - c(E_{t-1}P_{t+1} - E_{t-1}P_t) \tag{2.77}$$

where $b = 1 + \frac{c}{\alpha}(1-T)$

We can also substitute for y_t, from equation (2.73) and for m_t from equation (2.74), to obtain

$$\varepsilon_t + \bar{m} + \rho\beta(P_{t-1} - E_{t-2}P_{t-1})$$

$$= P_t + b[\bar{y} + \beta(P_t - E_{t-1}P_t)] - \frac{c}{\alpha}(1-T)\bar{y}$$

$$- c(E_{t-1}P_{t+1} - E_{t-1}P_t) \tag{2.78}$$

We look for a Muthian solution of the form

$$P_t = \bar{P} + \sum_{i=0}^{\infty} \pi_i \varepsilon_{t-i} \tag{2.79}$$

and substitute this into equation (2.78). Details are given in appendix 5 of this chapter (2.12, below). The solution is

$$P_t = \bar{P} + \frac{\varepsilon_t}{1 + b\beta} + \frac{\rho\beta}{(1+c)(1+b\beta)}\varepsilon_{t-1}$$

for prices, and from equation (2.73) the solution for output is

$$y_t = \bar{y} + \frac{\beta}{1 + b\beta} \, \varepsilon_t$$

or, from equation (2.74)

$$y_t = \bar{y} + \frac{\beta}{1 + b\beta} \, (m_t - E_{t-1} m_t) \tag{2.80}$$

ε_t is thus the difference between the actual money supply and its expected value. Now equation (2.80) illustrates the startling conclusion first put forward by Sargent and Wallace – in a model embodying rational expectations and a Sargent–Wallace supply curve (or augmented Phillips curve), with our implied information assumptions of identical information for both private and public agents, government stabilisation policy is unable to influence movement of output around its normal (or equilibrium) level. That is, changing ρ does not affect y.

Of course if in the model given above agents form their expectations adaptively, then systematic monetary policy will influence movements of output around its normal level. This is easily illustrated by considering

$$m_t^s = m_t^d = P_t + y_t$$

$$y_t = \bar{y} + \beta(P_t - E_{t-1} P_t)$$

and

$$E_{t-1} P_t - P_{t-1} = P_{t-1} - P_{t-2}$$

a simple expectations scheme. The solution for output in this model is given by

$$y_t = \frac{\bar{y}}{1 + \beta} + \frac{2\beta}{1 + \beta} \, y_{t-1} - \frac{\beta}{1 + \beta} \, y_{t-2}$$

$$+ \frac{\beta}{1 + \beta} \, (m_t - 2m_{t-1} + m_{t-2})$$

Here, the government can change the movement of output by choosing an appropriate monetary rule (for example, equation (2.74)) – see Black (1975), Peel (1977), Peel and Metcalfe (1979) for a number of more complicated models in which this point is illustrated. It is also important to note that the Sargent–Wallace result relates to stabilisation policy, and not to the determinants of the normal level of output ($\bar{y}$). It is quite possible that the steady-state growth of output may vary with the steady-state growth of the money stock – see Burmeister and Dobell (1970) who provide an introduction to the money and growth literature, and also Calvo and Peel (1983).

Returning to equation (2.80), we can see that only unanticipated changes in the money supply ($m_t - E_{t-1} m_t$) can influence the variation of output around its normal level $\bar{y}$. However, by definition, unanticipated changes by the government cannot constitute a systematic policy (given the assumption of identical information sets of public and private agents). Clearly in this model the more predictable the government's monetary policy, the lower the variance of output. The Sargent–Wallace model suggests that, from the standpoint of stabilisation of output, all monetary stabilisation rules are equally ineffective (the interested reader can show that this is not true for prices). The Sargent–Wallace model consequently gives support to the Friedman view that a monetary rule should be chosen which has simple operating characteristics. The most simple rule is to choose a fixed rate of monetary growth which has the most desirable properties with respect to steady-state inflation (see Friedman, 1969). We note from equation (2.80) that automatic stabilisers such as tax rates (given in this model by T), do influence the variance of output since the coefficient b, which includes the tax parameter, appears in the solution for output. This result is due to McCallum and Whittaker (1979). However, it may not be general, because if agents completely capitalise the future value of the tax burden, anticipated changes in T will not alter output (see Barro, 1974).

Since the Sargent–Wallace paper much research has shown that their result for stabilisation policy must be regarded as a very special case. In the context of models embodying a Sargent–Wallace supply curve, Turnovsky (1980) and Weiss (1980) have shown that if there are any information asymmetries between public and private agents then systematic monetary stabilisation policy will alter the variance of output.

Of course, there is no reason why a model in which agents form their expectations rationally should be typified by a Sargent–Wallace supply curve. Phelps and Taylor (1977) and Fischer (1977) show that in models in which there are multi-period overlapping wage or price contracts the authorities are able to influence the variance of output by systematic stabilisation policy. This occurs because the authorities can change their behaviour in response to new information more quickly than some agents who are locked into the multi-period contracts (to understand this point, re-solve the model above, where the expectation in the supply curve is dated $E_{t-2}P_t$ rather than $E_{t-1}P_t$). Minford and Peel (1983) show that if the supply function is modified to allow for anticipations of future prices, then stabilisation policy can once again be effective.

The general conclusion which emerges is that rational expectations *per se* cannot be assumed to rule out the possibility of the effectiveness of stabilisation policy. This will depend on the nature of the behavioural equations in which the assumption of rational expectations is embodied. There is no reason in principle why a 'Keynesian disequilibrium model' cannot embody rational expectations. Consequently, the general case for activist stabilisation policy must be based on a consideration of the welfare properties of such a policy, and not on the sole consideration of how the expectations are formed – see Sargent (1979a), Minford and Peel (1983).

Of course, if expectations are formed rationally rather than in some mechanistic manner this can dramatically change the nature of the evolution of an economy in response to changes in government policy. The potential importance for model builders of this point has become known as the Lucas critique of policy evaluation, and it is to this issue we now turn.

2.5 Lucas critique of policy evaluation

In a paper of great importance Lucas (1976) pointed out how the assumption of rational expectations may have major implications for the evaluation of alternative government policies by macroeconomic model builders. His basic insight is that unless the estimated equations within a macroeconomic model are genuinely behavioural, or structural, simulations of alternative government policies in such a model may be misleading. We can illustrate the Lucas point by consideration of the basic multiplier/accelerator model discussed in 2.2, above

$$y_t = C_t + I_t + G_t \tag{2.27}$$

$$C_t = cy_t + \varepsilon_t \tag{2.28}$$

$$I_t = d(E_{t-1}y_t - y_{t-1}) \tag{2.29}$$

$$G_t = \bar{G} \tag{2.30}$$

The rational expectation solution for output in this model (as shown earlier) is

$$y_t = \frac{-e}{1-e} y_{t-1} + \frac{\bar{G}}{(1-c)(1-e)} + \frac{\varepsilon_t}{1-c} \tag{2.36}$$

where $\quad e = \dfrac{d}{1-c}$

After substituting for $E_{t-1} y_t$ from equation (2.36) into equation (2.29) the investment equation can be written as

$$I_t = \frac{-d}{1-e} y_{t-1} + \frac{d\bar{G}}{(1-c)(1-e)} \tag{2.81}$$

This will be our 'true' model of the economy. Now assume our model builders construct a model of the economy which is given by equations (2.27), (2.28), (2.81) and (2.30) – that is, the 'reduced-form' equation (2.81) replaces the structural equation (2.29). As long as government policy continues to be defined by equation (2.30), the model will give good forecasts. Suppose now the model builder conducts a policy simulation exercise by looking at the effects of the new feedback stabilisation rule

$$G_t = \bar{G} + \rho(y_{t-1} - \bar{y}) + \rho_1(y_{t-2} - \bar{y}) \tag{2.82}$$

where $\quad \rho, \rho_1$ and $\bar{y} = $ constants

The rational expectations solution for y_t of the model given by equations (2.27), (2.28), (2.29) and (2.82) is

$$y_t = \frac{(\rho - d)}{1-c-d} y_{t-1} + \frac{\rho_1}{1-c-d} y_{t-2}$$
$$+ \frac{\bar{G} - \rho\bar{y} - \rho_1\bar{y}}{1-c-d} + \frac{1}{1-c} \varepsilon_t \tag{2.83}$$

Consequently the 'reduced'-form investment function for the new policy rule (equation (2.82)) is

$$I_t = \frac{-d(1-(c+\rho))}{1-c-d} y_{t-1} + \frac{d\rho_1}{1-c-d} y_{t-2}$$
$$+ d\left[\frac{\bar{G} - \rho\bar{y} - \rho_1\bar{y}}{1-c-d} \right] \tag{2.84}$$

This new reduced form is quite different from equation (2.81). If a modeller uses equation (2.84) to simulate the effects of the new government stabilisation rule when equation (2.81) is the correct equation, the simulations will give misleading results. Lucas's insight is that if equations within a model are not structural or behavioural, and expectations are formed rationally, then the coefficients in such equations will not be invariant to changes in the policy regime. Alternative policy evaluations will consequently be misleading. The solution to the problem is, of course, quite simple in principle. Model builders should endeavour to make sure that equations within the model are genuinely structural, and that expectations are formally modelled. Obviously, this problem may be difficult to solve in practice since it is not always clear what constitute 'behavioural' as opposed to 'reduced-form' parameters in a model (see, for example, Lucas, 1976). It would appear that for a correct resolution of this problem it is necessary to estimate the parameters of technology and tastes, the only parameters that might be regarded as stable across changes in policy regime. However, the formidable problems that are encountered in attempting to do this are illustrated by the recent research of, for example, Hansen and Sargent (1980).

An alternative approach (as we will see in chapter 6), which has been pursued by the Liverpool Model builders, is to model expectations rationally, but to treat the parameters of such a model as *constant*. This may be reasonably accurate for 'small' changes in policy regime, since changes in parameters may be of secondary importance to the explicit modelling of expectations.

The conclusion from the Lucas critique is that if agents allow for anticipated changes in government policy when they form their expectations then this should be taken into account in building a model. Also, simulations of changes in government policy from models in which expectations are represented in a mechanistic manner are largely worthless. However, it is also true that forecasting agencies may in part meet the Lucas critique when they make 'judgemental' adjustments to their forecasts to allow for induced changes in the behaviour of the economy, rather than simply taking simulation results at face value.

2.6   Criticisms of the rational expectations hypothesis

The purpose in this section is to consider some of the criticisms of the rational expectations hypothesis. We will not be concerned with the empirical evidence relating to the hypothesis as this will be summarised in later chapters, but rather *a priori* limitations. The most poweiful criticisms of the rational expectations hypothesis are based on the implicit information requirements of the assumption – agents are assumed to know the correct model of the economy, and solve it appropriately. This assumption is obviously not literally valid. As Shiller (1978) writes, 'while it may sometimes be useful as an expositional device to assume that agents have this much information, the assumption cannot be taken seriously. If economists are only now discovering these models, we cannot seriously propose that everyone else knew them all along'.

Given that Shiller's point is obviously formally correct, the issue we consider is how far, from an *a priori* viewpoint, the assumption of rational expectations would appear to depart from a correct description of the expectations formation mechanism. One approach is to suggest that we are trying to model explicitly the imperfect 'hunches' of smart operators or agents in markets. Another promising approach to this issue must be from a consideration of the marginal costs and benefits of processing information for forecasting purposes. This is the basis of the work of Feige and Pearce (1976), who introduced the concept of economically rational expectations. They suggest that where the marginal costs of information gathering (and processing) are non-trivial, the economically rational individual may opt for a less expensive forecasting framework even at the cost of a larger error of forecast. The time-series methodology of Box and Jenkins (1970) (as discussed in chapter 1) is also a low marginal cost method of forecasting, and therefore must be considered as a candidate for an economically rational expectation. However, it seems to us that whilst Box–Jenkins forecasts may well be part of the information set conditioning the expectation of some agents, they are unlikely to be the only information source. We suggest this for two reasons. First, economists know (following the analysis of Taylor, 1975; and Lucas, 1972) that a time-series model will give inefficient forecasts following a change in policy regime, for example when a new government is elected or there is a move from fixed to floating exchange rates.

This is illustrated in appendix 6 of this chapter (2.13, below). The new policy regime changes the time-series model of the economy, so that non-random forecast errors result. The problem for agents is how to forecast under the new policy regime until sufficient observations are available to estimate the new time-series process. Clearly, if the forecaster continues to take into account observations from the previous regime then the resulting forecast errors will be serially correlated.

The second reason for doubting that time-series methods meet the criteria for economically rational expectations for many agents is based on a consideration of their implicit marginal costs relative to some readily available alternative forecasts. Most agents in an economy are not expert statisticians, and are not therefore able to produce their own time-series forecasts. Since time-series forecasts are not typically published in the media it is difficult to see how they could condition many agents' forecasts. However, there is access through the media in most developed economies to the public forecasts from many econometric models, such as the National Institute, the London Business School, the Treasury and the Liverpool Research Group, in the UK, the Wharton model, DRI, Chase, etc., in the USA. Summaries of the forecasts are discussed in the press, and so their direct marginal cost is extremely low. In fact such forecasts have essentially the same marginal costs as the information on the previous period's inflation rate which is required for an agent to form his expectations adaptively. For many agents, these forecasts represent informed expert opinion. Given the differences between the forecasting groups an economically rational agent might wish to diversify risk and combine the public forecasts of the various institutions, or combine them with other information to produce his own forecast (see chapter 7).

From a general consideration of the costs and benefits of information gathering and processing for forecasting purposes, it is clear that equating the marginal costs and benefits will generally imply that different agents will devote different amounts of resources to forecasting. *A priori*, the returns to reducing the forecasting errors of (say) inflation will be quite different, in general, for a housewife, a student, a trade union negotiator and the manager of a pension fund. It is this type of consideration which has led authors such as Fleming (1976) to propose that the rational expectations hypothesis is more appropriate to markets dominated by experts and professionals – such as financial markets – rather than, say, labour markets (see Peel and Metcalfe, 1979). However, it is unlikely that the marginal costs and benefits of forecasting, say, inflation for a wage negotiator will differ substantially from those faced by an agent in financial markets. All things considered, the relatively low marginal costs of public forecasts and time-series forecasts (compared with their potential marginal benefits) make it difficult to see how an adaptive forecasting mechanism can be an appropriate way of modelling expectations formation.

A formal analysis of the properties of public forecasts relative to the alternatives is discussed in chapter 7. However, we can say at this point that since the majority of macroeconomic model builders do not currently model expectations in the (hopefully) structural equations in an *ex ante* consistent (or unbiased manner) (see chapter 6) it is unclear how, if regime changes occur, their public forecasts could have the property of unbiasedness.

The final issue we consider relates to the costs of processing data, and hence to the possibility that model builders will ultimately converge on the same (hopefully true) structural model of the economy. In recent years there has been much theoretical work which has considered how agents might learn to improve their forecasts (see, for example, Blume, Bray and Easley, 1982). The theoretical problem addressed is whether agents, who in the absence of rational expectations will be making systematic mistakes, can modify their behaviour until their expectations become rational. In appendix 7 (2.14, below) of this chapter we demonstrate De Canio's (1979) point that when expectations influence the actual outcome, whether or not there is a convergence to a rational expectations equilibrium depends on the specific learning process assumed, the parameter values in the model, and agents' prior beliefs. From this literature it appears that convergence on a rational expectations equilibrium is in no sense assured. The conclusions of a study by De Canio are worth stating in full. He writes:

> The conclusion to be drawn from these examples is that purely theoretical arguments will never be able to settle the question as to whether economic agents in reality modify their forecasts so as to approximate the rational expectations.
>
> The only general statement that can be made about rationality in expectation formation is that maximising behaviour will lead to forecasting methods that depend on the cost of information, the intrinsic difficulty of the forecasting problem, and the benefits to be obtained from actual predictions (p. 55).

The general implications of this section are that the information assumptions demanded by the rational expectations hypothesis are too stringent for the hypothesis to be literally true. Rather, the hypothesis has the obvious merits of focusing our attention on the costs and benefits of information gathering and processing. From this perspective we suggest that both public forecasts and time-series methods offer relatively low-cost methods of forecasting. *A priori*, they would appear likely to condition expectation formation and, in general, dominate mechanistic alternatives such as adaptive expectations.

However, if the economy is subjected to changes in policy regimes, then expectations based on these methods will generally exhibit serially-correlated errors *ex post*. Nevertheless, it is difficult to see how a typical agent in an economy can *ex ante* improve on these methods of forecasting.

2.7 Conclusions

The purpose in this chapter has been to provide an introduction to the concept of rational expectations and some of the issues raised by this method of expectations formation. We reiterate that our coverage of issues has necessarily been selective, and the interested reader is directed to more specialised texts for further reading.

In 2.1, the concept of rational expectations was defined as being that agents derive their expectations of the future values of variables from the underlying true economic model by using all the available relevant information. The resulting expectations have three important properties. First, they are both unbiased (see equation (2.17)) and efficient predictors (in other words, the variance of the forecasting error is smaller than that of any other predictor). Second, agents are unable to predict how the expectations will be revised (see equation (2.19)). Third, in linear models, rational expectations satisfy the chain rule of forecasting.

Three alternative methods of solving rational expectations models were outlined in 2.2 – first, taking expectations of the reduced form, second the Muthian method and third the Lucas method. Each of these gave the same solution to the model. In general, when a model contains expectations of the future value of a variable (rather than the current value) there is no unique solution. However, a unique solution can be obtained by imposing additional criteria such as stability, minimum variance or terminal conditions.

In 2.3 the effects of having incomplete current information were considered. As well as affecting the solution it affects the serial-correlation properties of *ex post* forecast errors. Serial correlation will occur up to a level which reflects the forecast horizon − 1 plus the lag on global information. Only in the special case of a one-period ahead forecast with full current information will the forecast error have no serial correlation.

When the role of stabilisation policy under rational expectations was discussed in 2.4, we found that rational expectations *per se* do not render monetary policy impotent. The effectiveness of stabilisation policy will depend on the nature of the behavioural equation in which rational expectations occur.

The Lucas critique of policy evaluation was considered in 2.5. Unless all the equations in a model are behavioural and expectations are formed rationally then the equations will not be invariant to policy changes and model simulations will be subject to error.

Finally in 2.6 the main criticism of the rational expectations hypothesis – namely the onerous information requirement that agents both know the true structure of the model and can forecast the future course of the exogenous variables – was presented. This criticism obviously has some validity. The information assumptions of the rational expectations hypothesis are so stringent that in general it cannot be taken as being literally true. Perhaps the great strength of the hypothesis, however, is that it forces the model builder to give consideration to the information set possessed by agents. Anticipated changes in policy following (say) general elections or announced changes in future policy (if believed), must be given explicit attention in the modelling of expectations. The crucial implications of this for model building and policy simulation were illustrated by consideration of the Lucas critique of policy evaluation.

Some of the empirical evidence relating to the issues raised in this chapter are discussed later. In the next chapter we consider surveys of expectations, and see if these provide any empirical support for the rational expectations hypothesis.

2.8 Appendix 1: illustration of Wold's decomposition theorem

Consider the following simple macroeconomic model

$$y_t = C_t + I_t \tag{2.85}$$

$$I_t = 100 \tag{2.86}$$

$$C_t = a y_{t-1} + \varepsilon_t \tag{2.87}$$

where y_t = real income
       C_t = real consumption
       I_t = investment
       ε_t = a random shock (white noise)
       a = a constant (less than unity)

Substitution of equations (2.86) and (2.87) into equation (2.85) gives

$$y_t = ay_{t-1} + 100 + \varepsilon_t \tag{2.88}$$

and by substitution for y_{t-1} we obtain

$$y_t = a(ay_{t-2} + 100 + \varepsilon_{t-1}) + 100 + \varepsilon_t \tag{2.89}$$

and eventually, by repeated substitution

$$y_t = 100(1 + a + a^2 + a^3 + \ldots) + \varepsilon_t + a\varepsilon_{t-1} + a^2\varepsilon_{t-2}$$
$$+ a^3\varepsilon_{t-3} + \ldots \tag{2.90}$$

$$= \frac{100}{1-a} + \varepsilon_t + a\varepsilon_{t-1} + a^2\varepsilon_{t-2} + a^3\varepsilon_{t-3} + \ldots \tag{2.91}$$

(using $(1-x)^{-1} = 1 + x + x^2 + x^3 \ldots$ given $0 < x < 1$)

Hence, equation (2.91) has the form given by equation (2.2), with $\bar{y} = 100/(1-a)$ and $\pi_i = a^i$.

2.9   Appendix 2: rationality of adaptive and regressive expectations

First, suppose the series to be forecast has the time-series representation

$$y_t = y_{t-1} + \pi_0\varepsilon_t + \pi_1\varepsilon_{t-1} \tag{2.92}$$

This is an autoregressive integrated moving-average (ARIMA) process of order $(0,1,1)$. The rational expectation $E_{t-1}y_t$ of equation (2.92) is given by

$$E_{t-1}y_t = y_{t-1} + \pi_1\varepsilon_{t-1} \tag{2.93}$$

Since equation (2.92) can be written

$$y_t - y_{t-1} = (\pi_0 + \pi_1 L)\varepsilon_t \tag{2.94}$$

where L = the lag operator $(L\varepsilon_t \equiv \varepsilon_{t-1})$, then

$$\varepsilon_t = \frac{y_t - y_{t-1}}{\pi_0 + \pi_1 L} \quad \text{and} \quad \varepsilon_{t-1} = \frac{y_{t-1} - y_{t-2}}{\pi_0 + \pi_1 L}$$

Thus, substituting for ε_{t-1} in equation (2.93) gives

$$E_{t-1}y_t = y_{t-1} + \frac{\pi_1}{\pi_0 + \pi_1 L}(y_{t-1} - y_{t-2}) \tag{2.95}$$

Multiplying by $\pi_0 + \pi_1 L$ gives

$$\pi_0 E_{t-1}y_t + \pi_1 E_{t-2}y_{t-1} = (\pi_0 + \pi_1)y_{t-1} \tag{2.96}$$

and subtracting $\pi_0 E_{t-2} y_{t-1}$ from both sides results in

$$E_{t-1} y_t - E_{t-2} y_{t-1} = \left(\frac{\pi_0 + \pi_1}{\pi_0}\right)(y_{t-1} - E_{t-2} y_{t-1}) \tag{2.97}$$

That is

$$E_{t-1} y_t - E_{t-2} y_{t-1} = K(y_{t-1} - E_{t-2} y_{t-1}) \tag{2.98}$$

which is an adaptive expectations scheme of forecasting as seen in equation (1.12) above. Consequently if a series has the time-series representation of equation (2.92), then by appropriate choice of parameter (K) the adaptive expectations scheme can be rational. Interestingly, many series do appear to have this time-series representation (see, for example, Bomhoff, 1980).

Next consider a series with the following time-series representation (as obtained, for example, in equation (2.88))

$$y_t = (1 - \mu)\bar{y} + \mu y_{t-1} + \varepsilon_t \tag{2.99}$$

where $\quad 0 \leqslant \mu < 1 =$ a constant

Taking expectations at time t

$$E_t y_{t+1} = (1 - \mu)\bar{y} + \mu y_t \tag{2.100}$$

or

$$E_t y_{t+1} - y_t = (1 - \mu)(\bar{y} - y_t) \tag{2.101}$$

Equation (2.101) defines a regressive expectations adjustment mechanism (see equation (1.3)). In other words, if the mean or equilibrium value of y is above (below) the current level of y_t, then expectations of the future level are revised upwards (downwards). Consequently if the rational expectations solution for a variable has the time-series representation given by equation (2.99), a regressive expectations scheme for the variable, with suitable choice of parameter $(1 - \mu)$, will be rational.

2.10 Appendix 3: further example of the Muthian and Lucas solution methods

We now give another example of the Muthian and Lucas solution methods involving a slightly more complicated model. Consider the following, where the variables are defined as previously

$$y_t = C_t + I_t + G_t \tag{2.27}$$

$$C_t = cy_t + \varepsilon_t \tag{2.28}$$

$$I_t = d(E_{t-1} y_{t+1} - y_t) \tag{2.102}$$

$$G_t = fy_{t-1} \tag{2.103}$$

Comparing this with equations (2.27)–(2.30), the accelerator mechanism in equation (2.102) includes *future* rather than current expectations, and government expenditure in equation (2.103) depends on past output instead of being a constant. The reduced form of this model is

$$y_t = cy_t + d(E_{t-1}y_{t+1} - y_t) + fy_{t-1} + \varepsilon_t \tag{2.104}$$

We can rewrite equation (2.104) as

$$y_t = \alpha_0 E_{t-1}y_{t+1} + \alpha_1 y_{t-1} + u_t \tag{2.105}$$

where $\alpha_0 = d/(1 - c + d)$
$\alpha_1 = f/(1 - c + d)$
$u_t = \varepsilon_t/(1 - c + d)$

Assuming the Muthian solution, ignoring the mean value of $\bar{y}$ for ease of exposition

$$y_t = \sum_{i=0}^{\infty} \pi_i u_{t-i} \tag{2.37}$$

and equating coefficients on the errors, the coefficient of u_t gives

$$\pi_0 = 1 \tag{2.106}$$

u_{t-1} gives

$$\pi_1 = \alpha_0 \pi_2 + \alpha_1 \pi_0 \tag{2.107}$$

u_{t-2} gives

$$\pi_2 = \alpha_0 \pi_3 + \alpha_1 \pi_1 \tag{2.108}$$

and therefore

$$\alpha_0 \pi_i - \pi_{i-1} + \alpha_1 \pi_{i-2} = 0 \qquad \text{for } i \geqslant 2 \tag{2.109}$$

Equation (2.109) defines a second-order difference equation, and consequently has a solution (see Baumol, 1970)

$$\pi_i = A(\mu_1)^i + B(\mu_2)^i \tag{2.110}$$

where $A, B = $ constants, and
μ_1 and $\mu_2 = $ the roots of the quadratic equation (in μ)

$$\alpha_0 \mu^2 - \mu + \alpha_1 = 0 \tag{2.111}$$

Now equation (2.110) is simply a different but equivalent way of writing each of the conditions (2.107), (2.108) and in general (2.109). Consequently, the solution (equation (2.110)) must run from a value of i which implies the condition (2.107). Since the general equation (2.109) commences from a value which begins at π_0, so equation (2.110) must be valid for $i \geqslant 0$. The roots μ_1 and μ_2 are stable if their modulus is less than 1. The three possibilities are two unstable roots, one unstable and one stable root, or two stable roots. As our solution method rules out unstable roots by setting them to 0, we cannot have two unstable roots since equation (2.110) then puts $\pi_0 = 0$ which contradicts equation (2.106). Thus two unstable roots implies that the model is misspecified. Similarly, if two roots are stable there is a non-uniqueness problem. We therefore assume one stable root (μ_1, say) and one unstable root. For the solution of this model we therefore set μ_2 to 0, and equation (2.110) gives

$$\pi_i = A(\mu_1)^i \qquad \text{for } i \geqslant 0 \tag{2.112}$$

and hence

$$\pi_i = \pi_0(\mu_1)^i \qquad \text{for } i \geqslant 0$$

Conditions (2.106), (2.107) and (2.112), define the rational expectation solution for y_t, which is

$$y_t = \sum_{i=0}^{\infty} \mu_1^i u_{t-i} \tag{2.113}$$

Alternatively, using the Lucas method, we guess the solution to equation (2.105) as

$$y_t = Fy_{t-1} + Ju_t \tag{2.114}$$

where F and J = constants

From equation (2.114), taking expectations timed at $t-1$

$$E_{t-1}y_{t+1} = FE_{t-1}y_t \tag{2.115}$$

also

$$E_{t-1}y = Fy_{t-1} \tag{2.116}$$

and therefore, using the chain rule

$$E_{t-1}y_{t+1} = F^2 y_{t-1} \tag{2.117}$$

Substituting equation (2.117) into equation (2.105), we obtain

$$y_t = \alpha_0 F^2 y_{t-1} + \alpha_1 y_{t-1} + u_t \tag{2.118}$$

which can be written

$$y_t = (\alpha_0 F^2 + \alpha_1)y_{t-1} + u_t \tag{2.119}$$

Equating coefficients between equations (2.119) and (2.114), we obtain for y_{t-1}

$$F = \alpha_0 F^2 + \alpha_1 \tag{2.120}$$

which is equivalent to equation (2.111), and for u_t, $J = 1$.

The stable root for $F(|F| < 1)$ would be chosen from equation (2.120), and the result is that the solution given by the Lucas method is precisely the same as that from the Muthian method.

2.11   Appendix 4: model with incomplete current information

Suppose the behavioural equations are given by a variant of the basic model

$$y_t = C_t + I_t + G_t \tag{2.27}$$

$$C_t = cy_t + \varepsilon_t \tag{2.28}$$

$$I_t = d(E_t y_t - y_{t-1}) - eR_t \tag{2.121}$$

$$\bar{m} + m_t = p_t + y_t - fR_t \tag{2.122}$$

$$G_t = \bar{G}, \; p_t = \bar{p} \tag{2.123}$$

where R_t = the current interest rate

m_t, ε_t = both random variables with mean 0 and variances respectively σ_m^2 and σ_ε^2

p_t, the price level, is assumed fixed, as is government expenditure, G_t, and the mean level of money supply $\bar{m}$

$E_t y_t$ is the expectation of y_t conditional on an information set in which the only currently observed variable is R, and all other information has a one-period lag

As well as the different timing of expectations in equation (2.121) compared with equation (2.102), the investment function includes the nominal interest rate, as does the demand for money equation (2.122). The variables other than y and R can be eliminated by substituting equations (2.28), (2.121) and (2.122) into equation (2.27), to give

$$y_t = \alpha_0(E_t y_t - y_{t-1}) - \alpha_1 R_t + G^0 + \varepsilon_t / 1 - c \tag{2.124}$$

where $\alpha_0 = d/1 - c$, $\alpha_1 = e/1 - c$, $G^0 = \bar{G}/1 - c$

For simplicity, we assume $\bar{m} = \bar{p}$, and hence write equation (2.122) as

$$m_t = y_t - fR_t \tag{2.125}$$

The equations (2.124) and (2.125) are to be solved for y and R. We now suppose that R_t has a Muthian solution of the form

$$R_t = \bar{R} + \sum_{i=0}^{\infty} \pi_i \varepsilon_{t-i} + \sum_{i=0}^{\infty} \gamma_i m_{t-i} \tag{2.126}$$

where π_i and γ_i = constants to be determined from the model

We also assume that y_t has a Muthian solution of the same form

$$y_t = \bar{y} + \sum_{i=0}^{\infty} d_i \varepsilon_{t-i} + \sum_{i=0}^{\infty} h_i m_{t-i} \tag{2.127}$$

where d_i and h_i = constants to be determined from the model

From equation (2.126) and the information assumption, our optimal expectation of m_t and ε_t, given the observation of $R_t, \bar{R}$ and all previous errors, is

$$E(\varepsilon_t) = \frac{\phi}{\pi_0} (\pi_0 \varepsilon_t + \gamma_0 m_t) \tag{2.128}$$

$$E(m_t) = \frac{(1-\phi)}{\gamma_0} (\pi_0 \varepsilon_t + \gamma_0 m_t) \tag{2.129}$$

where $\phi = \dfrac{\pi_0^2 \sigma_\varepsilon^2}{\pi_0^2 \sigma_\varepsilon^2 + \gamma_0^2 \sigma_m^2}$

These use the fact that

$$\pi_0\varepsilon_t + \gamma_0 m_t = R_t - \bar{R} - \sum_{i=1}^{\infty} \pi_i\varepsilon_{t-i} - \sum_{i=1}^{\infty} \gamma_i m_{t-i}$$

is the unobserved part of equation (2.126). It follows from equations (2.127), (2.128) and (2.129) that

$$E_t y_t = \bar{y} + \frac{d_0\phi}{\pi_0}(\pi_0\varepsilon_t + \gamma_0 m_t) + \frac{h_0}{\gamma_0}(1-\phi)(\pi_0\varepsilon_t + \gamma_0 m_t)$$

$$+ \sum_{i=1}^{\infty} d_i\varepsilon_{t-i} + \sum_{i=1}^{\infty} h_i m_{t-i} \tag{2.130}$$

Substitution of equation (2.125) into equation (2.124) to eliminate R_t yields

$$y_t(1+\alpha_2) = \alpha_0(E_t y_t - y_{t-1}) + G^0 + \alpha_2 m_t + \frac{\varepsilon_t}{1-c} \tag{2.131}$$

where, for convenience, $\alpha_2 = \alpha_1/f$

We can now eliminate y and Ey from equation (2.131) by using equations (2.127) and (2.130). This gives an expression in ε and m. By equating coefficients, the constant term gives

$$\bar{y}(1+\alpha_2) = G^0 \tag{2.132}$$

The coefficient of ε_t is

$$d_0(1+\alpha_2) = \alpha_0\left(d_0\phi + \frac{h_0}{\gamma_0}(1-\phi)\pi_0\right) + \frac{1}{1-c} \tag{2.133}$$

that of ε_{t-1} is

$$d_1(1+\alpha_2) = \alpha_0(d_1 - d_0) \tag{2.134}$$

that of ε_{t-2} is

$$d_2(1+\alpha_2) = \alpha_0(d_2 - d_1) \tag{2.135}$$

and, for $i \geqslant 1$

$$d_i(1+\alpha_2-\alpha_0) = -\alpha_0 d_{i-1} \tag{2.136}$$

Similarly, m_t gives

$$h_0(1+\alpha_2) = \alpha_0\left(\gamma_0\frac{d_0}{\pi_0}\phi + h_0(1-\phi)\right) + \alpha_2 \tag{2.137}$$

and m_{t-1} gives

$$h_1(1+\alpha_2) = \alpha_0(h_1 - h_0) \tag{2.138}$$

and

$$h_i(1+\alpha_2-\alpha_0) = -\alpha_0 h_{i-1} \qquad \text{for } i \geqslant 1 \tag{2.139}$$

The same approach is applied to equation (2.125), where we substitute equations (2.126) and (2.127) to eliminate y and R, and obtain

$$m_t = \bar{y} + \sum_{i=0}^{\infty} d_i \varepsilon_{t-1} + \sum_{i=0}^{\infty} h_i m_{t-i}$$
$$- f \left(\bar{R} + \sum_{i=0}^{\infty} \pi_i \varepsilon_{t-i} + \sum_{i=0}^{\infty} \gamma_i m_{t-i} \right) \tag{2.140}$$

From equating coefficients on the constant ε_t and ε_{t-1}, we get

$$0 = \bar{y} - f\bar{R} \tag{2.141}$$
$$0 = d_0 - f\pi_0 \tag{2.142}$$
$$0 = d_1 - f\pi_1 \tag{2.143}$$

and

$$d_i = f\pi_i \qquad \text{for } i \geqslant 0 \tag{2.144}$$

Also from the coefficients on m_t and m_{t-i}

$$1 = h_0 - f\gamma_0 \tag{2.145}$$
$$0 = h_i - f\gamma_i \tag{2.146}$$

and

$$h_i = f\gamma_i \qquad \text{for } i \geqslant 1 \tag{2.147}$$

The various equations (2.132)–(2.147) are now to be solved for the unknown d_i and h_i. Using conditions (2.133) and (2.137) to eliminate ϕ, we obtain

$$d_0\gamma_0(1+\alpha_2) - \frac{1}{1-c}\gamma_0 = h_0\pi_0(1+\alpha_2) - \alpha_2\pi_0 \tag{2.148}$$

Using equation (2.142) for d_0 and equation (2.145) for h_0, substituting into equation (2.148) gives

$$\pi_0 = \frac{-1}{1-c}\gamma_0 \tag{2.149}$$

From equation (2.149) and the definition ϕ, we have immediately that

$$\phi = \frac{\sigma_\varepsilon^2}{\sigma_\varepsilon^2 + (1-c)^2\sigma_m^2} \tag{2.150}$$

Also, we can substitute into equation (2.137) from equation (2.142) for d_0/π_0 and from equation (2.145) for f, to obtain

$$h_0(1+\alpha_2) = \alpha_0((h_0-1)\phi + h_0(1-\phi)) + \alpha_2 \tag{2.151}$$

Rearranging equation (2.151) gives

$$h_0 = \frac{\alpha_2 - \alpha_0\phi}{1 + \alpha_2 - \alpha_0} = \frac{(e/f) - d\phi}{1 - c - d + (e/f)} \tag{2.152}$$

from using the definitions of α_0 and α_2. Thus h_0 is expressed in terms of the original parameters of the model in equations (2.27)–(2.28), (2.121)–(2.123). The solution for γ_0 immediately follows from equations (2.152) and (2.145). We obtain the solution for π_0 from equation (2.149), and that for d_0 by appropriate substitution in equation (2.133). From the values of d_0, h_0, π_0 and γ_0, the full solution is readily given by equations (2.126), (2.127), (2.136), (2.139), (2.144) and (2.147).

Next we consider the effect of the assumptions about the information set on the impact of shocks. In this model, the impact effect of a current monetary shock on output is given by h_0 (see equation (2.152)). If the information conditioning expectations were to be dated at $t-1$, then the impact effect using equation (2.131) with $E_{t-1}y_t$ replacing $E_t y_t$ becomes

$$h_0 = \alpha_2/(1 + \alpha_2) \tag{2.153}$$

Similarly, if agents have complete current information ($E_t y_t = y_t$), the impact coefficient is given by

$$h_0 = \alpha_2/(1 + \alpha_2 - \alpha_0) \tag{2.154}$$

It is clear from equations (2.152), (2.153) and (2.154) that for particular values of the parameters, the impact effect of a monetary shock can be quite different under the various information assumptions.

We now show how incomplete current information modifies the *ex post* serial-correlation properties of rational expectations. Our analysis is based on that of Minford and Peel (1983). Suppose the series to be forecast, y_t, which is not currently observed, is given the representation in equation (2.127). Thus

$$y_t = \bar{y} + \sum_{i=0}^{\infty} d_i \varepsilon_{t-i} + \sum_{i=0}^{\infty} h_i m_{t-i} \tag{2.127}$$

Suppose further that agents observe some current information given by R_t as in equation (2.126). The rational expectation of y_{t+1} will be

$$E_t y_{t+1} = \bar{y} + d_1 E_t(\varepsilon_t) + \sum_{i=2}^{\infty} d_i \varepsilon_{t-i+1} + h_1 E_t(m_t)$$

$$+ \sum_{i=2}^{\infty} h_i m_{t-i+1} \tag{2.155}$$

Now given observation of R_t and using the signal extraction formulae (2.128)–(2.129), we have that

$$E_t(\varepsilon_t) = \frac{\phi}{\pi_0} (\pi_0 \varepsilon_t + \gamma_0 m_t) \tag{2.128}$$

and

$$E_t(m_t) = \frac{(1 - \phi)}{\gamma_0} (\pi_0 \varepsilon_t + \gamma_0 m_t) \tag{2.129}$$

The difference between y_{t+1} and its expectation (equation (2.155)) is the forecast error

$$k_{t+1} = y_{t+1} - E_t y_{t+1} = d_0 \varepsilon_{t+1} + h_0 m_{t+1} + d_1(1 - \phi)\varepsilon_t + h_1 \phi m_t$$

$$- \frac{d_1 \gamma_0 \phi m_t}{\pi_0} - \frac{h_1 \pi_0 (1 - \phi)\varepsilon_t}{\gamma_0} \tag{2.156}$$

If we take expectations of two successive errors, we find that

$$E(k_{t+1}, k_t) = \frac{\sigma_\varepsilon^2 \sigma_m^2}{\pi_0^2 \sigma_\varepsilon^2 + \gamma_0^2 \sigma_m^2} (d_1\gamma_0 - h_1\pi_0)(d_0\gamma_0 - h_0\pi_0) \tag{2.157}$$

which is unlikely to be 0. Consequently, as noted in the main text, incomplete current information will add to the serial correlation of the *ex post* rational expectation forecast errors. In fact, in general there will be serial correlation up to the level of the forecast horizon -1 plus the lag on global information relevant for forecasting future values of y.

2.12 Appendix 5: solution of equation (2.78)

$$\varepsilon_t + \bar{m} + \rho\beta(P_{t-1} - E_{t-2}P_{t-1})$$
$$= P_t + b[\bar{y} + \beta(P_t - E_{t-1}P_t)]$$
$$- \frac{c}{\alpha}(1-T)\bar{y} - c(E_{t-1}P_{t+1} - E_{t-1}P_t) \tag{2.78}$$

The Muthian form of solution is

$$P_t = \bar{P} + \sum_{i=0}^{\infty} \pi_i \varepsilon_{t-i} \tag{2.79}$$

Lagging one period

$$P_{t-1} = \bar{P} + \sum_{i=0}^{\infty} \pi_i \varepsilon_{t-i-1} \tag{2.158}$$

Taking expectations timed at $t-2$

$$E_{t-2}P_{t-1} = \bar{P} + \sum_{i=1}^{\infty} \pi_i \varepsilon_{t-i-1} \tag{2.159}$$

since $E_{t-2}\varepsilon_{t-1} = 0$. Subtracting equation (2.159) from equation (2.158)

$$P_{t-1} - E_{t-2}P_{t-1} = \pi_0 \varepsilon_{t-1} \tag{2.160}$$

Taking expectations (timed at $t-1$) of equation (2.79)

$$E_{t-1}P_t = \bar{P} + \sum_{i=1}^{\infty} \pi_i \varepsilon_{t-i} \tag{2.161}$$

and subtracting equation (2.161) from equation (2.79) gives

$$P_t - E_{t-1}P_t = \pi_0 \varepsilon_t \tag{2.162}$$

Leading equation (2.79) one period

$$P_{t+1} = \bar{P} + \sum_{i=0}^{\infty} \pi_i \varepsilon_{t-i+1} \tag{2.163}$$

and taking expectations timed at $t-1$

$$E_{t-1}P_{t+1} = \bar{P} + \sum_{i=2}^{\infty} \pi_i \varepsilon_{t-i+1} \tag{2.164}$$

Subtracting equation (2.161) from equation (2.164) gives

$$E_{t-1}P_{t+1} - E_{t-1}P_t = \sum_{i=1}^{\infty} (\pi_{i+1} - \pi_i)\varepsilon_{t-i} \tag{2.165}$$

We can now substitute equations (2.160), (2.79), (2.162) and (2.165) directly into equation (2.78)

$$\varepsilon_t + \bar{m} + \rho\beta(\pi_0 \varepsilon_{t-1})$$

$$= \bar{P} + \sum_{i=0}^{\infty} \pi_i \varepsilon_{t-i} + b\bar{y}$$

$$+ b\beta(\pi_0 \varepsilon_t) - \frac{c}{\alpha}(1-T)\bar{y} - c\left(\sum_{i=1}^{\infty} (\pi_{i+1} - \pi_i)\varepsilon_{t-i}\right) \tag{2.166}$$

Rearranging this, and collecting terms together

$$\left(\bar{m} - \bar{P} - b\bar{y} + \frac{c}{\alpha}(1-T)\bar{y}\right) + \varepsilon_t(1 - \pi_0 - b\beta\pi_0)$$

$$+ \varepsilon_{t-1}(\rho\beta\pi_0 - \pi_1 + c(\pi_2 - \pi_1))$$

$$= \sum_{i=2}^{\infty} \varepsilon_{t-i}(\pi_i - c(\pi_{i+1} - \pi_i)) \tag{2.167}$$

The first term simplifies, using the definition of b

$$b = 1 + \frac{c}{\alpha}(1-T)$$

to $\bar{m} - \bar{P} - \bar{y}$, which, when set to 0 is

$$\bar{P} = \bar{m} - \bar{y} \tag{2.168}$$

and the coefficients of ε_t, ε_{t-1} and ε_{t-2} give

$$\pi_0(1 + b\beta) = 1 \tag{2.169}$$

$$\rho\beta\pi_0 = \pi_1 - c(\pi_2 - \pi_1) \tag{2.170}$$

$$0 = \pi_2 - c(\pi_3 - \pi_2) \tag{2.171}$$

and, in general

$$\pi_i = \frac{(1+c)}{c}\pi_{i-1} \qquad \text{for } i \geqslant 3 \tag{2.172}$$

Assuming that we rule out unstable roots, equation (2.172) implies (since $c > 0$) that $\pi_i = 0$ for $i > 1$. Consequently, from equations (2.169) and (2.170)

$$\pi_0 = 1/(1 + b\beta) \tag{2.173}$$

$$\pi_1 = \frac{\rho\beta}{(1+c)(1+b\beta)} \tag{2.174}$$

Also, from equation (2.79), using $\pi_i = 0$ for $i > 1$

$$P_t = \bar{P} + \pi_0\varepsilon_t + \pi_1\varepsilon_{t-1}$$

By taking expectations and subtraction

$$P_t - E_{t-1}P_t = \pi_0\varepsilon_t$$

Using this and equation (2.173) in equation (2.73) gives the following solution for output

$$y_t = \bar{y} + \frac{\beta}{1+b\beta}\varepsilon_t \quad \text{or} \quad y_t = \bar{y} + \frac{\beta}{1+b\beta}(m_t - E_{t-1}m_t) \tag{2.80}$$

2.13 Appendix 6: effects of a change in policy regime on time-series forecasts

Consider the model discussed earlier

$$y_t = C_t + I_t + G_t \tag{2.27}$$

$$C_t = cy_t + \varepsilon_t \tag{2.28}$$

$$I_t = d(E_{t-1}y_t - y_{t-1}) \tag{2.29}$$

$$G_t = \bar{G} \tag{2.30}$$

where   variables = defined as previously, and
         c and d = constants

The rational expectations solution for output in the model is

$$y_t = Ay_{t-1} + \frac{\bar{G}}{1-c-d} + \frac{\varepsilon_t}{1-c} \tag{2.175}$$

where

$$A = \frac{-e}{1-e} = \frac{-d}{1-c-d} \tag{2.176}$$

Let us assume that the policy regime defined by equation (2.30) has been in operation for a long time. If agents were to forecast output ($E_{t-1}y_t$) using time-series methods, and had discovered the ARIMA (1, 0, 0) representation (equation (2.175)), they would obtain good forecasts since equation (2.175) is obviously consistent with the model structure. Suppose now the authorities change their policy rule from equation (2.30) to

$$G_t = \bar{G} + \rho(y_{t-1} - \bar{y}) \tag{2.177}$$

where ρ = a constant

Substitution of equations (2.28), (2.29) and (2.177) into equation (2.27) gives

$$(1-c)y_t = dE_{t-1}y_t + (\rho-d)y_{t-1} + \bar{G} - \rho\bar{y} + \varepsilon_t \tag{2.178}$$

Taking expectations timed at $t-1$

$$(1-c)E_{t-1}y_t = dE_{t-1}y_t + (\rho-d)y_{t-1} + \bar{G} - \rho\bar{y}$$

and rearranging

$$E_{t-1}y_t = \frac{(\rho-d)y_{t-1}}{(1-c-d)} + \frac{(\bar{G}-\rho\bar{y})}{(1-c-d)} \tag{2.179}$$

Substituting equation (2.179) into equation (2.178) to eliminate the expectations term

$$(1-c)y_t = \frac{d(\rho-d)y_{t-1}}{(1-c-d)} + (\rho-d)y_{t-1} + \frac{d(\bar{G}-\rho\bar{y})}{(1-c-d)} + \bar{G} - \rho\bar{y} + \varepsilon_t$$

This can be rearranged to give

$$(1-c)y_t = \frac{(1-c)(\rho-d)y_{t-1}}{(1-c-d)} + \frac{(1-c)(\bar{G}-\rho\bar{y})}{(1-c-d)} + \varepsilon_t$$

This simplifies to

$$y_t = \frac{(\rho-d)}{(1-c-d)} y_{t-1} + \frac{(\bar{G}-\rho\bar{y})}{(1-c-d)} + \frac{\varepsilon_t}{1-c} \tag{2.180}$$

Comparing this with equation (2.175), both are ARIMA $(1, 0, 0)$ models but the parameters differ. If agents continue to use the original solution (equation (2.175)) with the new structure, then the actual path of output will be given by the solution of equations (2.27)–(2.29) and (2.177), with expectations from equation (2.175). Thus, taking expectations of equation (2.175) timed at $t-1$

$$E_{t-1}y_t = \frac{-d}{(1-c-d)} y_{t-1} + \frac{\bar{G}}{(1-c-d)} \tag{2.181}$$

Substituting equations (2.28), (2.29), (2.177) into equation (2.27) gives

$$y_t = cy_t + \varepsilon_t + d(E_{t-1}y_t - y_{t-1}) + \bar{G} + \rho(y_{t-1} - \bar{y})$$

and using equation (2.181)

$$(1-c)y_t = \varepsilon_t - \frac{d^2 y_{t-1}}{(1-c-d)} + \frac{d\bar{G}}{(1-c-d)} - dy_{t-1} + \bar{G} + \rho(y_{t-1} - \bar{y})$$

Collecting terms together with $\rho_1 = \rho(1-c-d)$

$$y_t = \frac{\varepsilon_t}{(1-c)} - \frac{(d-cd-\rho_1)y_{t-1}}{(1-c)(1-c-d)} + \frac{\bar{G}(1-c)-\rho_1\bar{y}}{(1-c-d)(1-c)} \tag{2.182}$$

This gives the actual path of output, and it differs from the time-series forecast (equation (2.175)). The forecast errors will therefore be *non-random*. To summarise this argument:

1. if the true model is equations (2.27)–(2.30), the solution is equation (2.175)
2. if the true model is equations (2.27)–(2.29) with (2.177), the solution is equation (2.180)

3. if the true model is equations (2.27)–(2.29) with (2.177), and agents form expectations using equation (2.175), then output follows equation (2.182) and forecasts from equation (2.175) (and also equation (2.180)) will be wrong.

2.14 Appendix 7: learning and the convergence to rational expectations

Consider a good with demand schedule as in equation (2.183) and supply schedule as in equation (2.184), where

$$Q_t = -\alpha_1 P_t + \alpha_2 X_t + u_t \tag{2.183}$$

$$Q_t = \beta_1 E_{t-1} P_t + \beta_2 Y_t + v_t \tag{2.184}$$

and Q and P are actual quantity and price, X and Y are exogenous variables, $E_{t-1} P$ is the expected price at t based on information at $t-1$, $\alpha_1, \alpha_2, \beta_1, \beta_2$ are parameters and u and v are independent random disturbances.

With market clearing, the reduced form for prices is

$$P_t = a E_{t-1} P_t + b X_t + c Y_t + w_t \tag{2.185}$$

where $a = -\beta_1/\alpha_1$, $b = \alpha_2/\alpha_1$, $c = -\beta_2/\alpha_1$, and $w = (u-v)/\alpha_1$

Treating X and Y as constants, the rational expectations solution of equation (2.185) is

$$E_{-1} P_t = \frac{b X_t + c Y_t}{1-a} \tag{2.186}$$

To illustrate the possibility of learning, suppose that agents believe that expectations are formed by

$$E_{t-1} P_t = d P_{t-1} + e X_t + f Y_t \tag{2.187}$$

where d, e and $f = $ constants

Expectations are thus partly adaptive, but include the correct exogenous variables (with incorrect weights). The actual evolution of prices is then given by combining equation (2.187) with equation (2.185), so that

$$P_t = a d P_{t-1} + (ae + b) X_t + (af + c) Y_t + w_t \tag{2.188}$$

Thus equation (2.188) differs from equation (2.187) in the values of the parameters. De Canio (1979) investigates the effects of agents realising that equation (2.187) is incorrect and modifying their expectations to be based on equation (2.188). Thus

$$E_{t-1} P_t = a d P_{t-1} + (ae + b) X_t + (af + c) Y_t \tag{2.189}$$

However, if this is the way expectations are formed then, combining equation (2.189) with equation (2.185), the (new) actual path of prices will be

$$P_t = a^2 d P_{t-1} + (a^2 e + ab + b) X_t + (a^2 f + ac + c) Y_t + w_t \tag{2.190}$$

which again differs from the assumed expectations mechanism (equation (2.189)). The agents will eventually realise that equation (2.189) is incorrect, and base their expectations on equation (2.190), so that

$$E_{t-1}P_t = a^2 dP_{t-1} + (a^2 e + ab + b)X_t + (a^2 f + ac + c)Y_t \qquad (2.191)$$

which combines with equation (2.185) to give the new actual path of prices.

This process of agents modifying their expectations, the actual path of prices changing, and agents again modifying their expectations continues, and after n such steps expectations are given by

$$E_{t-1}P_t = a^n dP_{t-1} + [a^n e + b(1 + a + a^2 + \ldots + a^{n-1})]X_t$$
$$+ [a^n f + c(1 + a + \ldots + a^{n-1})]Y_t \qquad (2.192)$$

For convergence $|a| < 1$, and as n tends to infinity a^n tends to 0 and

$$1 + a + a^2 + a^3 + \ldots = \frac{1}{(1-a)}$$

so that

$$E_{t-1}P_t = \frac{bX_t}{(1-a)} + \frac{cY_t}{(1-a)}$$

which is the rational expectations solution in equation (2.186). If $|a| > 1$ then this convergence to rational expectations does not occur. The critical assumptions for convergence are thus the agents' prior belief on how expectations are formed (equation (2.187), above), the value of the parameter a and the way agents learn to modify their expectations generation process. Should any of these be inappropriate, there will be no convergence to the rational expectations solution.

3

Survey Evidence on Expectations Formation

3.1 Test procedures

We now turn to the results of surveys of expectations. As outlined in
1.2 above, there are a large number of surveys of agents' views about
the future. While many are limited to the expected change in
consumer prices, others refer to wholesale prices, wages or interest
rates. In this chapter we review ways of testing for the various
expectations mechanisms described in chapters 1 and 2, and then go
on to consider the evidence from a number of individual surveys to see
which explanations are supported by the data. Surveys are the only
way of measuring expectations directly and so, while we must bear in
mind the various weaknesses discussed in 1.2 above, they can still
provide evidence in favour of (or against) the alternative expectations
mechanisms. One particular area of interest is the rational expectations hypothesis. As was seen in chapter 2, this hypothesis has many
attractions, and immediately raises the question of whether it is an
accurate description of agents' actions. Much of the literature on
expectations surveys has tried to answer this question, as we will see
below. First, however, we will look at the techniques available for
assessing the evidence.

The rational expectations hypothesis has several implications. One
is that, on average, agents' expectations have the same mean as the
actual outcomes. In our exposition we will refer to expectations about
inflation but, of course, the same approach applies generally.

We will also consider initially expectations over a one-period horizon before going on to the multi-period horizon case. If we let $E_t P_{t+1}$ be the expectation formed at time t, of the rate of inflation from t to $t+1$, and let P_{t+1} be the actual rate of inflation from t to $t+1$ (so that P_{t+1} is backward-looking), then equation (2.12) can be written

$$P_{t+1} = E_t P_{t+1} + \varepsilon_t \tag{3.1}$$

where $\varepsilon_t =$ a random residual which, under the rational expectations hypothesis, will be white noise

This is known as the *unbiasedness* property, and is usually tested by estimating the regression equation

$$P_{t+1} = \alpha + \beta E_t P_{t+1} + \varepsilon_t \tag{3.2}$$

Two tests are then performed – the first to see whether the observed equivalent of ε_t (say, e_t) are white noise, and the second to check the joint hypothesis $\alpha = 0$ and $\beta = 1$. There are various ways of testing for white noise. As we saw in 1.6 above, white noise is defined as a random variable with a mean of 0, a constant variance and 0 covariances. The least-squares method ensures that the mean of e_t is 0. Tests for a constant variance, such as the Goldfeld–Quandt test (see Pindyck and Rubinfeld, 1981, pp. 148–9) are seldom reported because the number of observations on expectations series is generally limited, giving the tests low power. If covariances are divided by the variance then autocorrelations result, so a test for 0 autocorrelations is equivalent to one for 0 covariances. The usual test for first-order autocorrelation (or correlation between ε_t and ε_{t-1}) is the Durbin–Watson statistic

$$DW = \frac{\sum (e_t - e_{t-1})^2}{\sum e_t^2} \tag{3.3}$$

which has a mean value of 2 in the absence of autocorrelation. If the observed value of DW lies in the rejection region, the hypothesis of no first-order autocorrelation is rejected. Formally the hypothesis is that ρ_1, the first-order autocorrelation coefficient, is 0. A more general test of the first K autocorrelations $\rho_1 \rho_2 \ldots \rho_K$ is provided by the Box–Pierce statistic

$$BP = n \sum_1^K r_i^2 \tag{3.4}$$

where $n =$ the number of observations in the series, and
$r_i =$ the estimate of ρ_i

If the autocorrelations up to order K are all 0, then BP has approximately a chi-squared distribution with K degrees of freedom. This test requires n to be large, and it is usually recommended that K be 15 or 20, which limits its usefulness for short series. Further, several alternative versions of equation (3.4) have been suggested to improve the closeness of the approximation to the chi-squared distribution.

Ljung and Box (1978), for example, suggest using

$$Q = n(n+2) \sum_{i=1}^{K} (n-i)^{-1} r_i^2 \tag{3.4a}$$

in place of equation (3.4).

The second test of equation (3.2) is of the joint hypothesis $\alpha = 0$ and $\beta = 1$. If ε_t is white noise, then a standard F-test (see, for example, Johnston, 1972, pp. 28–9) can be used and, putting $X = E_t p_{t+1}$

$$F_0 = \frac{(n\hat{\alpha}^2 + 2n\bar{X}\hat{\alpha}(\hat{\beta}-1) + \sum X^2)(\hat{\beta}-1)^2/2}{\sum e^2/(n-2)} \tag{3.5}$$

which has an F-distribution with 2 and $n-2$ degrees of freedom if the joint hypothesis is true. Here $\hat{\alpha}$ and $\hat{\beta}$ are the least-squares estimators of α and β, and $\bar{X}$ is the mean of $E_t P_{t+1}$. If the observed value of F_0 exceeds the critical value, the hypothesis will be rejected and the survey-based expectation will be a biased estimate of the actual rate of inflation.

Next we examine what happens when the forecast horizon is more than one time period. Suppose, for example, that data are available quarterly and the expectation formed at time t refers to the year ahead from period $t-t+4$. The unbiasedness property requires modification since, as was shown by equation (2.15), successive forecast errors will be correlated and the error in, for example

$$P_{t+4} = E_t P_{t+4} + \varepsilon_t \tag{3.6}$$

will not be white noise. This can easily be seen by considering two successive observations and splitting the four-quarter error term into its four components. For example

$$P_5 = E_1 P_5 + (\varepsilon_1' + \varepsilon_2' + \varepsilon_3' + \varepsilon_4') \tag{3.7}$$

where $\varepsilon_i' =$ the error for period $i-i+1$
Also

$$P_6 = E_2 P_6 + (\varepsilon_2' + \varepsilon_3' + \varepsilon_4' + \varepsilon_5') \tag{3.8}$$

It is clear that the errors in equations (3.7) and (3.8) will be correlated, and more generally, the error at time t will be correlated with the errors at $t+1, t+2$ and $t+3$, but not $t+4$ when a four-period horizon is used. Thus the requirement that ε_t in equation (3.1) is white noise is replaced by the new requirement that in equation (3.6) ε_t will have 0 autocorrelations of order 4 or higher, but may have non-0 auto-correlations of order 1, 2 or 3. This readily generalises for an s-period horizon to

$$P_{t+s} = E_t P_{t+s} + \varepsilon_t \tag{3.9}$$

where   the rational expectations hypothesis requires autocorrelations of order s or higher to be 0

The Box–Pierce statistic (equation (3.4)) can be modified to test the hypothesis that $\rho_s \rho_{s+1} \ldots \rho_K$ are all 0. In this case

$$BP^* = n \sum_{s}^{K} r_i^2 \tag{3.10}$$

has approximately a chi-squared distribution with $K - s$ degrees of freedom.

Problems occur with the estimation of the multi-period version of equation (3.2). It might appear that estimating this subject to an appropriate moving-average error term will allow unbiasedness to be tested. However, McDonald and Darroch (1983) show that such estimators will be inconsistent (that is, even with a very large sample the average values of $\hat{\alpha}$ and $\hat{\beta}$ will differ from α and β) if the disturbances ε_t' are aggregates of other disturbances – as when there are random shocks in goods, money and labour markets. In these circumstances Brown and Maital (1981) suggest using ordinary least squares to get consistent estimates of α and β, and then use the methods of Hansen and Hodrick (1980) to estimate the variances. Unbiasedness can then be tested.

The property of unbiasedness is really a minimal requirement for expectations to be rational. It is necessary, but not sufficient, since the rational expectations hypothesis also requires *efficiency*. This was defined formally in equation (2.16). It means that the expectations must utilise *all the relevant information available* at the time they are formed. If this were not the case, their accuracy could be improved by using the extra information.

The difficulty in testing for efficiency is in defining the 'relevant' information. Pesando (1975) suggests that the past history of inflation is an obvious component of the relevant information, and proposes a test based on the regressions

$$P_{t+1} = \beta_0 + \sum_{i=1}^{N} \beta_i P_{t-i+1} + \varepsilon_t \tag{3.11}$$

$$E_t P_{t+1} = \beta'_0 + \sum_{i=1}^{N} \beta'_i P_{t-i+1} + \varepsilon'_t \tag{3.12}$$

where N = an appropriate lag

In equation (3.11), actual inflation is related to its past values while in equation (3.12) the inflation expectations are related to past actual inflation. If the inflation expectations utilise all the information contained in past inflation, then the coefficients in equations (3.11) and (3.12) will be the same, and the null hypothesis of efficiency is

$$H_0: \beta_i = \beta'_i \qquad \text{for } i = 0, \dots N \tag{3.13}$$

which can be tested by a Chow (1960) test. This requires three regressions to be estimated – equations (3.11) and (3.12), and a pooled regression in which the dependent variable consists of the observations on P_{t+1} and also those on $E_t P_{t+1}$. Let the residual sum of squares from these regressions be respectively $RSS(1)$, $RSS(2)$ and $RSS(3)$, then the appropriate test uses the statistic

$$F = \frac{(RSS(3) - RSS(1) - RSS(2))/(N+1)}{(RSS(1) + RSS(2))/(2n - 2N - 2)} \tag{3.14}$$

which under the hypothesis in equation (3.13) has an F-distribution with $(N+1, 2n-2N-2)$ degrees of freedom, where n is the number of observations in the series and N is the number of lags in equations (3.11) and (3.12). A large value of F leads to a rejection of the hypothesis, and hence of the property of 'efficiency'.

There are two aspects of this test which are of interest. The first is that the omission of variables from equations (3.11) and (3.12) leads to the same bias in both sets of estimated coefficients and so the test is still valid. This was pointed out by Friedman (1980). Second, Mullineaux (1978) argues that the error variance in equation (3.11) is larger than that in equation (3.12) under rational expectations, since the error in equation (3.11) has both a systematic and random component whilst that in equation (3.12) has only the random one.

This heteroscedasticity invalidates the Chow test. Mullineaux suggests that an alternative approach is to subtract equation (3.12) from equation (3.11), to give

$$P_{t+1} - E_t P_{t+1} = \beta_0 - \beta'_0 + \sum_1^N (\beta_i - \beta'_i) P_{t-i+1} + (\varepsilon_t - \varepsilon'_t)$$

(3.15)

and, for efficiency, all the estimated coefficients on the right-hand side will be insignificant. In equation (3.15), the dependent variable is the error in the expectation. The significance test is performed by comparing the residual sum of squares from equation (3.15) – $RSS(1)$, say – with that of the dependent variable – $RSS(2)$, say – and

$$F = \frac{(RSS(2) - RSS(1))/(N+1)}{RSS(1)/(n-N-1)}$$

(3.16)

has an F-distribution with $(N+1, n-N-1)$ degrees of freedom. A large value of F leads to the hypothesis of efficiency being rejected.

These tests of efficiency easily generalise for an s-period forecast horizon. An obvious modification also allows forecasts for different periods to be related. In the case of a two-period horizon, if forecasts for both one and two periods ahead are available then, following equation (3.12), we have

$$E_{t-1} P_{t+1} = \beta''_0 + \beta''_1 E_{t-1} P_t + \sum_2^N \beta''_i P_{t-i+1} + \varepsilon''_t$$

(3.17)

and subtracting equation (3.17) from equation (3.12) gives

$$E_t P_{t+1} - E_{t-1} P_{t+1}$$
$$= \beta'_0 - \beta''_0 - \beta'_1 P_t - \beta''_1 E_{t-1} P_t + \sum_2^N (\beta'_i - \beta''_i) P_{t-i+1} + \varepsilon'_t - \varepsilon''_t$$

(3.18)

The property of *consistency*, as Mullineaux (1978) calls it, is satisfied if all $\beta'_i = \beta''_i$, so that equation (3.18) reduces to

$$E_t P_{t+1} - E_{t-1} P_{t+1} = \beta'_1 (P_t - E_{t-1} P_t) + \varepsilon'_t - \varepsilon''_t$$

(3.19)

This is tested by estimating equation (3.18) to give the residual sum of squares $RSS(1)$, and equation (3.19) to give $RSS(2)$, and the resulting F-statistic is equation (3.16). In equation (3.19) the way in which an expectation is revised depends only on new information. Notice the similarity to the adaptive expectations model (equations (1.12), above).

An alternative interpretation of efficiency is the property of *orthogonality* of the errors to information which is available at minimal cost. Friedman (1980) explains that the test of efficiency resulting from equations (3.11) and (3.12) relates to autoregressive structures. But rational expectations are efficient in the wider sense that errors in expectations will be due to unpredictable shocks, and so will be unrelated to any information freely available. Orthogonality between the errors and an information set I_t can thus be checked by the regression

$$P_{t+1} - E_t P_{t+1} = \beta_0 + \sum_{i=1}^{N} \beta_i I_{t-i+1} + \varepsilon_t \tag{3.20}$$

and testing the joint hypothesis $\beta_i = 0$ by the F-test as in equation (3.16). Friedman suggests using relevant macroeconomic variables as elements of I. Obviously, equation (3.15) results if I consists solely of past inflation rates. Figlewski and Wachtel (1981) say that one important variable in I is the most recent forecast error, so that equation (3.20) becomes

$$P_{t+1} - E_t P_{t+1} = \beta_0 + \beta_1 (E_{t-1} P_t - P_t) + \varepsilon_t \tag{3.21}$$

Again, these tests readily generalise to the s-period horizon case.

Yet another interpretation of the efficiency property – known as *relative efficiency* – is the way the expectations series performs relative to time-series models. If the expectations series efficiently utilises all the available information, it should be a better predictor than a time-series model, and so should have a smaller error variance.

So far we have been concerned with testing whether survey-based expectations data satisfy the rational expectations hypothesis. However, it is also interesting to examine the alternative mechanisms discussed in chapter 1 to see if they provide an adequate explanation of the data. The most commonly-used models are the extrapolative (equation (1.6)), the simple adaptive (equation (1.12)) and the generalised adaptive (equation (1.23)). These three are presented in Table 3.1, along with a summary of the different tests for rational expectations, limited to the one-period forecast horizon.

Next we turn to the application of these expectations formations models to particular survey results. We will consider first the Livingston data, which has attracted most attention in the literature,

Table 3.1 Summary of expectations formation tests

A Tests of rational expectations hypothesis (REH) (with one-period forecast horizon)

1 Unbiasedness

$$P_{t+1} = \alpha + \beta E_t P_{t+1} + \varepsilon_t \tag{3.2}$$

REH requires $\alpha = 0$, $\beta = 1$ and ε to be white noise

2 Efficiency

(a)
$$P_{t+1} = \beta_0 + \sum_{i=1}^{N} \beta_i P_{t-i+1} + \varepsilon_t \tag{3.11}$$

$$E_t P_{t+1} = \beta'_0 + \sum_{i=1}^{N} \beta'_i P_{t-i+1} + \varepsilon'_t \tag{3.12}$$

REH requires $\beta_i = \beta'_i$ for all i

(b)
$$P_{t+1} - E_t P_{t+1} = (\beta_0 - \beta'_0) + \sum_{1}^{N} (\beta_i - \beta'_i) P_{t-i+1} + \varepsilon_t - \varepsilon'_t \tag{3.15}$$

REH requires $\beta_i = \beta'_i$ for all i

3 Orthogonality

$$P_{t+1} - E_t P_{t+1} = \beta_0 + \sum_{i=1}^{N} \beta_i I_{t-i+1} + \varepsilon_t \tag{3.20}$$

REH requires $\beta_i = 0$ for all i

B Alternative expectations mechanisms

1 Generalised extrapolative

$$E_t P_{t+1} = \sum_{i=0}^{N} \beta_i P_{t-i} + \varepsilon_t \tag{1.6}$$

2 Simple adaptive

$$E_t P_{t+1} - E_{t-1} P_t = (1 - \lambda)(P_t - E_{t-1} P_t) + \varepsilon_t \tag{1.12}$$

3 Generalised adaptive

$$E_t P_{t+1} = \sum_{i=1}^{N} \alpha_i E_{t-i} P_{t-i+1} + \sum_{i=0}^{N} \beta_i P_{t-i} \tag{1.23}$$

and then examine consumer and business expectations, econometric forecasts, wage, interest rate and finally money supply expectations.

3.2   The Livingston series

In 1.3 above, we gave details of the Livingston inflation expectations series, and mentioned some of the problems of interpretation. The fact that the respondents include leading academic economists in America means that the series has been the focus of attention by the profession – a large number of articles have been written attempting to check whether the series is rational, or whether another model of expectations formation is more appropriate. Much of this work has either not used the original data, or has ignored the multi-period time-horizon complications.

Here we will concentrate on two studies which attempt to deal with these various problems. The first is by Brown and Maital (1981), and uses the results of the survey averaged across the panel membership. Both half-year and full-year forecasts of inflation are analysed. The second study is that of Figlewski and Wachtel (1981), which uses the original individual responses (rather than averages) to examine both the time-series and cross-section behaviour of the expectations. The references at the end of these two papers list the other important research work on the Livingston data.

Brown and Maital take data for 1961–77, and perform various tests of the rational expectations hypothesis. In testing for unbiasedness they recognise the problem of the time horizon and its effect (as in equation (3.9)) on the random error. For the six-month forecast they expect the error term to be a first-order moving-average process since the forecast for, say, January–June is made in October or November, so the forecast error of the July–December prediction is not known. Similarly, when the twelve-month forecasts are made, neither of the two previous errors are known so a second-order moving-average error process is expected. They therefore estimate equation (3.9) subject to the moving-average process, and their results for the six-month forecast for consumer prices is

$$P_{t+2} = 0.99 + 0.91 E_t P_{t+2} \qquad (3.22)$$
$$(1.3) \quad (5.4)$$

with $\varepsilon_t = w_t + 0.2 w_{t-1}$

where   the numbers in parentheses $= t$-values

        $w =$ a white-noise disturbance

Their estimation method for the parameters is ordinary least squares, but the variances are estimated by generalised least squares because of the moving-average errors. The hypothesis of unbiasedness is accepted for equation (3.22). The result for the twelve-month forecast is

$$P_{t+4} = 0.97 + 1.01 E_t P_{t+4} \qquad (3.23)$$
$$\phantom{P_{t+4} = }(0.9) \quad (4.0)$$

with $\varepsilon_t = w_t + 0.92 w_{t-1} - 0.44 w_{t-2}$

Again the hypothesis of unbiasedness is accepted, so that the averaged Livingston data satisfy this aspect of the rational expectations hypothesis.

The second test applied by Brown and Maital is the orthogonality test (equation (3.20)), generalised for the forecast horizon. For the information set I_t, the variables used were lagged values of the percentage changes in money supply, public interest-bearing debt, consumer prices and wholesale prices, and the levels of weekly wages, industrial production, business investment and the unemployment rate. For the six-month forecasts (with a first-order moving-average error as in equation (3.22)), only the growth in money supply was significant but it was enough to lead to the rejection of the orthogonality property. This was confirmed with the twelve-month forecasts where both changes in money supply and wholesale prices were significant.

Brown and Maital perform these tests for eight other expectations series from the Livingston survey, and conclude that, in general, the unbiasedness property was accepted but orthogonality rejected. The presence of under-utilised information thus did not support the rational expectations hypothesis.

Figlewski and Wachtel (1981) prefer to examine the individual responses in Livingston's survey so that the distribution of inflation expectations across respondents and the differences between them can be analysed. For the period 1947–75 more than 100 individuals took part in the survey. Responses were included in the data set only if the previous survey had been answered, in order that changes in expectations could be obtained. This gave 1 864 observations. The authors focus on the six-months ahead forecasts, and define their 'actual' rate of inflation to be the change in prices from October–April for the December surveys, rather than the December–June change. This is because they want to make sure the actual rate of inflation *known to respondents* is being used. The effect of this is to remove the time-horizon problem (if their procedure is accepted as valid). The ordinary least-squares estimate of equation (3.2) showed widely differing residual variances for different time periods. The authors then re-estimated the equation using weighted least squares, where each observation is divided by the standard error of the residuals for that time period, and obtained

$$P_{t+1} = 1.017 + 0.772 E_t P_{t+1} \qquad R^2 = 0.54 \qquad (3.24)$$
$$\quad (36.3) \quad (55.1)$$

where   the numbers in parentheses $=$ t-values
$R^2 =$ the multiple correlation coefficient

The hypothesis of unbiasedness is rejected. Next, Figlewski and Wachtel perform the orthogonality test (equation (3.20)), using the previous period forecast error as the information set I. The estimated equation is

$$E_t P_{t+1} - P_{t+1} = -0.898 + 0.297(E_{t-1} P_t - P_t) \qquad (3.25)$$
$$\qquad (14.3) \quad (15.4)$$
$$R^2 = 0.113$$

Here the intercept term and slope coefficients are both significant, so that information contained in past forecast errors is not fully utilised in forming the expectation. The rational expectations hypothesis is therefore rejected.

The simple adaptive model (equation (1.12)) is estimated by Figlewski and Wachtel with a constant term included to give

$$E_t P_{t+1} - E_{t-1} P_t = -0.386 + 0.362(P_t - E_{t-1} P_t) \qquad (3.26)$$
$$\qquad (8.2) \quad (25.2)$$
$$R^2 = 0.54$$

and the constant term is significant. The authors re-estimate equation (1.12) using the mean expectation for each time period, and obtain a similar result but with smaller coefficients. They also test whether the adaptive parameter ($(1 - \lambda)$ in equation (1.12)) is constant for different individuals and different time periods. They find that it does in fact vary between individuals, and over different time periods, so that the restricted model in equation (1.12) is unsatisfactory.

Finally, they use the Livingston series to test a version of regressive expectations which is based on equation (1.3), but includes P^N, the actual long-run 'normal' inflation rate. This is defined as the mean inflation rate over the five years prior to the survey. The estimated equation is

$$E_t P_{t+1} - P_t = -1.302 + 0.451(P_t^N - P_t) \qquad (3.27)$$
$$(23.9) \quad (19.8)$$
$$R^2 = 0.175$$

This equation is satisfactory, but when the parameters are allowed to vary between individuals and for different time periods, equation (3.27) is rejected in favour of the more flexible version. Examining the adjustment parameter (the equivalent of θ in equation (1.3)), they find that in the majority of cases it is either negative (implying the inflation rate is expected to move away from the 'normal' rate) or greater than unity (implying overshooting the 'normal' rate). The authors therefore reject their regressive expectations model.

Figlewski and Wachtel conclude that the Livingston data on individuals are inconsistent with rational expectations because of the presence of biases and the serial correlation of the forecast errors, and that a flexible adaptive expectations model is more appropriate.

Comparing the results of these two papers, it is clear that the treatment of the data has important implications for their conclusions. Brown and Maital, using averaged data, and providing an explicit allowance for the time-horizon problem, obtain weak support for the rational expectations hypothesis. Figlewski and Wachtel, using individual data and considering only six month-ahead forecasts, reject the rational expectations formulation. The crucial importance of the assumptions made in empirical studies is emphasised by these results.

3.3 Consumers' expectations data

Now we consider expectations of consumers – the Carlson–Parkin series for the UK, the Survey of Consumer Finances (University of Michigan) for the USA, the Institute of Applied Economic and Social Research (IAESR) University of Melbourne series for Australia, and the EEC Consumer Survey. As we saw in 1.2 and 1.3 above, the Carlson–Parkin series is derived from the responses of consumers to a question about whether prices will go up, stay the same, or go down, over the next six months. Before turning to models of expectations formation some points about the series require clarification. The technique used by Carlson and Parkin requires an assumption about the difference limen (*a* in 1.2, above). They chose *a* so as to make the average expected inflation figure equal the average actual inflation figure over their data period; the effect of this is that their expected inflation series is unbiased, so that equation (3.2) cannot provide evidence of rationality. The second point about this series is that while the question refers to 'the next six months', the published series is at an *annual* rate. In order to compare actual and expected inflation, the same time horizon should be used. Carlson and Parkin use a twelve-month change for the actual inflation series, whereas it might be argued a six-month change is more appropriate. Alternatively, if consumers interpret the question as to mean the next six months, allowing for seasonal fluctuations, the authors' interpretation may be correct. Third, unlike the Livingston series and the surveys to be discussed in the rest of this chapter, the respondents are a stratified quota sample, rather than a panel. It is thus very unlikely that the same respondent will answer two consecutive monthly questions. Any interpretation of adaptive expectations as an error-learning mechanism must be viewed with caution; the respondents would not know the previous month's expected inflation figure, so could not adapt to it. Similarly, the information set of respondents could not include lagged values of expected inflation.

Carlson and Parkin attempt to explain their series by means of adaptive models. They consider the simple adaptive form (equation (1.12)) and second-order model (equation (1.13)), which they estimate in the unrestricted form (equation (1.23)). For their full data period 1961–73 they find there is severe autocorrelation for both adaptive models, even when a dummy variable is introduced to allow for the effects of the devaluation in November 1967. When the data are split into the low-inflation period 1961–June 1967, and the high-inflation period July 1967–1973, they find the autocorrelation disappears, and the results are rather different. For the low-inflation period, lagged actual inflation has no impact on expectations, while for the high-inflation period both lagged actual and lagged expected inflation has an impact. They conclude that these are satisfactory models of expectations formation.

Carlson and Parkin did not attempt to test the rationality of their series, but they provided enough information for some of the tests to be carried out. Our own estimate of equation (3.2) with a fifth-order moving-average error (because of the six-month horizon) gave values of 5.3 and 0.007 for α and β, and a significant value for BP^* (see equation (3.10)) for autocorrelations 6–24. The estimates of α and β differ from 0 and 1 because observations are lost when a moving-average error is estimated. There is no support for the unbiasedness property, even though the expectations are scaled (as explained above).

Next we estimated equation (3.15) with three lagged values of actual inflation, and a fifth-order moving-average error. The F-test (equation (3.16)) gives a highly significant result, so that the hypothesis of efficiency is rejected. The expectations of inflation could have been improved by taking account of *past* inflation.

Our conclusion from these tests is that the Carlson and Parkin data do not support the rational expectations hypothesis.

The US Survey of Consumer Finances gives a directly-observed quantitative expectations series which has been tested for rationality by Gramlich (1983). Estimation of equation (3.2) for 1956–80 led to the rejection of $\alpha = 0$ and $\beta = 1$ using the F-test (equation (3.5)). Also, severe first-order autocorrelation, measured by the Durbin–Watson statistic (equation (3.3)), showed a non-randomness of residuals. Gramlich concludes that this series is not rational.

In the IAESR survey the original question is qualitative, asking whether prices will rise, stay the same, or fall, over the next twelve months. But if a price change is expected, a further question asks for a percentage estimate. The series results from the quarterly mean levels of consumer price expectations from this data. As the series is quarterly, a four-period ahead forecast horizon is implied, and so non-randomness of residuals up to third order is expected. Horne (1981) tests the IAESR series (also referred to as the Defris–Williams series) for rationality. Using quarterly data for 1974–80, the unbiasedness test gives

$$P_{t+4} = 10.6 + 0.1 E_{t-4} P_t \qquad (3.28)$$
$$(2.99) \ (0.4)$$
$$\bar{R}^2 = -0.13, \ DW4 = 0.98,$$
$$F = 1\,235$$

where $DW4 =$ the fourth-order equivalent of equation (3.3)
             F is from equation (3.5) and tests $\alpha = 0$ and $\beta = 1$

The hypothesis of unbiasedness is rejected. Horne then proceeds to add extra variables to equation (3.28) to test for efficiency. The argument is that if extra information significantly improves the fit, then the expectations series is inefficient. The function to be estimated is thus

$$P_{t+4} = \alpha + \beta E_{t-4} P_t + \gamma I_t + \varepsilon_t \tag{3.29}$$

where I = the information set and if $\gamma = 0$ the expectations series is efficient

Comparing equation (3.29) with the orthogonality test (equation (3.20)), the two are equivalent if $\alpha = 0$ and $\beta = 1$. The test proposed by Horne is therefore more general than the orthogonality test. Horne tries a number of variables as the information set including lagged values of inflation, monetary growth (M), growth of government spending, growth in nominal wages, growth of import prices, unemployment and a dummy variable for wage awards from 1975 (Z). The preferred specification is

$$P_{t+4} = 7.05 + 0.17 E_{t-4} P_t + 0.34 M_{t-5} - 0.17 M_{t-6}$$
$$(2.97) \ (1.08) \qquad (2.35) \qquad (0.85)$$

$$+ 0.32 M_{t-7} - 0.15 M_{t-8} - 2.62 Z_{t-4} \tag{3.30}$$
$$(1.40) \qquad (1.00) \qquad (2.68)$$
$$\bar{R}^2 = 0.70, \ DW4 = 2.21$$

The extra variables have increased the degree of explanation, compared with equation (3.28), so that the efficiency property is rejected.

   It is also clear that $\alpha = 0$ and $\beta = 1$ is not satisfied. The predictions from equations (3.28) and (3.30) are compared with the actual inflation rate by Horne in a graph, and the improvement of equation (3.30) over equation (3.28) is considerable. Horne concludes that the IAESR series of expected inflation is not rational, and that the forecasts of inflation could be improved by including economic variables.

   Defris and Williams (1979a) also investigate the properties of the IAESR series, but over the shorter period 1973–7, giving a maximum of twenty observations. They do not consider the time-horizon problem (and, in fact, with so few observations would have had difficulty dealing with it). They fit various forms of equation (1.6), and choose as the best

$$E_t P_{t+4} = 6.59 + 0.58 P_{t-1} \qquad (3.31)$$
$$(3.34) \ (3.84)$$
$$\bar{R}^2 = 0.43, \ DW = 1.77$$

where $\quad P_{t-1} = $ the most recently-available measure of inflation

Next, they estimate the simple adaptive model (equation (1.12)), with an intercept term which is not significant, and find that the adjustment coefficient is not significantly different from unity. Unrestricted estimation (as in equation (1.23)) gives a poorer fit than in equation (3.31), so the simpler model is preferred. They find some support for a modified form of the second-order error-learning process (equation (1.13))

$$E_t P_{t+4} = \beta_0 + \beta_1 P_{t-1} + \beta_2 (P_{t-2} - E_{t-2} P_{t+2}) \qquad (3.32)$$

but note that the line-up of expectations and actuals in the final term is incorrect. Defris and Williams go on to examine the influence of other economic variables and measures of consumer sentiment (such as the percentage of respondents who regard the current level of inflation as serious). They conclude that expectations are determined mainly by recent rates of actual inflation.

The results of the EEC Consumer Survey for Belgium, Denmark, France, Germany, Holland, Italy and the UK are analysed for rationality by Papadia (1983). Since the question relates to price changes over the next twelve months and the survey is conducted in January, May and October there is the same problem over the forecast horizon as with the Livingston data. Papadia follows Brown and Maital (1981) and combines ordinary least-squares estimation of equation (3.2) with generalised least-squares estimation of the variances. When the countries are considered individually the hypothesis of unbiasedness is rejected for Denmark, France and Italy while it is accepted for Belgium, Germany, Holland and the UK. However, Papadia goes on to consider whether the data from different countries can be pooled so as to increase the sample size. As a result of further tests and of comparisons between the survey series and autoregressive models, he concludes that the expectations for Belgium, France, Germany and Holland are unbiased and efficient, while those for Denmark, Italy and the UK are not.

The conclusion from these various studies of consumer expectations is that only in the case of the EEC Consumer Survey is there any evidence in support of the rational expectations hypothesis.

3.4 Business expectations data

Now we turn to surveys of expectations of businessmen and consider surveys in the EEC, Australia, New Zealand and the USA. The EEC survey was discussed briefly in 1.3 above, and here we are interested in the monthly survey of expected inflation and expected growth. The questions refer to changes in the firm's own prices and production over the next 'three or four months' so that there is uncertainty over the precise time horizon relevant. Batchelor (1982) uses a version of the Carlson–Parkin technique to give a quantitative expectations series and then tests for rationality using the unbiasedness property. For Belgium, France, Germany and Italy he estimates equation (3.9) using the Hildreth–Lu procedure (see, for example, Pindyck and Rubinfeld, 1981, p. 157) to remove first-, second- and third-order autocorrelation. His result for inflation for Belgium is

$$P_{t+4} = 2.50 + 0.32 E_t P_{t+4} \qquad (3.33)$$
$$(1.30)\ (1.73)$$
$$BP^*(4-12) = 7.7$$

where t-values are in parentheses, and
        BP^* = the Box–Pierce statistic (equation (3.10)) for auto-correlations from 4–12

The results of the joint test $\alpha = 0$ and $\beta = 1$ are not given, but the hypothesis $\beta = 1$ is rejected. Batchelor concludes that for all four countries expectations of both inflation and growth are biased so that rationality is rejected.

Batchelor also provides comparisons between the expectations series and both extrapolative and ARIMA models. The extrapolative models are simply

$$E_t P_{t+4} = P_t \qquad (3.34)$$

so that the current (backward-looking) rate of inflation is expected to continue, and the ARIMA (p, d, q) models are selected with $d = 1$ and $p + q \leqslant 6$. By comparing root-mean square errors, that is

$$RMSE = \sqrt{\frac{\sum (P_{t+4} - E_t P_{t+4})^2}{n}} \qquad (3.35)$$

or the square root of the average squared error, Batchelor finds a ranking, from best (smallest $RMSE$) to worst of ARIMA, survey data, and extrapolative model. The survey data, while dominating the simple extrapolative model, are thus inferior to the ARIMA models. They cannot therefore be rational, since they are not efficient. Batchelor concludes that the rational expectations hypothesis is not supported by the EEC survey data.

Agenor (1982) analyses the expectations of French businessmen derived from the monthly INSEE survey (part of the EEC enquiry) which gives qualitative responses to a question about the level of industrial prices over the next three or four months. He uses three different assumptions about the distribution of responses to transform the qualitative data into a quantitative series. These are a normal distribution (as in 1.2 above), a Cauchy distribution and an asymmetric log-normal distribution. Agenor found that these three assumptions gave similar results: the expectations are biased (as tested by equation (3.2)) and inefficient (as tested by equation (3.15)) but the errors are orthogonal to previous errors (as tested by equation (3.20)). Thus, again, there is only weak support for rationality. Agenor also checked adaptive and extrapolative models, and rejected these.

Using a rather different approach, Nerlove (1983) examines the individual responses to the INSEE survey, together with the German counterpart of the EEC enquiry, conducted by the Ifo-Institut, Munich. The data are analysed in the three groups – increase, the same, and decrease. Simple extrapolative, adaptive and error-learning models are compared, and in general there is support for the third of these.

The Confederation of British Industry (CBI) survey (see 1.3 above) is tested for unbiasedness by Pesaran (1984). Instead of using equation (3.2) directly, he estimates it in the form

$$P_{t+1} - E_t P_{t+1} = \alpha + \beta E_t P_{t+1} + \beta_1 (E_t P_{t+1})^2 + u_t$$

and tests $\alpha = \beta = \beta_1 = 0$. The unbiasedness hypothesis is rejected both for the series derived by the Carlson–Parkin method and by Pesaran's own method.

The two surveys of business expectations in Australia that we consider are the Australian Chamber of Manufacturers/Bank of New South Wales Survey of Industrial Trends (ACM), and the Department of Industry and Commerce Survey of Manufacturing Activity (SOMA) which were referred to in 1.3 above. The ACM survey is quarterly and the questions refer to changes over the next three months of selling prices; a one-period forecast horizon can thus be assumed. Danes (1975) transformed the qualitative survey results into a quantitative series, and tested various models of expectations formation for 1967–74. In testing for unbiasedness, the estimate of equation (3.2) is

$$P_{t+1} = 0.102 + 0.811 E_t P_{t+1} \qquad (3.36)$$
$$\quad (0.3) \quad (4.2)$$
$$\bar{R}^2 = 0.38, \; DW = 1.72$$

where t-values are in parentheses
          $\bar{R}^2$ = the corrected multiple-correlation coefficient, and
          DW = the Durbin–Watson statistic (equation (3.3))

Danes concludes that this result supports the rationality hypothesis. However, it should be noted that in his derivation of the expectations series he chose the difference limen (a in 1.2 above) on the basis of the actual inflation rate so that the expectations series must be unbiased.

Danes also estimated several versions of the extrapolative expectations model, and found autocorrelation was a problem. An example of his results is

$$E_t P_{t+1} = 0.8 + 0.381 P_t + 0.394 P_{t-1} \qquad (3.37)$$
$$\quad (3.2) \; (2.8) \qquad (2.6)$$
$$\bar{R}^2 = 0.50, \; DW = 1.39$$

He also estimated the simple adaptive model (equation (1.12)), and found the estimate of λ to be 0.029 when allowance was made for autocorrelation. When the second-order adaptive model was estimated in the restricted form (equation (1.13)), none of the parameters was significant.

Danes's conclusion is that the different expectations hypotheses he tested were not adequate explanations of the expectations series. This could be partly due to the lack of inflation in Australia from 1967–73, resulting in the returns to accurate forecasting being small.

Saunders (1983) has tested the rationality of the SOMA data. This is a quarterly survey and the question refers to the next six months. Saunders transferred the data on to a quarterly basis, but left the possibility of first-order autocorrelation being present as an empirical matter. The original data at the firm level are aggregated to total manufacturing industry and twelve sub-categories. The test for unbiasedness gave the estimate of equation (3.2) for total manufacturing industry as

$$P_{t+1} = 0.810 + 1.019 E_t P_{t+1} \qquad (3.38)$$
$$\phantom{P_{t+1} = }(1.29) \quad (4.79)$$
$$R^2 = 0.51, \ F = 10.16,$$
$$BP = 4.84$$

where t-ratios are in parentheses

F from equation (3.5) and tests $\alpha = 0$ and $\beta = 1$, and

$BP =$ the Box–Pierce statistic (equation (3.4)) with eight lags

Here the hypothesis of unbiasedness is rejected. In fact, it is accepted for only three of the thirteen groups. Saunders also estimated equation (3.15) to test for efficiency; lags of up to five quarters were allowed. In this case, the hypothesis of efficiency was rejected in only two of the thirteen groups.

Finally, Saunders tests orthogonality by estimating equation (3.20) using unit cost variables, unanticipated inventory changes and the level of capacity utilisation as the information set I. In three cases out of thirteen, the hypothesis of orthogonality is rejected. Saunders concludes that while unbiasedness is generally rejected, efficiency and orthogonality are generally accepted. As a result the rational expectations hypothesis is neither fully supported nor decisively rejected by the SOMA data. In a different study using the same data, Saunders (1981) carries out the tests for unbiasedness and efficiency for each of the different quarters from September 1973–March 1976. He finds the unbiasedness hypothesis is rejected for all eleven quarters, and the efficiency hypothesis is rejected for eight of the eleven. However, in Saunders (1980), the unbiasedness hypothesis is accepted for these data at the aggregate level. The conclusion on the SOMA series is that the way the data are examined seems to be crucial in the tests for rationality.

The New Zealand Institute of Economic Research's Quarterly Survey of Business Opinion results have been transformed into a quantitative expectations series by Hall and King (1976). The question of interest concerns changes in selling prices over the next three months, and so a one-period forecast horizon is used. Hall and King fitted various models of expectations formation for 1964(1)–1973(3) for the distribution sector. They estimated the extrapolative expectations model (equation (1.3)) both in the restricted form

$$E_t P_{t+1} - P_t = \theta (P_t - P_{t-1}) \qquad (3.39)$$

and in the unrestricted form

$$E_t P_{t+1} = \beta_1 P_t + \beta_2 P_{t-1} \tag{3.40}$$

and rejected the restrictions $\beta_1 = 1 + \theta, \beta_2 = -\theta$. The simple adaptive scheme (equation (1.12)) also did not satisfy the implied restrictions, and the only acceptable model is the version of equation (1.2) which was estimated as

$$E_t P_{t+1} = 0.88 P_t \tag{3.41}$$
$$(22.1)$$
$$DW = 1.45$$

Hall and King did not test the rational expectations hypothesis with their data. However, their paper provides enough information for unbiasedness and efficiency tests. Our own estimate of equation (3.2) for their data is

$$P_{t+1} = 0.46 + 0.78 E_t P_{t+1} \tag{3.42}$$
$$(3.6) \quad (8.2)$$
$$F = 50.3, \ DW = 2.05,$$
$$R^2 = 0.64$$

and the F-statistic (from equation (3.5)) leads us to reject the unbiasedness hypothesis. Next we test for efficiency with equation (3.15), using three lagged actual inflation figures

$$P_{t+1} - E_t P_{t+1} = 0.02 + 0.47 P_t$$
$$(0.1) \quad (4.0)$$
$$-0.73 P_{t-1} + 0.41 P_{t-2} \tag{3.43}$$
$$(5.1) \qquad (3.5)$$
$$F = 7.4, \ DW = 1.68, \ R^2 = 0.44$$

where   the F-statistic (from equation (3.16)) is highly significant

The hypothesis of efficiency is also rejected. Finally, we tested for the orthogonality of past errors by estimating equation (3.20) in the form

$$P_{t+1} - E_t P_{t+1} = 0.23 - 0.19(P_{t+1} - E_t P_{t+1}) \tag{3.44}$$
$$(3.5) \quad (1.2)$$
$$F = 0.2, \ DW = 2.03, \ R^2 = 0.04$$

where   the F-statistic (from equation (3.16)) tests that the coefficients are all 0

Here this hypothesis is accepted and so orthogonality is the only rational expectations property supported by this data.

De Leeuw and McKelvey (1981) analyse the US Bureau of Economic Analysis survey of businessmen. As the questions refer to annual price changes there is no problem with the time horizon. They report the errors in the expectations and find wide variations between different industries, for different years, and between sales (output) prices and capital goods (input) prices. To test for rationality, equation (3.2) is estimated with pooled time-series and cross-section data. The hypothesis of unbiasedness (as tested by equation (3.5)) is rejected. The orthogonality of capacity utilisation and past money supply data is tested by adding these variables to equation (3.2). Each is found to be significant, implying that the expectations could have been made more accurate by utilising this extra information. The conclusion is that this survey provides little support for the rational expectations hypothesis.

For each of these surveys of businessmen, there is some weak support for the rational expectations hypothesis, but not enough to conclude that it is a useful description of how businessmen form their expectations.

3.5 Econometric forecasts as expectations

McNees (1978) examines the *ex ante* forecasts of three prominent US econometric models to see if they satisfy the rational expectations hypothesis. The forecasts are from the Chase, DRI and Wharton models, and are quarterly for 1970–5, with one-, two-, three- and four-quarter ahead forecast horizons. The variables considered are the implicit GNP price deflator, real GNP, and the unemployment rate. McNees first tests for unbiasedness by estimating equation (3.2). He recognises the problem of non-randomness of residuals and so as well as ordinary least squares he uses generalised least squares (GLS) to take account of this problem. He presents estimates of equation (3.2) for the three models, for three variables and four forecast horizons, giving thirty-six regressions. The null hypothesis $\alpha = 0$ and $\beta = 1$ is accepted for twenty out of the thirty-six cases when GLS is used. Of the sixteen rejections of the hypothesis, nine are for the implicit GNP price deflator, and six for the four-quarter ahead forecast horizon. The evidence does not, therefore, provide strong support for the rational expectations hypothesis. Notice, however, that there is no test for randomness of the residuals, which is required by equation (3.2).

Next, McNees relates the current forecast errors to previous forecast errors. This is the orthogonality test (equation (3.20)) with the information set limited to the latest forecast error known when the current forecast is made. The equation he estimates is

$$P_{t+s} - E_t P_{t+s} = \gamma(P_t - E_{t-s}P_s) + \varepsilon_t \qquad (3.45)$$

where $s = 1, 2, 3$ and 4, so there is no intercept term

Again both ordinary least squares and GLS are used, and the hypothesis $\gamma = 0$ is tested. For the GLS results this hypothesis is rejected in twelve out of the thirty-six regressions, with six of these twelve being from the implicit GNP price deflator, and nine for one- or two-quarter ahead horizons. The forecasts could thus have been improved by incorporating recent forecast errors in the information set.

Two of the present authors (Holden and Peel, 1984) have tested the rationality of the forecasts for the UK economy from the National Institute econometric model. The forecasts are published quarterly for one–four quarters ahead, and the series examined are rates of change of consumer prices, real gross domestic product (GDP), consumers' expenditure, investment, imports and exports. Because of the delays in the availability of official statistics, when a forecast is published in quarter t it is based on information relating to quarter $t - 2$. This means that in testing for unbiasedness, equation (3.2) is modified by the addition of a two-period moving-average error. Unbiasedness is rejected only once out of the twenty-four cases examined, for the four periods ahead forecast of the rate of inflation. It is interesting to note that in seven out of twenty-four the hypothesis $\beta = 0$ is accepted, implying that there is no relationship between the forecasts and the actual values.

Efficiency is tested in relation to the data available when the forecasts were made. It is important to realise that national income statistics are generally published in a preliminary form, and are subsequently revised. From the point of view of rationality, it is the data known when the forecasts were *made* which matters, rather than any revised figures. The forecast errors are related to the four most recently available one-quarter actual rates of change (as in equation (3.15)), and the hypothesis of efficiency is accepted.

Finally the property of consistency is tested by examining the relationship between successive forecasts for the same period. In the case of forecasts for $t + 1$ using information dated at $t - 2$ and $t - 3$, for example, the equation estimated is

$$E_{t-2}P_{t+1} = \alpha + \beta E_{t-3}P_{t+1} + u_t \tag{3.46}$$

Consistency requires the intercept to be 0 and the slope to be unity, and is rejected in only four out of eighteen tests, twice each for GDP and consumer prices.

The conclusion from these studies is that – as with much of the evidence from surveys of expectations – forecasts from these econometric models are not fully rational; there is evidence of both bias and under-utilisation of previous forecast errors. These partial tests of the rational expectations hypothesis do not provide support for the rationality of econometric forecasts

3.6 Wage, interest rate and money supply expectations

Leonard (1982) tests the Endicott survey of employers' wage expectations for rationality. The survey covers half-year ahead forecasts of average starting salaries of new graduates in eight specialities. The raw data are weighted by expected hires for each firm to give a mean for each year. The tests are applied to these means for 1962–78 or 1965–78. Leonard estimates equation (3.2), and finds that $\alpha = 0$ and $\beta = 1$ is accepted only for three subjects – chemistry, mathematics and sales. There is no evidence of autocorrelation for any of the eight subjects other than sales. The unbiasedness property is therefore rejected, except for chemistry and mathematics.

To test for efficiency, Leonard estimates equations (3.11) and (3.12), but finds heteroscedasticity so instead turns to equation (3.15), with lags of either one or two periods. The null hypothesis of 0 coefficients is rejected for six out of the eight subjects, being accepted for chemistry and mathematics. Leonard also tests for orthogonality using equation (3.20) with the information set including real wages lagged four or five years (not significant), the number of graduates lagged one year (significant for chemistry and sales), the current and past rate of inflation (not significant), expected money supply and unanticipated money supply as defined by Barro (1978) (not significant except for engineering), and other variables. He does not give details of these tests, and concludes that the orthogonality property is not satisfied by the data. Leonard proposes a model of labour-market activity which suggests that the forecasters under-estimate demand.

In his conclusions, Leonard argues that the Endicott wages data indicate that the expectations of experienced personnel executives are not rational, and hence that the rational expectations hypothesis is not applicable to the labour market as a whole. Strictly, for the eight specialities considered, rationality is rejected for seven of them, with mathematics being the only one for which unbiasedness, efficiency and orthogonality are accepted. However, since this study relates to averaged data (rather than data from individual agents), aggregation problems need to be explicitly considered before a final decision is made.

Next we turn to the quarterly survey of interest-rate expectations conducted by Goldsmith–Nagan Inc. Market professionals are asked their expectations for a number of interest rates both one quarter ahead and two quarters ahead, and the mean responses are reported. Friedman (1980) presents tests for the rationality of expectations of six rates – federal funds, three-month US Treasury bills, six-month Eurodollar certificates of deposit, twelve-month US Treasury bills, new issues of high-grade long-term utility bonds, and seasoned issues of high-grade long-term municipal bonds. The data are quarterly for 1969–76. Friedman notes the problem of the forecast horizon, and in particular that the error in the unbiasedness test may be non-random. He estimates equation (3.2) for a one- and two-period horizon by both ordinary least squares and also Zellner's (1962) 'seemingly unrelated regression' method. This latter method requires estimation of equation (3.2) for all six interest rates simultaneously, and is a form of GLS. The method is particularly appropriate when the disturbances in different equations are correlated. In each case the Zellner estimation method gives $\alpha > 0$ and $\beta < 1$ in equation (3.2), and the hypothesis $\alpha = 0$ and $\beta = 1$ is always rejected. There is also evidence of non-random residuals. The data thus do not support the unbiasedness property.

Friedman then tests for efficiency using equations (3.11) and (3.12) with lags of up to six quarters previously. A significant difference between the two sets of coefficients is found for all of the two-quarter ahead expectations and for three of the one-quarter ahead expectations. Friedman confirmed these results by using equation (3.15). Next, he applied the consistency test by comparing equations (3.12) and (3.17) for the two-quarter horizon data; the hypothesis of consistency is rejected for three of the six series. Finally, Friedman applies the orthogonality test (equation (3.20)), using lagged values of the unemployment rate, the growth rate of industrial production and price inflation as indicators of macroeconomic activity, and the lagged growth of money stock and the lagged federal government deficit as monetary and fiscal variables. The results split into two groups. The four short-term interest rates appear to be rational in that they efficiently utilise data in the information set. For the two long-term interest rates this is not the case, and each macroeconomic variable and the federal government deficit are all significantly related to the interest-rate expectations; better forecasts of these two interest rates could have been made by using this information. Interestingly, the rate of growth of money stock is orthogonal to all the errors in expectations.

Friedman summarises his results on the rational expectations hypothesis as varying from mixed to unfavourable. The predictions are generally biased, did not always utilise all the available information efficiently, and were not consistent. He concludes that the evidence from this survey is that interest-rate expectations are not rational.

Next we turn to the properties of the Money Market Services Inc. data on expected change in money supply. As explained in 1.2 above, these are the expectations of money-market participants on Tuesdays and Thursdays concerning the weekly Friday announcement of the money supply change. Grossman (1981) examines these series. He estimates equation (3.2) for both the Tuesday data and the Thursday data for September 1977–September 1979, and the two sub-periods split at September 1978. In each case the hypothesis $\beta = 1$ is accepted, but the estimate of α is significantly negative for the full period and the later period. The F-statistic (equation (3.5)) is insignificant for the two sub-periods and, together with the randomness of residuals indicated by the Durbin–Watson statistic (equation (3.3)), the conclusion is that the expectations are unbiased.

Grossman then goes on to examine the orthogonality of errors in expectations to the available information. From regression equation (3.2) a series of errors are obtained which are then related to changes in lagged money, the monetary base, the Federal fund rate and bank deposits data. There is no evidence that any of these are related to the expectations errors, so the conclusion is that the expectations are efficient. Finally, the relative efficiency of the expectations is tested by comparing their errors with those from an autoregressive model estimated with data from 1973–September 1977. This model is used to predict the next weekly money supply change and is then re-estimated using the extra actual value to make the following week's prediction. In this way a sequential one-step ahead predicted series is obtained. This series has a larger mean square error than the expectations series, and so the expectations incorporate information in addition to a simple extrapolative model.

Grossman concludes from his results that the Money Market Services Inc. data series for 1977–9 satisfies the requirements of the rational expectations hypothesis. This conclusion is confirmed by Smith and Goodhart (1983) for the period 1977–83. They also examine the properties of a series produced by L. Messel and Co. (a London firm of stockbrokers), giving their assessment of the market's expectation of the growth of M3 in the UK. This is published prior to the monthly announcement of the money supply figures. The unbiasedness hypothesis (tested by equation (3.2)) is accepted, and the authors point out that for both the UK and the USA, the degree of explanation ($\bar{R}^2$) is below 50 per cent. Smith and Goodhart then test for efficiency or orthogonality (see equation (3.20)) by relating errors in the expectation to past actual changes in money, and find the series is efficient. Thus, for both the USA and the UK the expectations of changes in the money supply satisfy the requirements of the rational expectations hypothesis.

3.7 Conclusions

In this chapter, the empirical evidence from surveys of expectations has been reviewed. Particular emphasis has been placed on whether the various series satisfy the rational expectations hypothesis. This requires expectations to be unbiased and to use the available information efficiently, and also that any errors in expectations should be orthogonal to the known information set. Failure to satisfy any of these requirements means that the series is not strictly rational. On this basis only the Endicott wages series for mathematics, some of the econometric forecasts, and the USA and UK money supply expectations series are rational. All the other series fail one or more of the criteria. The conclusion must thus be that, in general, surveys of expectations do not support the rational expectations hypothesis.

However, there are three points which must be remembered

concerning expectations. First, as was mentioned in our discussion of economically rational expectations (1.5 and 2.6 above), agents will use the available information until the marginal cost of producing and processing it is equal to the marginal benefit derived from the improvement in the forecast. When an agent is asked to complete a questionnaire (and is usually guaranteed anonymity) there are few costs in making large errors. It is not clear that those completing surveys of expectations have any incentive to give an accurate answer; if the cost of an error is small a 'rational' agent might happily make an inaccurate response. This reasoning does not explain why survey responses are biased, but might justify a lack of efficiency and orthogonality.

The second point concerns the relationship between the definition of rationality and how it is tested. The definition of rationality concerns agents' subjective probability distributions of future outcomes being the same as the actual probability distributions when the expectations are formed; these probability distributions are not observed. The survey records a single drawing (presumed to be the mean) at successive time intervals. By aggregating over different individuals and different time periods, the various tests of rationality can be performed. If the world was unchanging this aggregation would not matter. However, the development of economic theory and improvements in data availability should mean that the characteristics of the expectations formation mechanism change over time; in these circumstances the aggregation process requires careful analysis.

The final point concerning surveys is made by Sheffrin (1983), who argues that in many market situations the *marginal participant* plays a key role. If transactions costs are low, a few sophisticated agents could make a market appear rational even though the average expectations were biased and inefficient.

4

The Efficient Markets Hypothesis

4.1 Econometric implications of expectations

The importance of expectations in economic theory has been emphasised in chapters 1 and 2, and this importance is reflected in the empirical literature in economics involving expectations variables. In this chapter and the next we consider single-equation studies while macroeconomic models as a whole are examined in chapter 6. Because of the volume of published material covering expectations, we are necessarily selective in our review. Our emphasis is on breadth of coverage of results and methodology with special reference to the rational expectations hypothesis. First we review the econometric implications of expectations variables, and then consider in detail the efficient markets hypothesis. This is an example of *implicit* expectations where inferences about expectations are made from the data series. Applications to short-term interest rates, the term structure of interest rates and the foreign exchange market are presented. Other single-equation studies are reviewed in chapter 5 and cover the consumption function (where expectations are again implicit), and the wage equation and expected capital gains (where expectations are explicitly modelled).

As noted at the beginning of chapter 2, we will not be concerned with the detail of how rational expectations models may be estimated. Nevertheless, given the weaknesses of survey measures of expectation discussed in chapter 3, we need to examine how to infer expectations for which no data series exists. Great care is necessary concerning the interpretation of econometric evidence derived from economic models containing expected future values of variables. Failure of the model concerned to satisfy statistical tests may be due to one of three causes. First, the economic structure of the model may be mis-specified. Second, the hypothesis of how expectations are formed may be wrong. Third, the method of inferring the unobservable expectations from observable data may be incorrect. Conversely, successful completion of the tests may be due to errors offsetting each other. Econometric evidence can therefore provide only guidance, not conclusive proof, thus accounting for the continuing controversy and conflicting evidence in the topics examined in this chapter and the next.

Three broad methods to overcome the problem of the unobservable nature of expectations have been extensively used in the literature. First, recourse may be made to information derived from surveys. Second, expectations about future values of a variable may be inferred from its own past behaviour. Third, it may be possible to build a series of the expected values from other variables which are in effect used as instruments.

We have discussed survey data both in chapters 1 and 3 so it is now necessary only to note that many of the studies surveyed in this chapter use survey material, especially that derived from the Livingston and the Carlson–Parkin series. It is of course necessary to remember that, in the latter case, the data are transformed from qualitative responses to quantitative data, as discussed in chapter 1 (section 1.2).

The second method of obtaining estimates of expectations is by utilising the past history of the variable itself. In 1.4 above, we discussed the various methods involved with particular reference to the adaptive expectations mechanisms and to 'Almon' lags. In 1.6, we also discussed time-series modelling and use of an 'optimal' time-series predictor based on this methodology appears frequently in the literature on the term structure of interest rates. A formulation similar in principle to 'adaptive expectations' is the error correction model suggested by Hendry amongst others (see, for example, Hendry, 1979). The basic rationale is that a long-run relationship exists between the dependent variable (Y) and the independent variable (X). In the short run, however, the desired long-run relationship may not be attained. Consider, for example, the following short-run equation

$$\Delta Y_t = \beta_0 + \beta_1 \Delta Z_t - \beta_2 (Y/X)_{t-1} \qquad (4.1)$$

where $Z =$ a vector of relevant variables

Long-run static equilibrium requires ΔZ and ΔY to equal 0, so that

$$Y = (\beta_0/\beta_2)X \qquad (4.2)$$

or

$$Y = kX \qquad (4.2a)$$

In the case of steady-state growth equilibrium the solution is similar to equation (4.2a), but the value of k will be constant only for particular rates of growth. This is easily seen if equation (4.1) appears in logarithmic form

$$\Delta \log Y_t = \beta_0 + \beta_1 \Delta \log Z_t - \beta_2 \log (Y/X)_{t-1} \qquad (4.3)$$

Steady-state growth equilibrium requires

$$g = \Delta \log Y = \Delta \log Z \qquad (4.4)$$

Hence

$$g = \beta_0 + \beta_1 g - \beta_2 \log (Y/X) \qquad (4.5)$$

that is

$$\log Y = (1/\beta_2)((\beta_1 - 1)g + \beta_0) + \log X \qquad (4.6)$$

or, taking antilogs

$$Y = k'X \qquad (4.6a)$$

where $k' =$ the exponential $(1/\beta_2)((\beta_1 - 1)g + \beta_0)$

Clearly, then, k will vary with the value of g.

In effect, the error correction method side-steps the problem of assessing how expectations are formed, and concentrates instead on how agents move towards a desired long-run relationship. It therefore requires only 'minimal assumptions about the rationality and/or intelligence of agents' (Davidson and Hendry, 1981, p. 191). Of course, since expectations do not appear explicitly in the behavioural functions when the Hendry methodology is utilised but are encapsulated in the dynamic structure, the Hendry procedure would appear to be highly vulnerable, in principle, to the 'Lucas' critique discussed in 2.5 above.

The third method of modelling expectations to be discussed refers to the use of instrumental variables. As we have seen, rationality implies that agents will form their estimates of an expected variable (say, X) in the light of all relevant information available at the time of expectations formation. Consequently consistent estimates of, say, $E_t X_{t+1}$ may be obtained by regressing X_{t+1} on the variables contained in the information set Ω and using the resultant regression equation to predict values of X_{t+1} given information available in period t. These predicted values serve as consistent estimators of $E_t X_{t+1}$. The problem is to ascertain which variables are to be included in the information set. This can be achieved by trial and error having recourse to criteria provided by economic theory and regression analysis such as, for example, goodness of fit. The resultant series can be tested for rationality as in chapter 3, with due allowance being made for the forecasting horizon. A variation of this method is proposed by McCallum (1976a, b). This involves substituting *ex post* realisations for the expected variables. Because this substitution introduces an 'error in variables' problem, McCallum proposes the use of instruments not only for the endogenous but also for the exogenous variables appearing in the equation.

A further problem occurs with respect to the identification of the model. Standard econometric texts (see, for example, Pindyck and Rubinfeld, 1981; and Johnston, 1972) provide detailed coverage of the identification problem, so we merely indicate its relevance to models containing expectations. A model is identified if we can obtain estimates of the individual parameters. Consideration of the following very simple and unreal two-equation model used purely for illustrative purposes demonstrates the problem

$$Y_t = \delta_1 X_t + \delta_2 E_{t-1} Y_t + U_t \tag{4.7a}$$

$$X_t = \alpha X_{t-1} + e_t \tag{4.7b}$$

Solving for Y in the manner discussed in chapter 2, gives

$$Y_t = \delta_1 X_t + \frac{\alpha \delta_1 \delta_2}{1 - \delta_2} X_{t-1} + U_t \tag{4.7c}$$

Estimation of equation (4.7c) by standard regression methods produces

$$Y_t = b_1 X_t + b_2 X_{t-1} \tag{4.7d}$$

Clearly it is not possible to obtain estimates of the original parameters α, δ_1 and δ_2 from the estimated regression coefficients b_1 and b_2. Furthermore, equation (4.7c) is consistent with a model which merely states that Y depends on current and lagged values of X because of slow adjustment. In this case, the rational expectations model (equations (4.7a) and (4.7b)) and the slow adjustment model are said to be *observationally equivalent* – it is not possible to distinguish between them. This problem often arises in rational expectations models because lagged values of the exogenous variables can enter models for two reasons. First, they may convey that the dependent variable responds only slowly to changes in the exogenous variables; second, they may provide forecasting information for expected future values of that variable (in equation (4.7b), for example, if X_t follows an autoregressive model so that $E_{t-1}X_t = \alpha X_{t-1}$).

4.2 Efficient markets hypothesis

The term 'efficiency' can be applied to various aspects of market behaviour. Does the market, for example, operate at low cost – is it operationally efficient? Alternatively, we may be concerned with the role of the market in the allocation of resources – allocative efficiency. In fact, in this section we are concerned with neither of these two concepts but a third aspect – *informational* efficiency. Financial assets are 'durable' assets, and are held not only for the interest they bear but also for expected future capital gain. Continuous trading is a feature of financial markets so the market price is free to move to eliminate any imbalance between supply and demand. In this context, a market can be described as 'efficient' if the prices of the assets traded instantaneously reflect all the information contained in a defined information set. The theory of market efficiency therefore comprises two components – first, the idea that an equilibrium price exists, and second that actual prices adjust quickly to the equilibrium. Two predictions follow directly from our description of an efficient market. First, prices will change only in response to new information – 'news' in the technical jargon. Second, since market prices reflect the assumed information set, all opportunities for 'knowable' super-normal profits with respect to the postulated information set will have been eliminated by market trading.

The incentive for market trading has been the subject of discussion in the literature. Grossman and Stiglitz (1976) show that if asset prices do reflect all available information, then market agents would have no incentive to collate and process information since it is already reflected in the market price. Obviously, it is the possibility of obtaining *abnormal* profits which provides the incentive to collect and process information. In equilibrium, an individual is indifferent between remaining uninformed or collecting information (or, for that matter, buying expertise) since after allowance for costs each action offers the same prospective return. Hellwig (1982) demonstrates that the Grossman and Stiglitz result occurs because all agents are assumed to observe current market prices prior to trade. If this untenable assumption is relaxed, Hellwig shows that the market price will approximate full informational efficiency arbitrarily closely as the time period is reduced, but that the return to 'being informed' is never 0. Following Begg (1982), since we observe data at discrete intervals (end-of-day trading price, for example) we might assume that the process of arbitrage has occurred *within* the period of our data observations, in which case the implications of different information structures can be analysed without modelling the process of arbitrage itself.

Tests of market efficiency take the form of examining actual market prices – normally end-of-trading – to ascertain whether the implications of market efficiency are apparent. Fama (1970) usefully categorises three types of informational efficiency:

1. weak efficiency – the requirement that the asset price reflect fully the information contained in the past history of prices of the asset concerned
2. semi-strong efficiency – the requirement that the asset price reflect all publicly available information
3. strong efficiency – the requirement that the asset price reflect all information whether public or private (including information which is restricted to some individuals due to their position, commonly called 'insider' trading)

Most of the early literature in connection with the efficient markets hypothesis was concerned with equity prices. Excellent summaries of this literature already exist (see, for example, Fama, 1970; and Firth, 1977), so we concentrate on other markets namely short-term rates of interest (4.3 below), the market for government bonds (4.4) and foreign currency markets (4.5).

4.3 Short-term rates of interest and expected inflation

In a world of perfect certainty containing perfect capital markets, it is hypothesised that an equilibrium relationship will exist so that the one-period nominal rate of return is equal to the one-period real rate of return plus an allowance for the fully-anticipated rate of inflation. Therefore

$$(1+R)=(1+i)(1+P) \tag{4.8}$$

where R = nominal rate of interest
         i = real rate of interest
         P = 'known' rate of inflation
         all variables refer to the same time period (or holding period)

If this relationship did not exist, there would be an imbalance between the real rate of return (determined in classical economic theory by the forces of productivity and thrift) and the nominal rate of interest. Noting that the term iP is small relative to the other terms (since both i and P are normally relatively small decimals) equation (4.8) may be approximated by the 'Fisher' identity, that is

$$R = i + P \tag{4.9}$$

In a world of uncertainty, the terms P and i would have to be replaced by their expectations – the rate of inflation or real rate of interest expected to occur during the period concerned. Equation (4.9) then becomes

$$R_t = i + E_{t-1}P_t \tag{4.9a}$$

where R is measured at the end of period $t-1$. Consequently, the efficient markets hypothesis predicts that the nominal rate of interest responds to changes in the expected rate of inflation with a unit coefficient provided the real rate (i) is unaffected by price expectations. Testing the propositions summarised in equation (4.9a) is fraught with difficulty since it comprises three joint hypotheses. First, there is the hypothesis concerning the determination of the real rate of interest. Second, there is an underlying hypothesis concerning the method of expectations formation. Third, there is the hypothesis that nominal rates of interest respond to changes in price expectations with a unit coefficient. Failure of a test of equation (4.9a) may therefore be due to an incorrect specification of either of the first two hypotheses in the test rather than the main or third hypothesis.

Early tests tended to show that the markets did not perform efficiently in predicting the rate of inflation – for a survey of evidence see Roll (1972). Reasons advocated for this failure include:

1. poor commodity price data underlying the inflation series
2. representation of expected price changes by a distributed lag of past price changes

Contrasting results were reported in Gibson (1972). He estimated an equation of the form

$$R_t = \alpha_0 + \alpha_1 E_{t-1} P_t \qquad (4.10)$$

using US data for a variety of interest rates over the period 1952–70; the inflation expectations series was derived from the Livingston series referred to in chapters 1 and 3. He also assumed that the expected real rate of interest was constant. Given these assumptions, several *a priori* assertions can be made about the values of α_0 and α_1. First, α_0 represents the 'constant' real rate of interest, and should therefore be positive. Second, a value for α_1 of unity indicates complete adjustment of the nominal rate of interest to inflation expectations – sometimes called the 'strong' Fisher hypothesis. A value between 0 and unity supports the 'weak' Fisher hypothesis that inflation expectations have some role to play in the determination of interest rates (the efficient markets hypothesis requires the strong hypothesis to be true). Gibson concluded that his results supported the hypothesis 'that the real rate is not affected by price expectations over a six-month period and that interest rates fully adjust to expectations within six months' (Gibson, 1972, p. 863). It also appeared that expectations had a stronger effect on interest rates after 1959. Gibson attributes this to growth in accuracy of predictions of inflation. One potential defect in Gibson's study arises from the fact that he fails to quote relevant Durbin–Watson statistics; there is therefore no evidence concerning the existence or absence of autocorrelation.

In line with earlier work by Darby (1975) and Feldstein (1976), Carlson (1979) studied the proposition that α_1 should exceed 1 due to the fact that nominal interest rates (including the inflation premium) are taxable, whereas the appreciation of real capital owned by firms is often not taxable – hence α_1 should equal $1/(1-t)$, where t is the tax rate. Carlson found it difficult to isolate this relationship and his estimates tended to support the hypothesis that $\alpha_1 = 1$.

The role of inflation expectations in the setting of short-term rates of interest was also examined by Fama (1975) using US data. This study provoked responses by Carlson (1977b), Hess and Bicksler

(1975), Joines (1977) and Nelson and Schwert (1977). Fama (1977) also responded to the criticisms made in these papers. We propose to treat the original paper and the various rejoinders together.

Fama's methodology was similar to that adopted by Gibson (1972) inasmuch as he assumed a constant real rate of interest. On the other hand, he tested the role of short-term rates of interest as predictors of inflation. Equation (4.10) was consequently transformed, to obtain

$$P_t = \alpha_1' R_t - \alpha_0/\alpha_1 \qquad (4.11)$$

where R_t = nominal rate of interest at end of period $t-1$
          P_t = the rate of inflation observed during period t
          $\alpha_1' = 1/\alpha_1$

The efficient markets hypothesis requires $\alpha_1' = 1$. Fama found that regressions involving a range of short-term interest rates yielded estimates for α_1' within two standard errors of 1. Inclusion of the lagged rate of inflation P_{t-1} as an additional independent variable failed to improve significantly the explanatory power of equation (4.11), or provide a statistically significant coefficient for that variable. This result provides weak support for the efficient markets hypothesis – that the variable R_t incorporates all information contained in the past history of inflation. The main grounds of the attack on the study were twofold. First, after obtaining time-series forecasts of future inflation rates (using the Box–Jenkins methods discussed in 1.6 above and designating the best such forecast as the optimal time-series predictor) it is possible to examine whether this predictor provides information on future rates of inflation additional to that contained in the nominal rate of interest. Hess and Bicksler, and also Nelson and Schwert, found that the optimal time-series predictor did provide additional information so that there is a failure to meet a 'weak' test of market efficiency. Second, additional lagged variables contribute – Joines (the wholesale price index) and Carlson (the ratio of employment to total population) – so there is a failure to meet a semi-strong test. With regard to the first point Fama concedes that the addition of the optimal time-series predictor produces a coefficient which is statistically significant. He also notes that the practical effect of the addition of this variable is quite small, since the coefficient of determination is raised only from 0.29–0.31. With regard to the second criticism it is argued that lagged values of the wholesale price index may proxy similar effects to those captured by the optimal time-series predictor. Inclusion of the lagged employment:population ratio in equation (4.11) produces a statistically significant coefficient, but again raises the coefficient of determination by only a fairly small amount (from 0.29–0.36). The conclusion drawn by Fama was that these objections to his study were not sufficiently strong to reject the joint hypothesis of an efficient market and a constant real rate of interest as a useful approximation to the real world. Finally in this connection, Durbin–Watson statistics provided in Carlson revealed no evidence of misspecification in Fama's study. Later Summers (1983) argues that Fama's results were restricted to the period studied (1953–71), and could not be considered as a general phenomenon.

A further interesting study of interest rates as predictors of inflation using US data was provided by Pearce (1979). He estimated equation (4.10) again assuming a constant real rate of interest and compared the results obtained by using the Livingston series and a time-series predictor (designated by him as the rational-expectations predictor) as the proxies for expected inflation. A variety of short-term rates of interest were used in conjunction with two time horizons – i.e. eight months and fourteen months. In each case, a better fit was obtained using the time-series rather than the Livingston data so that Pearce concludes that the Livingston data 'are not rational' (p. 455) – see 3.2 above for similar conclusions drawn by Brown and Maital (1981) and Figlewski and Wachtel (1981). Of more relevance to this section is the result that whilst all the estimated coefficients for α_1 are significantly different from 0 they are also significantly less than 1. This result of course conflicts with the earlier evidence of both Fama and Gibson.

We now turn to a study using UK data – Demery and Duck (1978). They estimated equation (4.10)

$$R_t = \alpha_0 + \alpha_1 E_{t-1} P_t$$

using three-month rates of interest (Treasury bill, commercial bill and local authority rates) and the Carlson–Parkin series to represent $E_{t-1}P_t$. In each case, the estimated coefficient for α_1 was significantly different from 0. However, very low Durbin–Watson statistics suggest misspecification. Incorporation of the lagged dependent variable, to represent gradual adjustment, increased the goodness of fit of the regression equation whilst still leaving the estimated coefficient for α_1 less than 1. Demery and Duck also investigated the assumption of a constant real rate of interest. They put forward a 'loanable' funds theory with the real rate of interest depending on the demand and supply of loanable funds. Additional variables such as the PSBR, the rate of increase of the real money supply, and the level of vacancies (acting as a proxy for the level of economic activity) are consequently incorporated in equation (4.10) to capture movements in the real rate of interest. The estimated results were encouraging, and Demery and Duck concluded that nominal rates of interest rise as expectations of inflation rise but probably by less than the full expected increase, even in the long run. They also find that adjustment is not instantaneous and that it takes about nine months for 75 per cent of any adjustment to take place.

More recent work by Mishkin (1981) and Symons (1983) is conducted under the explicit assumption that price expectations are formed in an unbiased manner. The anticipated real rate is found to be correlated with a variety of lagged variables such as inflation or the money supply. This evidence casts further doubt on studies in which the anticipated real rate of interest is modelled as a constant, and may therefore provide some explanation of a coefficient for expected inflation which is less than unity. On reflection it is clear that the conditions under which the anticipated real rate of interest will be constant are stringent. This can easily be demonstrated by examining the derivation of the actual or anticipated real rate of interest as the reduced forms of the structural model of the economy (see, for example, Minford and Peel, 1983). To demonstrate this proposition we use the following simple stylised model of an economy based on that of Sargent and Wallace (1975) and which is essentially a simplified version of equations (2.71–(2.75)

$$y_t^d = -\alpha(R_t - E_{t-1}P_t) + Z + U_t \tag{4.12}$$

$$y_t^s = \beta(P_t - E_{t-1}P_t) + \lambda y_{t-1}^s + e_t \tag{4.13}$$

where y^d = aggregate demand
          y^s = aggregate supply
          Z = exogenous determinants of aggregate demand
      P and $E_{t-1}P$ = actual and expected rates of inflation
          U and e = white noise disturbance
          α and β are positive coefficients
          y^d and y^s are measured as deviations from their means

Assuming equilibrium we can solve equations (4.12) and (4.13) to obtain the anticipated real rate of interest

$$R_t - E_{t-1}P_t = \lambda(R_{t-1} - E_{t-2}P_{t-1}) - \frac{\beta}{\alpha}(P_t - E_{t-1}P_t)$$

$$+\frac{Z_t}{\alpha} - \frac{\lambda}{\alpha}Z_{t-1} + \frac{1}{\alpha}U_t - \frac{\lambda}{\alpha}U_{t-1} - \frac{1}{\alpha}e_t \qquad (4.14)$$

We observe from equation (4.14) that the anticipated real rate of interest will be constant only if the degree of speculation in the goods market is infinite – $\alpha = \infty$ (notice that as α tends to ∞ so $R_t = E_{t-1}P_t$ and $R_{t-1} = E_{t-2}P_{t-1}$). More generally, the anticipated real rate of interest will be serially correlated and dependent upon a number of current and lagged variables (those incorporated in Z) as well as a complicated error process.

The critical simplifying assumption made in the previous work concerns the determinants of the anticipated real rate of interest. Errors in this assumption could well lead to estimated coefficients on anticipated inflation which are seriously biased. Clearly the question of the Fisher hypothesis is unresolved at the moment. From the USA we have the evidence of Fama which suggests support for the strong hypothesis. In contrast, Pearce finds a coefficient less than unity and Summers suggests that Fama's results are peculiar to the period of data observation. The evidence from the UK supports the weak hypothesis and then only with slow adjustment. As well as the inadequacy of the series representing expected inflation, the assumptions made about the determinants of the real rate of interest may constitute a severe weakness in these studies. More research is therefore necessary. One possible suggestion for this is that the determinants of the anticipated real rate of interest in the bond market should be considered jointly with the determinants of anticipated real rates of interest in other markets such as the stock market. Given the existence of arbitrage between the markets, the anticipated real rates of return on different assets will be equal after allowing for their different risk characteristics (see, for example, Copeland and Weston, 1979). As with the efficiency tests described in 3.1 above, we can examine the *ex post* properties of the real rates of return in the various markets to ascertain whether they have the same relationship to a given data set. Such joint tests may provide additional restrictions in identifying the real rates of return in the bond market.

4.4   Term structure of interest rates

Government bonds are securities with a fixed rate of interest based on the face or nominal value of the security. They are generally issued for a fixed term, at the expiry of which the bonds are redeemed by the authorities. Some securities are, however, non-redeemable (for example, consols). Since the interest payment (the coupon value in US terminology) is fixed, the market price of the bond responds to changes in interest rates. Assuming for ease of exposition that interest is paid once a year, calculation of the return on a bond (that is, the yield to maturity) given the market price and the coupon value therefore becomes a simple application of the discounting process

$$p_t = \frac{C}{(1+R)} + \frac{C}{(1+R)^2} + \frac{C}{(1+R)^3} + \frac{C}{(1+R)^4}$$

$$+ \ldots \frac{C}{(1+R)^n} + \frac{RV}{(1+R)^n} \tag{4.15}$$

where p_t = market price of the bond
          n = term of the bond
          RV = redeemable value of the bond
          R = yield to maturity (nominal)
          C = coupon value

In practice, yields differ because of a number of factors such as risk, cost of administering the loan, etc. In this section we are concerned with variations in the yield to maturity on bonds which differ only in respect of the term to maturity (the term structure of interest rates). It is for this reason that we concentrate on government bonds. Even then differences do occur. Reference to equation (4.15) reveals that securities with a low coupon value (small value for C) must possess a lower market price than issues with a high coupon value if equality of yields is to be maintained. A significant part of the yield of low-coupon value bonds therefore consists of capital gains. In most countries capital gains are taxed at lower rates than those levied on income and this would be reflected in yields observed in the market. We will ignore this complication.

In a world which all future rates of interest (or yields) are known with certainty, perfect capital markets and no transaction costs, arbitrage would ensure equal yields from investing funds for a given period (termed the holding period) irrespective of the maturity terms of the bonds purchased. If this were not the case, trading would bid up the price of the bonds offering higher rates of return and bid down the price of bonds offering lower rates of return. In this way, yields on the differing bonds would be equalised. In the real world complete certainty is absent, so the known future rates of interest must be replaced by their expectations. As a demonstration of this proposition, consider the simple case of two investment strategies open to an investor with a holding period of n years. The first strategy consists of buying a succession of one-year bonds and re-investing the proceeds as each one-year bond matures. The second strategy consists of buying a bond which matures in n years time. Assuming interest is paid once a year, equality of yields is captured by equation (4.16) where the right-hand side represents strategy 1 and the left-hand side strategy 2

$$(1 + {}_tR_n)^n = (1 + R_1)(1 + E_t\, {}_{t+1}R_1)(1 + E_t\, {}_{t+2}R_1)$$
$$\ldots (1 + E_t\, {}_{t+n-1}R_1) \tag{4.16}$$

where ${}_tR_n$ = known n-period yield to maturity ruling at time t
       ${}_{t+i}R_1$ = one-period rate ruling at time $t+i$ (with i running from 0 to $n-1$)
       E_t = expectations of future rates with expectations being formed at time t

Rearranging equation (4.16) shows that the n-period rate is the geometric mean of the current known and future expected short-term rates (in our example, one-period rates)

$$_tR_n = ((1 + {}_tR_1)(1 + E_t\, {}_{t+1}R_1)(1 + E_t\, {}_{t+2}R_1)$$
$$\ldots (1 + E_t\, {}_{t+n-1}R_1))^{1/n} - 1 \tag{4.17}$$

In fact in the rest of this section we follow the example of many authors, who on the practical grounds that $\log(1 + R)$ is close to R itself (given that R is a relatively small decimal), use the arithmetic approximation to equation (4.17)

$$_tR_n = (1/n)({}_tR_1 + E_t\, {}_{t+1}R_1 + E_t\, {}_{t+2}R_1 + \ldots$$
$$+ E_t\, {}_{t+n-1}R_1) \tag{4.17a}$$

The theory of the term structure of interest rates described above is called the *expectations theory*. Hicks (1939) amended the model by suggesting that the long-term rate would exceed the average of the current and expected short-term rates by a liquidity or risk premium. The premium arises because the market price of long-term securities fluctuates more than short-term securities, and holders may require an extra sum to compensate them for the extra risk involved. Note that agents are assumed to be *risk-averse* as compared with *risk-neutral* under the pure expectations theory. Risk-aversion refers to dislike of risk – a 'risk-averter' is a person who will accept additional risk only if compensated by a higher expected return.

The *preferred market habitat* theory of the term structure combines and generalises Hicks's liquidity premium and the market segmentation theory which in its extreme form treats markets for bonds of differing maturities as completely isolated from each other. On the assumption that the risk premium is constant, equation (4.17a) becomes

$$_tR_n = (1/n)(_tR_1 + E_{t\ t+1}R_1 + E_{t\ t+2}R_1 + \ldots$$
$$+ E_{t\ t+n-1}R_1) + L \tag{4.18}$$

where　　L is the assumed constant liquidity/risk premium

The efficient markets hypothesis predicts that there are no knowable opportunities for supernormal profits with reference to the assumed information set. The question arises: Is that prediction compatible with the existence of a liquidity/risk premium? To some extent, it is a question of degree. A very large L relative to the risk involved would call into question the efficiency of the bond market since *ex ante* above-normal profits could be made by switching from short- to long-term bonds. In contrast a small L leaves the efficient markets hypothesis unscathed (note that this distinction requires some notion of a normal reward for the degree of risk/uncertainty).

Early tests of the term structure concentrated on examining comparisons of the inferred expected rates of interest with those subsequently observed. To illustrate this point, consider adapting equation (4.18) for a two-year bond

$$_tR_2 = (1/2)(_tR_1 + E_{t\ t+1}R_1) + L \tag{4.19}$$

Given that $_tR_2$ and $_tR_1$ are observed in the market, it is possible to derive a value for $E_{t\ t+1}R_1$ consistent with equation (4.19), assuming that $L=0$

$$E_{t\ t+1}R_1 = 2(_tR_2) - _tR_1 \tag{4.20}$$

Comparison of the values of $E_{t\ t+1}R_1$ derived from equation (4.20) with the subsequently observed values of $_{t+1}R_1$ provides a test (albeit a weak one) of the 'efficiency' of the market. If the expected values are unbiased this then provides evidence of the pure expectations theory – $L=0$. On the other hand, if the forecasts (expected values) always over-state the subsequently-observed interest rates (the forecasts are biased upwards) then this is consistent with the existence of a liquidity premium. The early studies using mainly US data did not strongly support the pure expectations theory. An investigation by Hickman (1943), for example, found little explanatory power in a regression of expected values on those subsequently observed. Similarly Kessel (1963) found evidence of a positive bias compatible with the existence of a liquidity premium. In contrast, Meiselman (1962), using an error-correction model, found firm evidence of correlation between forecasting errors and changes in the expected one-year rates. Replication of this methodology for the UK by Grant (1964) failed to obtain similar support for the expectations hypothesis of the term structure.

An alternative form of testing hypotheses concerning the term structure examines the behaviour of the observed rates of interest in the market. Consider equation (4.18) lagged one period (following the analysis in Mishkin, 1980)

$$_{t-1}R_n = (1/n)(_{t-1}R_1 + E_{t-1\ t}R_1 + E_{t-1\ t+1}R_1 + \dots$$

$$+ E_{t-1\ t+n-2}R_1) + L \qquad (4.21)$$

Subtracting equation (4.21) from equation (4.18) to obtain the change in the interest rate gives

$$\Delta_t R_n = (1/n)[_tR_1 - E_{t-1\ t}R_1) + (E_{t\ t+1}R_1 - E_{t-1\ t+1}R_1 \dots]$$

$$+ (1/n)[E_{t\ t+n-1}R_1 - _{t-1}R_1] \qquad (4.22)$$

The last term in the second square brackets on the right-hand side of equation (4.22) is likely to be small given a relatively flat yield curve and a large n. We now consider the terms in the first square bracket. By the properties of rational expectations discussed in 2.1 above, the first term is 0 on average since it is pure forecasting error and hence unbiased. Similarly the second and subsequent terms also average 0 (see equation (2.17)). Consequently equation (4.22) approximates to

$$\Delta_t R_n = e_t \qquad (4.23)$$

where $E_{t-1}e_t = 0$
         $E(e_i e_j) = 0$ $i \neq j$

If equation (4.23) represents the bond market, R_n is said to follow a random walk, and the best forecast for R_n made in period $t-1$ is the value actually observed in that period $-_{t-1}R_n$. In other words, no information available in period $t-1$ should enable more accurate prediction of $_t R_n$ because that information will already have been processed by the market in the determination of $_{t-1}R_n$. Yet another way of stating the same proposition is that R_n will change only in response to unanticipated new information – 'news'. Support for the random walk hypothesis has been claimed by a number of studies including, for example, Bierwag and Grove (1971), Laffer and Zecher (1975) and Sargent (1979b) – using US data; Granger and Rees (1968) – using UK data; and Pesando (1978) – using data for Canada.

A further method of testing the efficient markets hypothesis was utilised by Modigliani and Shiller (1973), drawing on earlier work by Modigliani and Sutch (1966). Their approach was to obtain optimal forecasts of short-term rates of interest and examine how well these (in conjunction with a liquidity premium) explained the term structure. Modigliani and Shiller use forecasts of expected future short-term rates based on weighted averages of past observed values of nominal rates of interest and of inflation. They justify this decomposition on the grounds that the forecast 'could be thought of as the sum of the expected real rate and an expected rate of change of prices for that period' (p. 20). They also consider the possibility of a non-constant liquidity premium by including the moving standard deviation of a short-term rate of interest ($\bar{S}$). This term should capture changes in risk. Hence the form of the equation estimated was

$$R_n = \sum_{i=0}^{m} \alpha_i r_{t-i} + \sum_{j=0}^{n} \beta_j P_{t-j} + \delta \bar{S}_t \tag{4.24}$$

The estimated equations possessed a high degree of explanatory power. The coefficients were well determined according to standard significance tests; the only defects appeared in the rather low Durbin–Watson statistics.

Modigliani and Shiller next attacked the problem of whether the forecasts used were optimal in the sense of being the best. In order to understand the methodology adopted by Modigliani and Shiller it is necessary, first of all, to realise that the lagged values of r and P in equation (4.24) are the basis of forecasts of future values of the two variables. An alternative approach would be to derive forecasts of r and P from their lagged values and then estimate R_n directly as the average of these values. One-period forecasts were obtained for the real rate of interest and inflation, each being based on its own lagged values. Using the chain rule of forecasting discussed in chapter 2 (equations (2.23)–(2.26)), it is possible to build up forecasts of future expected values of r and P in terms of their own lagged values and the coefficients derived from the one-period forecasts. These forecasts represent optimal time-series predictors, and the coefficients from this method can then be compared with the weights (α_i and β_j) in equation (4.24). Modigliani and Shiller found that a close correspondence existed, and concluded that the hypothesis that the long-term rate is an average of expected short-term rates adjusted for the existence of a risk premium was supported by US data.

Subsequently Shiller (1979) has questioned the acceptance of market efficiency with respect to the bond market. His attack on market efficiency takes two forms. First, he suggests that the volatility of observed holding period yields is inconsistent with the averaging process inherent in the expectations theory. Reference to equation (4.17) suggests that the long-term yield should change only slowly as short-term rates respond to 'news'. Shiller calculated the *ex post* one holding-period yield based on the actual short-term rates of interest, and found that this produced a smooth series in complete contrast to the volatile series of actual yields. Second, for both the UK and USA Shiller estimates regressions of the form

$$_{t+1}R - _tR = \alpha + \beta(_tR - _tR_s) \tag{4.25}$$

where R = nominal long-term rate of interest
           R_s = nominal short-term rate of interest

According to the efficient markets hypothesis, the future change in long-term rates of interest should be independent of information known at period t. In other words, the coefficient β in equation (4.25) should be 0 – a semi-strong test in the Fama terminology. Shiller obtained statistically significant coefficients for α (positive) and β (negative) for both the UK and the US data. The negative coefficient β is particularly detrimental to the expectations theory of the term structure, since long-term rates should rise on average when long-term rates are high relative to short-term rates. This is essential to produce the capital loss necessary to offset the higher rate of interest and equalise holding-period yields.

Begg (1982) questions Shiller's interpretation of his regression results. Begg argues that equations of the form of (4.25) are consistent with a rising risk premium due to greater uncertainty over inflation forecasts. Furthermore the gap between $_tR$ and $_tR_s$ will be greatest when short-term rates and inflation are expected to increase significantly. Begg therefore concludes that the negative coefficient for β in equation (4.25) may be due to the existence of a risk premium which is greater when inflation is accelerating sharply. Finally in this connection we note that the random walk model depends on the assumption of a constant liquidity premium.

As in the previous section on short-term rates of interest, the question of whether the bond market is efficient remains open. Certainly recent evidence questions the efficient markets hypothesis. However, one feature which is lacking from this work is evidence that profitable trading rules can be formulated on data from outside the period in question.

4.5   Foreign exchange market

As Levich (1979) notes, empirical tests of the efficiency of foreign exchange markets are made difficult because of the absence of a model for equilibrium pricing which commands widespread acceptance. A further difficulty also arises because of government intervention which may alter the normal equilibrium pricing and return relationships ruling in the foreign exchange market. For these reasons the conclusions derived from the survey of empirical evidence is less satisfactory than that carried out in 4.3 and 4.4, above.

Weak tests concerning the efficiency of the spot market have taken two forms: (a) searching for evidence of serial correlation, and (b) examination of the profitability of filter rules. Turning to the first type of test, research (for example, Poole, 1967) has generally shown that serial correlation is present in series of spot exchange rates. Nevertheless it is not permissible to use this as evidence of market inefficiency in the absence of a model of exchange rate determination. If the determinants of the exchange rate are themselves serially correlated, then it would be expected that the equilibrium exchange rate itself will also be serially correlated. Filter rules take the general form of 'buy if the price of the security rises x per cent above the recent trough' and 'sell when the price falls Y per cent below the recent peak'. The weak form of the efficient markets hypothesis predicts that such rules should not lead to abnormal profits, otherwise the market price would not be reflecting all available information in the past history of that variable. Two important studies of filter rules were carried out by Dooley and Shafer (1976) and Logue and Sweeney (1977), both covering a number of currencies during the middle 1970s. The general results of these two studies were similar. Profits over and above a 'buy and hold' strategy were obtainable provided small filters were used. However, in some sub-periods losses were incurred, raising the possibility that such rules were not free from risk of losses so that the returns may represent a reward for such risk. Second, there is the important caveat regarding filter rules that for the market to be demonstrated to be inefficient it must be possible *ex ante* to select a filter that leads to above-normal profits.

A more promising avenue to test the efficiency of the foreign exchange markets may lie in the market for forward currency. Forward rates specify the price of foreign currency to be delivered at given time in the future; thus the one-month forward rate refers to the price of currency to be delivered in one month's time (in contrast to the spot rate, which refers to the price of foreign currency for immediate delivery). If, for example, the one-month forward rate (F_t) for dollars is £0.75 per \$1, the agent can obtain \$1.33 per £1 (1/0.75) which will be delivered in one month's time. Normally this exchange rate is quoted as a premium/discount on the current spot rate (S_t), that is $(F_t - S_t)/S_t$ (or 0.25 if, in this example, the spot exchange rate is £1 per \$1). A forward transaction does not involve immediate payment but rather only a small margin, with the balance to be paid on completion of the contract; consequently, no discounting is involved. The forward market is used for three types of transactions – first, covered interest arbitrage; second, speculation (that is taking an open position in foreign currency); and third, as a hedge against the risk of exchange rate fluctuations relative to future receipts/payments in foreign currency. The equilibrium forward rate will reflect all these influences, and the interested reader is referred to Grubel (1968) for a more detailed discussion.

We commence by examining covered interest arbitrage transactions. The return on a security denominated in foreign currency consists of two components – the nominal rate of interest and the change in value of the foreign currency during the period the security is held. In order to facilitate the exposition we shall assume that all securities are held for one period, so that the relevant rate of return can be specified as

$$\text{Return} = (1/S_t)(1 + R_f)S_{t+1} \tag{4.26}$$

where S is the spot exchange rate, units of domestic currency per unit of foreign currency (£ per $)
   R_f is the nominal one-period foreign rate of interest

To illustrate this point we provide a simple numerical example. Assume that the one-period rate of interest in New York (R_f) is 10 per cent and that the current spot rate is £0.5 per $1. For demonstration purposes we assume perfect foresight, so that the spot exchange rate one period later (S_{t+1}) is known to be £0.498 per $1. Hence the return from investing £100 in New York involves:

1. conversion of £100 into dollars – £100/0.5 = $200
2. the one-period return from investing dollars in New York – $200 (1.1) = $220
3. conversion of $220 into sterling at the known spot rate – $220 × 0.498 = £109.56

The profit from the transaction is therefore £9.56, or equivalently 9.56 per cent. This could equally be derived from equation (4.26)

$$\text{Return} = 1/(0.5)(1 + 0.1)0.498 = 1.0956$$

or 9.56 per cent profit.

In the absence of perfect foresight, S_{t+1} is unknown. However, the transactor can eliminate exchange rate risk (unforeseen fluctuations in the exchange rate during the life of the security) by selling foreign currency forward for the date of maturity of the security. Consequently the return in equation (4.26) is modified to

$$(1/S_t)(1 + R_f)F_t \tag{4.27}$$

where F_t = forward rate ruling at the beginning of the period for currency to be delivered at the end of the period
   other variables as before

Provided that all three transactions – the spot purchase of foreign currency, the purchase of the foreign security and the forward sale of foreign currency – are carried out simultaneously, all prices are known at time t so that the return specified in equation (4.27) is certain. This type of transaction is called *covered interest arbitrage*.

In view of the absence of exchange rate risk, the return obtainable in domestic and foreign centres should be equal if the market is efficient in the sense that market prices reflect all available current information. We note that by using this condition we have side-stepped the necessity of specifying a model of the equilibrium exchange rate. Equality of returns requires that

$$(1 + R) = (1/S_t)(1 + R_f)F_t \tag{4.28}$$

where R = the domestic one-period rate of interest
other variables as before

The condition specified in equation (4.28) is called *interest-rate parity*. Referring to our calculation in equation (4.26), interest-parity requires the relevant rate of interest in London to be 9.56 per cent.

An early survey of the literature carried out by Officer and Willett (1970) concluded that interest-rate parity failed to occur. Clearly this could be accepted as evidence of differences of characteristics of assets denominated in different currencies. On the other hand, growth of Eurocurrency markets provided further opportunities to test interest-rate parity, since (as Bilson, 1979, noted) these assets are 'identical in all respects other than currency denomination' (p. 267). A number of studies have since been carried out to test interest-rate parity, and hence market efficiency. We concentrate on two – by Frenkel and Levich (1975, 1977). In order to demonstrate their methodology, it is first of all necessary to modify equation (4.28). Dividing throughout by $(1 + R_f)$ gives

$$F_t/S_t = (1 + R)/(1 + R_f) \tag{4.29}$$

Subtracting 1 from both sides and rearranging produces

$$(F_t - S_t)/S_t = (R - R_f)/(1 + R_f) \tag{4.30}$$

Defining d as the deviation from interest-rate parity gives

$$d = (F_t - S_t)/S_t - (R - R_f)/(1 + R_f) \tag{4.31}$$

In the real world, deviations from interest-rate parity would still be compatible with the efficient markets hypothesis provided that the gains from carrying out transactions were outweighed by the relevant transaction costs. Consequently we can specify a neutral band given by $\pm$(the cost per transaction) in which arbitrage is not profitable.

Observation of deviations from interest-rate parity outside this neutral band would, however, provide *prima facie* evidence against the efficient markets hypothesis. The basis of the tests carried out by Frenkel and Levich was the examination of actual observed deviations from interest-rate parity in the market. An interesting dichotomy appears in the results between evidence derived from Eurocurrency markets and comparative rates on domestic or onshore assets.

Dealing first with the evidence from the Eurocurrency markets, a very high proportion of weekly observations of deviations for external securities (Eurodollars, Eurodeutschmarks and Euro-canadian dollars) fall within the neutral band for periods 1962–7, 1968–9 and 1973–5. It is consequently concluded that the Euro-currency markets are efficient in that there are few opportunities for above-normal profits. In contrast, the evidence for a wide range of countries is that a much smaller proportion of observations lie within the neutral band when arbitrage is between Treasury bills or commercial paper in different domestic markets. Reasons put forward for this failure of interest-rate parity between domestic markets are twofold. First, there is always the danger that the government of the host country will prevent repatriation of funds. In this case covered arbitrage is not completely risk-free, and the gap may represent a risk premium. Second, existence of known capital controls will raise the cost of investment in foreign securities. Finally in this connection Bilson (1979) raises the interesting point that 'there is no reason why arbitrageurs who maintain the parity relationships between Euro-currency rates should not also be at work in the onshore markets' (p. 268). Bilson consequently concludes that the evidence for Euro-currency markets is also circumstantial evidence in favour of the efficiency of domestic markets.

A second type of study examines the relationship between the forward rate and the subsequently-observed spot rate. The rational expectations hypothesis predicts that

$$S_t = E_{t-1}S_t + e_t \tag{4.32}$$

where e_t is white noise

If a gap exists between the known forward rate and the spot rate expected to occur at the maturity of the forward contract, inter-temporal arbitrage would be stimulated. If the forward rate exceeded the relevant spot rate expected to prevail in the market, for example, speculators would sell the currency forward and fulfil the contract by buying currency spot at the maturity of the forward contract. These transactions would eliminate the gap between the forward rate and the expected spot rate. Consequently, assuming the absence of any risk premium

$$F_{t-1} = E_{t-1} S_t \qquad (4.33)$$

Substitution of equation (4.33) into equation (4.32) gives

$$S_t = F_{t-1} + e_t \qquad (4.34)$$

It is possible to test equation (4.34) by running a regression of the general form

$$S_t = \alpha + \beta F_{t-1} + e'_t \qquad (4.35)$$

For equations (4.34) and (4.35) to be identical. it is necessary that $\alpha = 0$ and $\beta = 1$, and for the errors to be serially uncorrelated.

Alternatively, the result that $\alpha = 0$ and $\beta = 1$ can be interpreted as that the forward rate is an unbiased predictor of the spot rate. Tests of this nature have been carried out by a number of economists including *inter alia* Frenkel (1977, 1981) – respectively Deutschmark *v.* sterling during the German hyperinflation; dollar *v.* Deutschmark, sterling and the French franc during period 1973–9. The general conclusion reached is that the forward rate is an unbiased predictor of the spot rate. A minor qualification arises in the case of the study by Frenkel (1977) which indicates a slight bias which in any case may be outweighed by transaction costs.

In contrast Baillie, Lippens and McMahon (1983) using data for 1973–80 for the US dollar, sterling, the Deutschmark, lira and the French franc and for 1977–80 for the Canadian dollar reject the hypothesis that the forward rate is an unbiased predictor of the spot rate. Furthermore there is evidence of serial correlation in their results. Two explanations are possible. The first concerns the possible existence of a risk premium (*a*), so that equations (4.33) and (4.34) become

$$F_{t-1} = a + E_{t-1} S_t \qquad (4.33a)$$

$$S_t = -a + F_{t-1} + e_t \qquad (4.34a)$$

The forward premium is consequently a biased predictor of the spot rate. If in addition it is assumed that the risk premium has varied over time, serial correlation would be induced. A second possible explanation for the presence of serial correlation is that information is incomplete at the time the forward rate is set, so that overlapping information is introduced into the error term.

An alternative method of testing equations (4.33) and (4.34) is to calculate the forecast error $S_t - F_{t-1}$, and then examine this error against standard statistical criteria such as mean error, mean squared error, etc. or alternatively the proportion of errors falling within a neutral band. Work on these lines has been carried out by *inter alia* Cornell (1977) – sterling, Canadian dollar, Swiss and French franc, Deutschmark, guilder and the yen for 1973–7, and Giddy and Dufey (1975) – Canadian dollar, French franc and sterling for 1973–7. The general tenor of the results is that the mean errors are small, and even when statistically significant likely to be outweighed by transaction costs. Second, the forecast errors are generally not serially correlated, an exception being the study by Cornell (1977). Lastly, in some instances, the forward rate is not the best predictor of the spot rate.

The final type of test of forward exchange market efficiency to be considered is to examine the performance of the forward rate against the predictions of forecasting agencies. If the forward exchange market is efficient then the forward rate can be taken to be a market-consensus forecast. The test thus becomes one of whether experts can persistently outperform the market – that is, a strong test in Fama terminology. Information for this type of test may be difficult to obtain because of the reluctance of forecasting agencies to divulge information sold to clients. However, one such test is contained in Brasse (1983), comparing predictions provided by the forward rate against six forecasting agencies for a number of currencies against the dollar for periods between 1978–82. A variety of tests were carried out for three- and twelve-month horizons including comparison of average forecast errors, root-mean squares and the ratio of forecast error to the forward rate error. The conclusion reached was that 'taken as a group our results favour the foreign exchange market as providing its own best predictor and this despite the existence of forward rate bias for most currencies. In short our answer to the question, do the forecasters beat the market, must be no' (p. 44).

4.6 Conclusions

In this chapter, we have surveyed the evidence concerning the efficient markets hypothesis in relation to markets for short-term securities, government bonds and foreign currency. At the outset it was emphasised that the term 'efficiency' was restricted to informational efficiency. We also wish to emphasise that it is difficult to conceive of a market which is absolutely (that is, completely) efficient, even in this restricted sense. Some departures are likely to exist and the practical question to be answered is whether a market approximates an 'efficient' market. The evidence we have surveyed, whilst not conclusive in either direction, would be adequate to sustain the belief in the efficient markets hypothesis of any protagonist of that viewpoint.

5

Other Single-equation Studies

5.1 Introduction

In this chapter, we consider three areas where the modelling of expectations has played an important role in the development of economic theory. First, we discuss the modern theory of the consumption function, and show the simplifications resulting from adoption of the rational expectations hypothesis. Next, the evidence on the role of expectations in the wage equation is presented from a number of studies. Finally, the ways in which expected capital gains are modelled by use of instrumental variables are reviewed.

5.2 Expectations and the consumption function

The analysis underlying the rational expectations consumption function closely follows that utilised in our discussion of the efficient markets hypothesis in the previous chapter. Initially, however, it is necessary briefly to examine the development of the theory of the consumption function. Modern theories of aggregate consumption behaviour (such as permanent income and life cycle hypotheses) tend to denigrate the importance of current income as a determinant of current consumption. It is argued that the existence of financial institutions which accept deposits and make loans permits individuals to smooth consumption expenditure by borrowing during periods of relatively low income receipts. Conversely, during periods of relatively high income individuals may repay previously-incurred debt and/or make deposits with financial intermediaries. As a direct consequence of this reasoning, the concept of income relevant to consumer expenditure is income expected over some future period. More rigorously, the maximum available for expenditure at time t may be specified by equation (5.1)

$$w_t + y_t + \sum_{i=1}^{\infty} \frac{E_t y_{t+i}}{(1+r)^i} \qquad (5.1)$$

where w = real wealth

         y_t = current real disposable income

         $E_t y_{t+i}$ = future real disposable income with expectations being formed at time t

         r = real rate of interest at which the individual may borrow or lend

Note that we have assumed an infinite life for sake of ease of exposition. It is also important to realise that the assumption of a single rate of interest implies a perfect capital market in which the individual may borrow (or lend) without restriction. This assumption is often attacked on the grounds that individuals experience liquidity constraints due to credit rationing.

We can define permanent income as the *constant* annual income stream whose expected present discounted value just equals the sum of the values of present wealth and discounted future income. Using equation (5.1)

$$w_t + y_t + \sum_{i=1}^{\infty} \frac{E_t y_{t+i}}{(1+r)^i}$$

$$= {}_t y^p \left(1 + \frac{1}{(1+r)} + \left(\frac{1}{(1+r)} \right)^2 + \ldots \left(\frac{1}{(1+r)} \right)^{\infty} \right) \qquad (5.2)$$

where ${}_t y^p$ = the individual's assessment at time t of his permanent income

         other variables as before

Noting that the right-hand side is the sum of a geometric series

$$w_t + y_t + \sum_{i=1}^{\infty} \frac{E_t y_{t+i}}{(1+r)^i} = {}_t y^p \left(\frac{1+r}{r} \right) \qquad (5.3)$$

Hence

$$_ty^p = \frac{r}{(1+r)}\left(w_t + y_t + \sum_{i=1}^{\infty} \frac{E_t y_{t+i}}{(1+r)^i}\right) \tag{5.4}$$

Clearly the amount of smoothing the individual will carry out depends on the relationship between the real rate of interest (r in equation (5.4)) and his or her rate of time preference. If the rate of time preference is less than the real rate of interest, for example, the individual will plan a rising rate of consumption because the return to saving now is greater than its cost in terms of consumption foregone. On the other hand, if these two rates (time preference and real interest) are approximately equal, then the individual will plan an approximately equal level of consumption so that in this case consumption will be a constant proportion of permanent income

$$c_t = k \, _ty^p \tag{5.5}$$

The remaining step necessary to model equation (5.5) is to specify how expectations of future income are formed. Ando and Modigliani (1963) tried a variety of functions to represent expected income, but found the simple form $E_t y = \beta y_t$ to be as good as any other representation. In contrast, Friedman (1957) represented permanent income by lagged values of current income extending back over a number of years

$$_ty^p = \lambda_0 y_t + \lambda_1 y_{t-1} + \lambda_2 y_{t-2} + \ldots \tag{5.6}$$

The values of λ_i were obtained from the data. Note that in his formulation $\sum \lambda_i$ exceeded unity, so as to allow for the trend of rising income.

Representation of permanent income by lagged values of current income has interesting implications for the sensitivity of the behaviour of the economy to changes in aggregate demand. If consumption is proportional to permanent income, as in equation (5.5), and

$$_ty^p = \sum_{i=0}^{n} \lambda_i y_{t-i} \tag{5.7}$$

then fiscal changes which alter current income will alter consumption (and therefore aggregate demand) only to the extent that they alter permanent income. In the case of long lags (large n in equation (5.7)) aggregate demand will exhibit considerable stability because consumption will respond only slightly to income changes in any one period. Fiscal policy changes will be therefore largely ineffective in stabilising aggregate demand.

The crucial point to note about the techniques used by both Ando and Modigliani and also Friedman is that, although expected income is itself a forward-looking variable, the proxies are essentially backward-looking. Hall (1978) examines the implication of adopting the alternative assumption that expectations about future income are themselves forward-looking and are formed in accordance with the rational expectations hypothesis. In this case consumers will process, at time t, information concerning current wealth and income and future earnings in order to arrive at their assessment of permanent income. Similarly in period $t-1$, economic agents would have processed all the information then available to assess permanent income. The only reason for these two assessments to differ is that new information ('news') has become available between time t and time $t-1$. From equation (5.4)

$$E_{t-1} y_t^p = \frac{r}{(1+r)} \left(E_{t-1} w_t + E_{t-1} y_t + \sum_{i=1}^{\infty} \frac{E_{t-1} y_{t+i}}{(1+r)^i} \right)$$

(5.8)

Consequently

$$_t y_t^p - E_{t-1} y_t^p = \frac{r}{(1+r)} \left(w_t - E_{t-1} w_t + y_t - E_{t-1} y_t + \sum_{i=1}^{\infty} \frac{(E_t y_{t+i} - E_{t-1} y_{t+i})}{(1+r)^i} \right)$$

(5.9)

The right-hand side of equation (5.9) is simply a forecasting error which, according to the rational expectations hypothesis property of unbiasedness (see 2.1), is 0. Hence

$$y_t^p - E_{t-1} y_t^p = u_t \qquad \text{with} \quad E_{t-1} u_t = 0$$

(5.10)

Equation (5.10) can be modified by noting that permanent income was earlier defined as a constant stream so that

$$y_{t-1}^p = E_{t-1} y_t^p$$

(5.11)

Substituting equation (5.11) into equation (5.10) provides

$$y_t^p - y_{t-1}^p = u_t$$

(5.12)

or

$$y_t^p = y_{t-1}^p + u_t \tag{5.12a}$$

Substituting for y_t^p in the proportional consumption function specified in equation (5.5) gives

$$c_t = k y_{t-1}^p + k u_t \quad \text{with} \quad E_{t-1} u_t = 0 \tag{5.13}$$

Since $c_{t-1} = k y_{t-1}^p$

$$c_t = c_{t-1} + k u_t \tag{5.14}$$

In other words, consumption expenditure follows a random walk in the same manner as that discussed for the government bond market (see equation (4.23)). This analysis leads to two striking predictions. First, the best predictor of next period's consumption is consumption expenditure in the *current* period. Second, the stability of the economy in response to demand shocks is questioned. According to the rational expectations hypothesis, receipt of 'news' (new information) will cause an immediate reappraisal of permanent income. The extent to which this affects the level of economic activity depends on two factors. First, the degree to which the level of permanent income is altered in response to the new information. At low real rates of interest the discount factor would be quite small, so that the response of permanent income to new information will be quite large. Second, the change in output will, as Bilson (1980) noted depend critically on the shape of the *supply curve*. If the aggregate supply curve is relatively flat following a typical Keynesian specification, the change in output (and therefore the multiplier) will be large despite the assumption of rational expectations. In contrast, adoption of the natural rate hypothesis as a short-run phenomenon even in conjunction with the rational expectations hypothesis will lead to the prediction of little change in the level of economic activity in response to new information.

Hall (1978) tested the empirical validity of the rational expectations/random walk consumption function hypothesis using a variation of the orthogonality test discussed in 3.1 above. A regression of the general form of equation (5.15) below was estimated

$$c_t = \beta_1 c_{t-1} + \beta_2 x_{t-1} \tag{5.15}$$

where c = non-durable consumption expenditure
x = vector of variables known in period $t-1$

Since the variables contained in x were known in period $t-1$, they should have been taken into account in assessing permanent income. According to the rational expectations hypothesis they should consequently not assist in the explanation of c_t, with the result that the coefficients in β_2 should all be 0. This hypothesis was examined by Hall using a standard 'F'-test (see equation (3.16)), and a variety of additional variables dated $t-1$ or earlier. First, lagged values of consumption for periods prior to $t-1$ were tried. These variables provided no statistically significant increase in the explanatory power of the estimating equation. Second, lagged values of real disposable income for period $t-1$ and earlier were introduced into equation (5.15). Again, the hypothesis that these variables provided no additional explanation of consumption in period t could not be rejected, but in this case the issue was less clear-cut. If the level of significance of the test had been 10 per cent instead of the customary 5 per cent then the hypothesis that these variables did not enhance the explanatory power of equation (5.15) would have been rejected. The final test introduced the market value of stock prices in period $t-1$ and earlier. In this case, these additional variables did contribute significantly to the explanation of consumption. The coefficients of the individual variables were also themselves significantly different from 0 according to customary 't'-tests. Hall, however, notes that whilst the improvement in predictive power is statistically significant, it is quantitatively quite small; furthermore, most of the improvement comes from the change in prices in the immediate past quarter. He therefore contends that this result is still consistent with the central tenet of the rational expectations life cycle/permanent income hypothesis.

Bilson (1980) also found support for the rational expectations life cycle/permanent hypothesis of the consumption function using quarterly data over the period 1963(1)–1978(4) for the UK, Germany and the USA. Unlike Hall, Bilson's data for consumer expenditure included expenditure on consumer durables. The starting point of the study was an estimate of expected income using the time series approach discussed in 1.6 above (or more precisely a ten-period moving average). In terms of equation (1.29)

$$\Delta y_t = \Delta \bar{y} + (1 + \theta_1 L + \theta_2 L^2 + \ldots + \theta_{10} L^{10}) e_t \tag{5.16}$$

where $\quad \Delta y =$ change in real income
$\quad\quad\quad e =$ random disturbance

The change in assessment of *permanent* income following a shock would be given by the discounted value of the sum of the moving-average coefficients. In other words

$$y_t^p = \alpha e_t \tag{5.17}$$

where $\quad \alpha = \sum \theta_i (1+r)^{-i} \quad$ with $\quad \theta_0 = 1$

It is apparent that the precise value of α will vary with the real rate of interest (r), so that the random walk model derived in equation (5.14) depends on a constant k which itself depends on a constant real rate of interest. An unanticipated change in income (an innovation, in Bilson's terminology) then follows as the gap between actual income and that predicted by the time-series analysis.

. Bilson used three types of test. First, he estimated an equation of the form

$$c_t - c_{t-1} = \beta_0 + \beta_1(y_t - y_t^p) + \beta_2 \Delta w_t + \beta_3 \Delta s_{t-1} \tag{5.18}$$

where $\quad w =$ real wage
$\qquad s =$ real stock price index
$\qquad$ other variables as before

The variable Δw_t was included because the relationship between consumption and transitory income (the innovation) may reflect the positive relationship between the real wage and transitory income. The variable s_{t-1} follows from the study by Hall. The estimated coefficient $\hat{\beta}_1$ should be consistent with the coefficient α in equation (5.17) derived from the time-series analysis. This was found to hold provided the real rate of interest was 2 per cent per quarter or less. It was felt by Bilson that the data met this test, since the real rate was unlikely to have exceeded this value during the observation period.

The rational expectations consumption function hypothesis predicts that consumption will be influenced by the current period's unanticipated changes in real income ($y_t - y_t^p$) in equation (5.18)) above but not by anticipated changes, since the latter will already have been taken into consideration in the assessment of permanent income. This suggests Bilson's second test – that is, to examine whether the addition of $E_{t-1} y_t^p$ (derived from the time-series analysis) to the independent variables on the right-hand side of equation (5.18) significantly improves the explanatory power of the equation. In the case of the UK and Germany the estimated coefficients were not significantly different from 0. This was not the case in respect of the data for the USA. A final test adopted was to regress the change in consumption on lagged values of unanticipated income which correspond to the 'income innovation'. The rational expectations consumption function hypothesis predicts that only *current* un-anticipated income should influence consumption, since past innovations will already have been taken into account in the assessment of permanent income. The appropriate null hypothesis was, therefore, that the coefficients on lagged innovations were all 0. This hypothesis was rejected at the 5 per cent level but not at the 1 per cent level in the samples for Germany and the USA; in the case of UK data, it was not possible to reject the hypothesis at either level of significance. Nevertheless, as in the case of the study by Hall, the inclusion of lagged income innovations resulted in only a small reduction in the residual standard error for data for the USA.

Bilson also noted the limitations of the tests discussed above. First, the definition of consumption used in the study includes durable consumption goods, which may be expected to respond to lagged income innovations via the accelerator mechanism. Second, his anticipated income series is generated entirely by past income. In view of these and other caveats, Bilson concludes that the rational expectations type of consumption functions estimated by him offer 'an empirically competitive alternative to the conventional consumption function' (p. 296).

Davidson and Hendry (1981) re-examined the results of an earlier study by Davidson, Hendry, Srba and Yeo (1978) in the light of the study by Hall (1978), and their evidence questions the rational expectations/random walk theory of the consumption function. To recapitulate, the earlier work by Davidson *et al.* provided a detailed study of various forms of the consumption function using quarterly data for the UK over the period 1958–76. The form of the selected 'best' equation used the error correction mechanism discussed in 4.1 above with a long-run steady state given by

$$c = ky \tag{5.19}$$

where k = constant for given rates of growth of both real income and rates of inflation

Davidson and Hendry re-estimated the selected 'best' equation over a different period from that adopted by Davidson *et al.* and reported that the results were 'closely similar to those of the original study'

(p. 183). Two further objections to the random walk/rational expectations consumption function were also advanced in Davidson and Hendry (1981). First, lagged values additional to c_{t-1} were tried in the estimating equation and found to be statistically significant. Second, 'Monte Carlo' experiments were used to demonstrate that even if the Davidson *et al.* model were the 'true' model of consumer behaviour, the random walk model would provide a reasonable description of the data and would therefore be unlikely to be rejected by standard statistical tests.

The final study on this topic to be surveyed is that by Muellbauer (1983), who examined the performance of the rational expectations consumption function in the explanation of consumer expenditure in the UK for period 1955(4)–1979(4). Over the entire period, the rational expectations model provided an acceptable model of consumer behaviour. This contrasts with the position if the total period is sub-divided into 1955(4)–1972(2) and 1972(3)–1979(4) – the rationale for this division being the change from a regime of fixed exchange rates to one of floating, with the consequent different responses of the economy to macroeconomic shocks. In this case, the Hall model was decisively rejected for both sub-periods, with Muellbauer arguing that the acceptance of the hypothesis for the total period was due to precisely offsetting effects in the two sub-periods. Muellbauer also investigated whether the assumptions of a constant real rate of interest or the absence of liquidity restraints were responsible for the rejection of the rational expectations consumption function hypothesis. On balance, he felt that these two factors were not responsible, and he argued that this suggested a more fundamental flaw in the model.

The important question is: Where does this leave the theory of the consumption function? For a long period of time this area was largely uncontroversial at least as far as the broad outlines were concerned. The rational expectations consumption function provides a radical alternative. As we have seen, the empirical evidence is ambiguous. There are, however, a number of reasons which may be responsible for researchers' findings that lagged values of economic variables are significant determinants of changes in consumption. The first is that agents do not have full current information on all variables relevant for forecasting current or future values of income, as has been assumed in the studies discussed so far. The assumption of incomplete current information is certainly typically made in other studies of the consumption function. For example, Deaton (1977) assumes that agents do not know current prices and hence current real income. If agents do not possess full current information, then changes in consumption will not be orthogonal to the variables which are not part of the current information set (see 2.3 above). Lagged values of economic variables (for example, income at time $t-1$) could consequently be significant determinants of current consumption. The second reason concerns the error term in the specification of the relevant equations. If a random error term is added to the basic hypothesis to allow for random deviations between actual and desired consumption expenditure, then changes in consumption will no longer follow a random walk but rather will have a time-series representation of the ARIMA $(0,1,1)$ form (see 1.6 above). This can easily be illustrated. Let

$$c_t = ky_t^p + e_t \tag{5.20}$$

where $\quad e =$ white noise error

Using equations (5.8)–(5.12), we can eliminate y_t^p, to obtain

$$c_t - c_{t-1} = ku_t + e_t - e_{t-1} \tag{5.21}$$

The composite error term can be written as a moving-average error term of order 1 (detailed explanation of this is beyond the scope of this text, but can be found in Harvey (1981). Consequently

$$c_t - c_{t-1} = \phi_t + j\phi_{t-1} \tag{5.22}$$

where $\quad \phi =$ random error
$\quad\quad\quad j =$ constant

Equation (5.22) thus shows consumption conforming to an ARIMA $(0,1,1)$ model. If the moving-average error is not allowed for in estimation, then lagged values of consumption could appear significant in regression equations, since the moving-error average term can be approximated by lagged terms in consumption. This can be illustrated by writing equation (5.22) in the following form using the lag operator L (see 1.4 above)

$$\left(\frac{c_t - c_{t-1}}{1 + jL}\right) = \phi_t \tag{5.23}$$

Recalling that $1/x \simeq 1 + x + x^2 + \dots$, equation (5.23) can be written as

or
$$(c_t - c_{t-1})(1 + jL + j^2 L^2 + \ldots) = \phi_t$$

$$c_t - c_{t-1} = -(j + j^2 L + \ldots)(c_{t-1} - c_{t-2}) + \phi_t \tag{5.24}$$

The final point to note is that estimates of the rational expectations hypothesis consumption function for different countries have been obtained as single-equation estimates. However, if (as seems likely) 'news' is correlated between countries, then more efficient estimates will be obtained using a systems estimator which allows for correlation between the error terms in the various consumption functions (see Judge *et al.*, 1980, chapter 6 for further analysis). Allowance for these three points and the possibility of a variable real interest rate (see, for example, Wickens and Molana, 1984) as discussed earlier may well have implications for previous tests of the 'rational expectations' consumption function. The type of expectations which best describes the formation of permanent income is still consequently an open question.

5.3 The wage equation

The wage equation purports to explain the behaviour of money wages. Much of the early theorising about the wage equation was based on the Phillips curve augmented by the expected rate of inflation

$$\Delta W_t = \beta_1 (U - U_n) + \beta_2 E_{t-1} P_t + e_t \tag{5.25}$$

where ΔW = proportionate change in money wages
U_n = natural rate of unemployment
U = actual level of unemployment
P = rate of inflation
e = random disturbance

An alternative approach to the wage equation follows the view that wage increases are the result of a wage-bargaining process, with the rate of change of money wages depending on such variables as the lagged real wage, the expected rate of inflation, the pressure of demand, the retention ratio (the proportion of wages retained after tax payments), and a target for growth of real wages (often proxied by a constant or time trend). Problems of 'observational equivalence' arise in distinguishing between the two approaches because incorporation of these variables in the traditional 'Phillips curve' wage equation can be justified. Incorporation of the real wage, for example, may be justified through an appeal to the neo-classical approach that excess demand for labour depends on the level of the real wage. Incorporation of the retention ratio can similarly be justified on the grounds that the wage relevant to the worker is the 'after-tax' real wage.

Our selection of studies from the considerable volume of literature on this topic concentrates on those studies based on UK data which are, for a variety of reasons, of particular interest. For a more detailed discussion of this topic the interested reader is referred to surveys by Gordon (1976) and Santomero and Seater (1978).

A particularly interesting study is that by Parkin, Sumner and Ward (1976). They commence from the basis that the wage level is set by a bargaining process between employees and unions with the aim of clearing the labour market. Both demand and supply of labour depend on the real wage, but the real wage appropriate to firms is different from that relevant to employees. In addition to the actual wage paid, firms have to pay social security contributions, so that the true nominal wage cost to the firm is the wage plus the social security contribution. In contrast, the wage concept relevant to the employee is the wage *less* the employee's social security contribution and direct taxes. The price levels to convert nominal wages into real wages are also different for the two parties. As far as firms are concerned, the appropriate price level is that referring to output – the wholesale price for domestic sales and a world price for foreign sales; the employees are concerned with the purchasing power of their wages so that the relevant price is the consumer price level plus indirect taxes. The assumption made is that wage levels are set so as to eliminate the excess demand for labour in the previous period, but in the light of the anticipated behaviour of tax rates and prices. These assumptions produce the following estimating equation

$$\Delta W = \beta_1 x_0 + \beta_2 E_{t-1} P^w + \beta_3 (E_{t-1} P^c + E_{t-1} T^i) + \beta_4 E_{t-1} P^f$$
$$+ \beta_5 E_{t-1} T^{fsc} - \beta_6 (E_{t-1} T^{sc} + E_{t-1} T^d) \qquad (5.26)$$

where x_0 = excess demand
           P = rate of change of prices
           T = rate of change of taxes
           superscripts w and f refer to wholesale and foreign prices, and c to consumer prices

> *i* and *d* refer to indirect and direct taxes
> *fsc* and *sc* refer respectively to firms and employees' social
>   security contributions
> $\Delta W =$ the proportionate rate of wage changes

A priori constraints on the size of the coefficients are:

1. $\beta_2 + \beta_3 + \beta_4 = 1$
2. $\beta_5 + \beta_6 = -1$

The three expectational price variables were derived from qualitative questionnaires by the Carlson–Parkin technique in the manner discussed in 1.2 above. Wholesale and foreign prices were derived from CBI (employers') surveys and consumer prices from the Gallup poll on consumer prices; the expected tax/social security variables were proxied by their actual values. Estimation was carried out in both free and restricted forms (in other words, subject to the *a priori* restrictions mentioned above), and the restrictions could not be rejected at the 5 per cent level of significance. Parkin, Sumner and Ward claim that the goodness of fit of the equations (as evidenced by the $\bar{R}^2$ values in the region of 0.45) compares favourably with other investigations of quarter-to-quarter changes and therefore provides 'strong support' for their model. The interesting feature of this study is the use of three price variables, in contrast to the other studies surveyed in this section which have a single price variable.

Two features distinguish Coutts, Tarling and Wilkinson (1976) from other studies in the literature. The first concerns the definition of the dependent variable (ΔW), and the second the role of price expectations in a model of the wage equation. They point out that an index of wage rates (or, for that matter, earnings) does not represent current wage bargaining behaviour. This is because the index covers wages currently being paid and is therefore a weighted average of settlements made in that period and those made in previous periods. They construct an index of wage settlements made in a period, and use this as the dependent variable in the estimated equations. Second, they examine the issue of expectation v. compensation. The augmented Phillips curve approach to wage determination holds that the expected rate of inflation is the relevant variable. An opposing view argues that the relevant variable is actual inflation, on the grounds that workers will endeavour to obtain compensation for inflation occurring during the current wage bargain. Coutts *et al.*

attempt to distinguish between these two models by estimating equations of the general form

$$\Delta WS = \beta_1(1/U) + \beta_2 P \qquad (5.27)$$

$$\Delta WS = \beta_1(1/U) + \beta_2 E_{t-1} P \qquad (5.27a)$$

where ΔWS = rate of change of wage settlement index
P = actual rate of inflation
$E_{t-1}P$ = expected rate of inflation based on Carlson/Parkin data

Greater explanatory power is obtained using equation (5.27) rather than equation (5.27a), which is interpreted by the authors as support for a real wage bargaining process. It is interesting to note that none of the other empirical work surveyed in this section had adopted the wage settlement approach.

In contrast to the empirical studies discussed so far, Batchelor and Sheriff (1980) examine the effects of unanticipated inflation on unemployment. To explain this, equation (5.25) can be written with the rate of inflation as the dependent variable assuming that $\beta_2 = 1$

$$P = \beta_1(U - U_n) + E_{t-1}P_t \qquad (5.28)$$

Rearranging this produces

$$U = \alpha(P_t - E_{t-1}P_t) + U_n \qquad (5.29)$$

where $\alpha = 1/\beta_1$ and since $\beta_1 < 0$, $\alpha < 0$

Actual unemployment is a function of the natural rate of unemployment and unanticipated inflation. Anticipated inflation was proxied in two ways. First, the Carlson–Parkin data on expected prices was available for the period 1961–73. Second, the series could be extended prior to 1961 and post-1973 using the function generating the expectations series as estimated by Carlson and Parkin. In turn, the equilibrium level of unemployment was hypothesised to depend on factors such as the real wage which represent movements along the demand and supply curves and factors which cause shifts in the two schedules, such as productivity, variability of inflation (demand side), benefits ratio (supply side) plus a time trend. In addition, the lagged dependent variable was incorporated into the estimating equation to allow for slow adjustment. Estimation was carried out using both quarterly and annual data and we concentrate on the quarterly data estimates. Substantial explanatory power was achieved with R^2 values in excess of 0.9. The coefficient relating unemployment to unexpected inflation was always significant with a magnitude in the region of 0.2, so that a sustained 5 per cent error in expectations would lead to a 1 per cent rise in unemployment. The evidence for the determinants of the equilibrium level of unemployment were more mixed. The industrial production and time trend coefficients were never significant at the 5 per cent level. The coefficient of the real wage was generally significant at the 5 per cent level, whereas the benefits ratio coefficient was significant only for the longer period. In contrast, the variability of inflation was found to exert a strong positive effect on unemployment. Finally, Batchelor and Sheriff argue that their equation explains the substantial increase in the equilibrium level of unemployment which appeared to occur in the early 1970s in the UK.

We now turn to empirical studies using the rational expectations hypothesis, of which three are surveyed. These are McCallum (1975), Minford and Brech (1981) and Ormerod (1982). This last study is of interest because it attempts to compare the relative performance of rational and non-rational expectations of inflation in wage equations.

McCallum (1975) estimates the augmented Phillips curve in logarithmic form

$$\Delta \log W_t = \alpha_1 + \alpha_2 x_{t-1} + \alpha_3 E_t P_{t+1} \tag{5.30}$$

where	$x_{t-1} =$ measure of excess demand for labour
	$P =$ inflation

Compared with traditional studies of the Phillips curve, McCallum's study is different in two respects. First, he eschews the use of unemployment as a proxy for excess demand for labour, setting x_t as the ratio of demand for labour to labour supply and specifying labour demand and supply schedules as follows

$$L^d/y = \beta_1 w^{\gamma_1} \tag{5.31}$$

where	$y =$ real output
	$w =$ real wage (nominal wage rate (W)/price level)
	$\gamma_1 < 0$

$$L^s/n = \beta_2 w^{\gamma_2} \tag{5.32}$$

where	$n =$ working population
	$\gamma_2 > 0$

Then

$$L^d/L^s = x = \frac{\beta_1}{\beta_2}\left(\frac{w^{\gamma_1}}{w^{\gamma_2}}\right)\left(\frac{y}{n}\right) \tag{5.33}$$

Taking logs and lagging one period

$$\log x_{t-1} = \log(\beta_1/\beta_2) + (\gamma_1 - \gamma_2)\log w + \log(y/n) \tag{5.34}$$

Substituting for x_{t-1} in equation (5.30) from equation (5.34)

$$\Delta \log W_t = \delta_0 + \delta_1 \log w + \delta_2 \log(y/n) + \delta_3 E_t P_{t+1} \tag{5.35}$$

where
$$\delta_0 = \alpha_2 \log(\beta_1/\beta_2) + \alpha_1$$
$$\delta_1 = \alpha_2(\gamma_1 - \gamma_2), \quad \text{so that} \quad \delta_1 < 0$$
$$\delta_2 = \alpha_2, \quad \text{so that } \delta_2 > 0$$
$$\delta_3 = \alpha_3$$

Estimates of equations similar to equation (5.35) were obtained using the rate of change both of wage rates and of nominal earnings. The second difference between this and the other studies concerns the estimation of the expected price variable. Instead of using survey data McCallum uses the instrumental variable technique (discussed in 4.1 above) with the instruments being those which on economic criteria might be expected to influence prices (money stock, government expenditure, import prices, etc.). McCallum claims that the results provide support for the natural rate hypothesis since five out of the six estimates of δ_3 in equation (5.35) are consistent with the hypothesis that $\delta_3 = 1$.

The interesting features of Minford and Brech (1981) are twofold. First is the adoption of the 'dual labour' market hypothesis – the existence of a unionised market side by side with a competitive or residual market for labour. Second, expectations are formed according to the rational expectations hypothesis.

The two labour markets are linked in two ways. The real equilibrium wage in the competitive sector influences the supply of labour to the unionised sector. Also (because the competitive sector is the residual labour market) employment in the unionised sector is an important determinant of the supply of labour to the competitive sector. In the unionised sector, trade unions are assumed to maximise permanent (long-run) wage receipts for their members. In addition, uncertainty is introduced by allowing for the effect of fluctuations in the rate of inflation and level of real income. Planned changes in real wages are assumed to adjust according to the gap between last period's actual real wage and the current permanent real wage. Wages in the competitive sector are determined freely by demand and supply. Substitution of the competitive wage equation into that for the unionised sector using the assumption that the unions' plans for changes in nominal wage prevail produces the following estimating equation

$$\Delta W = \alpha_0 + \alpha_1 E_{t-1} P_t + \alpha_2 b_{t-1} + \alpha_3 T X_{t-1} + \alpha_4 T$$
$$+ \alpha_5 E_{t-1} Q_t + \alpha_6 \operatorname{Var} P_{t-1} + \alpha_7 \operatorname{Var} E_{t-1}$$
$$+ \alpha_8 w_{t-1} + \alpha_9 \operatorname{Pres}_{t-1} \tag{5.36}$$

where
- P = rate of inflation
- ΔW = proportionate rate of change of nominal wages
- w = real wage
- TX = marginal tax rate
- Q = demand pressure
- $\operatorname{Var} P$ = variance of unanticipated inflation
- b = benefits:earnings ratio
- $\operatorname{Var} E$ = variance of unanticipated employment
- $\operatorname{Pres}_{t-1}$ = catching-up term representing unanticipated inflation during previous year

The expected variables were derived by regressing actual inflation and demand pressure on the variables which the relevant body of economic theory would predict to appear in a reduced form of a macroeconomic model. In the case of inflation, these variables were lagged values of money supply, and the money supply itself was related to the government budget deficit. A distinction was made between floating and fixed exchange-rate regimes. In the former case domestic money supply is the relevant variable, whereas in the latter case it is world money supply. In practice, this distinction is rather blurred because of intervention by the authorities in the foreign exchange markets; selection between the two variables was consequently made according to the characteristics of the resulting equation. Expected demand pressure was derived by regressing actual demand pressure on world trade and a fiscal measure. In broad outline, then, the approach is to follow the instrumental variable technique.

Equation (5.36) was estimated for nine countries (six European countries, USA, Canada and Japan) with the imposition of the restriction that $\alpha_1 = 1$. This restriction was tested using a standard 'F'-test, and in general the results were consistent with the constraint. Expected demand pressure entered the equations usually with the correct sign, though often the coefficients were not significant. The variance terms had some effect in almost all countries. The unemployment benefit term was not generally significant, whereas in contrast the lagged real wage entered the equation almost invariably with a correctly signed and significant coefficient.

As noted earlier, Ormerod (1982) attempts to compare the performance of different methods of expectation formation within the context of an estimated wage equation for the UK. The specification of this wage equation follows the general form often used in empirical work within the UK. The precise equation estimated was

$$\Delta W = \alpha_0 + \alpha_1 E_{t-1} P_t + \alpha_2 RR_{t-1} + \alpha_3 \Delta W_{t-1}$$
$$+ \alpha_4 (1/w)_{t-1} + \alpha_5 \text{ Time} \tag{5.37}$$

where RR = the proportionate change in the retention ratio (percentage of wages and salaries retained after deduction of income tax and national insurance contributions) other variables as before

Four hypotheses of expectations formation were tried

(a) a first-order autoregressive scheme

$$E_{t-1} P = \alpha_0 + \alpha_1 P_{t-1}$$

(b) a fourth-order autoregressive scheme

$$E_{t-1} P = \alpha_0 + \alpha_1 P_{t-1} + \alpha_2 P_{t-2} + \alpha_3 P_{t-3} + \alpha_4 P_{t-4}$$

(c) substitution or perfect foresight

$$E_{t-1} P = P_t$$

(d) rational expectations

In contrast to the other studies surveyed so far in this section, the rational expectations expected inflation series was derived from the predictions of a complete macroeconomic model (that of the National Institute of Economic and Social Research (NIESR). The methodology used was to choose a six-equation sub-system comprising equations for wage rates, consumer prices, short-term interest rates, government debt sales and exchange rates (both spot and forward).

These equations were estimated and substituted into the model, which was then solved to obtain predictions for the expected variables. These predicted values were used in the re-estimation of the sub-model and the whole process repeated until the parameters of the sub-model did not change between successive iterations by more than 0.001 per cent.

Estimation of the wage equation (5.37) proceeded, incorporating the four potential methods of expectation formation listed above. In terms of explanatory power, the rational expectations equation was marginally more successful – though this success was unlikely to be statistically significant. Ormerod was concerned about the value of the coefficient α_1 in the rational expectations estimate. This was not significantly different from unity, and he felt that this value – which implied that wage settlements incorporated both full compensation for expected inflation and partial compensation for any existing discrepancy between actual and desired wages – was not in accordance with any institutional description of wage bargaining during the period in question (1971–9). Equation (5.37) was therefore re-estimated subject to the constraint that $\alpha_1 + \alpha_3 = 1$. This constraint proved to be statistically valid, and the marginal superiority of the rational expectations approach was further reduced.

The conclusion reached by Ormerod was that in the context of the wage equation, the marginal gain through using the rational expectations hypothesis in modelling inflation expectations failed to compensate for the relatively large amounts of computing time and labour required. However, this comment should perhaps not be taken too seriously. If the purpose of a study is to discriminate between alternative expectations mechanisms which possess crucially different policy implications, then many would argue that the resources devoted to operationalising the rational expectations hypothesis would be well spent if that is the correct behavioural hypothesis.

In conclusion, the recent empirical results (Minford and Brech, 1981; and Ormerod, 1982) suggest that a rational or unbiased approach to expectations formation will generate results which are as good as those obtained from earlier studies using alternative methods. Future work on the wage equation must examine the behaviour of the function over known changes in the environment (such as fixed to floating exchange rates) in order to provide more powerful tests which can readily discriminate between the various possible expectational mechanisms.

5.4 Expected capital gains

As we noted in 4.5 above, the expected return on a bond consists of two components – the fixed-interest payment or coupon value, and the expected capital gain/loss during the holding period. An alternative approach to that considered in chapter 4 is to attempt to model expected capital gains. In particular, two studies (Spencer, 1981; and Grice and Bennett, 1981) are of interest in this connection as they both adopt the procedure of searching for instruments to estimate capital gains. The relevant instruments can be selected by trial and error according to criteria provided by economic theory and econometric considerations. A distinction can be made between those who regard the instruments purely as a solution to the econometric problem of obtaining a series of weakly rational predictors (or expectations), and those who also view the expectations equation as having some economic logic. Spencer (1981) tends towards the latter view, whereas Grice and Bennett (1981) adopt the former.

The *ex post* or realised differential return on bonds can be defined as

$$R + g - r \qquad (5.38)$$

where R = coupon value of the bond
g = realised capital gain during the holding period
r = nominal rate of interest on other financial assets

The pure expectations theory predicts that the expected value of equation (5.38) should be 0. Spencer examines the demand for gilt-edged securities by non-bank residents of the UK over the period 1967–77. He first of all examines whether the *ex post* differential return on long-term gilt-edged securities specified by equation (5.38) equalled 0 on average. This was found not to be the case, and can be considered as evidence against the pure expectations theory of the term structure. The next step in the study was to estimate the *ex post* differential return as a function of variables known at the time of expectations formation. A reasonable prediction of the differential return (as evidenced by the R^2 value of 0.624) was obtained using lagged values of the following variables:

1. autonomous balance of payments flows
2. Eurodollar rate of interest
3. weighted average of import and wage cost inflation

4. short-term rate of interest
5. real values of gilt-edged stocks
6. changes in real value of wealth attributable to savings and inflation

The predicted value of the differential return (including capital gains) is then used as the dependent variable in the demand-for-bonds equation estimated by Spencer. A number of equations were estimated, and we concentrate on just one of these in order to demonstrate the methodology adopted. An error-correction model (see 4.1 above) is assumed, with the real quantity of bond purchases expressed as a percentage of outstanding stock $(t - \Delta p)$ specified to be a function of capital gains, a constant term, the stock of bonds and a disequilibrium term (the growth of total final expenditure *less* the rate of inflation). The estimated equation was

$$t - \Delta p = 0.0819 + 0.0019(R + g - r)$$
$$+ 0.441(\Delta Y - \Delta p) - 0.2787(X/Y) \qquad (5.39)$$

where X = stock of gilts
Y = nominal total final expenditure (a scale variable)
Δ = percentage growth
other variables are as before

This can be solved to obtain the long-run static equilibrium relationship

$$X/Y = 0.2938 + 0.0043(R - r) \qquad (5.40)$$

A similar procedure is followed by Grice and Bennett for the period 1963–78, though in this case the variable of interest is the differential return on money over the total return on gilt-edged securities

$$R_m - (R + g) \qquad (5.41)$$

where R_m = return on money
other variables are as in equation (5.38)

As noted at the beginning of this section, Grice and Bennett adopt a broader approach than Spencer. It should be remembered that the McCallum technique entails using as instruments variables which economic theory predicts are related to the subsequently-realised capital gains. An alternative approach is to search out – using purely statistical criteria – instruments which are correlated with the variables subject to measurement error but uncorrelated with either the measurement error or the disturbance term. Grice and Bennett use a combination of the two approaches, searching over a large number of possible instruments including (in addition to the lagged value of the differential return on money) current and lagged values of:

1. gross real financial wealth
2. cumulated revaluations through changes in market prices of bonds
3. real total final expenditure
4. absolute return on money
5. real value of the money supply
6. Eurodollar rate of interest
7. various dummy variables

Again a reasonable prediction of capital gains is obtained, the R^2 value being 0.86. This figure could be further increased (to 0.96) by including the rank of the realised capital gain, though in this case it is far from clear that the rank of the capital gain is uncorrelated with the measurement error. The predicted differential return was then used in the equation estimated to explain the demand for sterling M3.

These two studies provide a good illustration of the use of instrumental variables as proxies for expected variables. It is, however, important to realise that these equations cannot be used to provide genuine *ex ante* forecasts within the sample period, since all the information would not be available to the forecaster.

5.5 Conclusions

We have surveyed a range of empirical studies involving expectational variables. These studies were classified into two categories, first, studies in which expectations were implicit rather than explicit. This category included the rational expectations consumption function which involved similar methodology to that used in the efficient markets literature discussed in the previous chapter. In both areas we examined evidence which supports the hypotheses and evidence which tends to cast doubt on their validity. A similar picture was obtained with regard to studies of the wage equation which forms the major component of the second class of studies. With respect to this function a variety of approaches to modelling expectations were considered, including survey data, lagged dependent variables, instrumental variables and model predictions. This range of approaches is in marked contrast to the position regarding macroeconomic models discussed in chapter 6. No doubt this difference is due in part to the difficulty in obtaining solutions to macroeconomic models which include expected values generated by the model as endogenous variables.

The verdict on the rational expectations hypothesis arising from the consideration of single-equation studies must therefore be one of *not proven*. There appears to be sufficient evidence to sustain the belief in the rational expectations hypothesis of its protagonists. On the other hand, there is not enough unambiguous evidence to convince those who doubt its adequacy. A similar verdict was, as we have already seen, reached in chapter 4 in relation to the efficiency of the various markets examined there.

6

Expectations in Econometric Models

6.1 Introduction

In this chapter, we examine the role of expectational variables in econometric models. In 6.2 we provide a brief comparison of the structure of four models of the UK economy, and in 6.3 go on to consider in more detail their treatment of expectational variables; some tentative conclusions concerning these models are reached in 6.4. In 6.5 we look at the use of expectation series in a number of models, and in 6.6 present conclusions on the role of expectations in macroeconometric models.

6.2 Models of the UK economy

There are a large number of macroeconomic models of the UK economy in current use. However, as many of these models are treated as confidential, we concentrate on those whose forecasts have been the subject of widespread comment in the news media. In our opinion, these are the models of the National Institute of Social and Economic Research (NIESR), the London Business School (LBS), the Treasury (HMT) and the Liverpool model (LM). We have not included the model used by the Cambridge Economic Policy Group because, as far as the role of expectations is concerned, the model is essentially the same as the NIESR model, with expectations being proxied by lagged values of variables.

The NIESR and HMT models are basically similar in construction. Both follow the traditional Keynesian income/expenditure approach augmented by a sophisticated financial structure and equations representing supply-side factors. In both models the most important determinant in the principal consumption equation is *lagged disposable income*. In the HMT model, the specification adopted for the manufacturing investment equation incorporates the error-correction mechanism discussed in 4.2 above with desired capital stock being dependent on output and the cost of capital. In the NIESR model, determination of manufacturing investment follows an accelerator type of relationship with an additional variable (company profitability) being incorporated. Much of government expenditure is exogenous in the sense of being forecast independently of the behavioural equations contained in the models. Finally, as far as the real sector is concerned, exports and imports depend on both activity variables and relative prices (including the exchange rate).

As noted above, the financial sectors of both models are quite sophisticated. In the NIESR model the main emphasis is placed on the explanation of credit flows arising from the finance of the PSBR and the flow of bank lending. These credit flows are mainly demand-determined, though there is some feedback from the financial variables to aggregate demand. The quantity of real balances, for example, is a determinant of consumption expenditure. In contrast, the financial sector of the HMT model is more closely integrated with the real sector of the model. The underlying process is one of allocating financial surpluses (gaps between income and expenditure of the different sectors) between the various assets and liabilities of the different sectors, whilst at the same time preserving the balance sheet identities. The returns on the assets/liabilities are determined within the model, and these in turn influence the size of the surplus/deficit of each sector. The HMT model includes a demand function for sterling M3, whereas in the NIESR model the explanation of M3 holdings is implicit since the quantity of money held must be consistent with the other asset demand functions. In both models, interest-rate determination follows a 'mark-up' relationship linked to the Treasury bill rate, which is treated as exogenous for estimation purposes.

As far as the supply side is concerned, the two models follow different approaches. In both cases the principal wage equation plays a crucial role, with prices being primarily a mark-up on costs. In the NIESR model, the rate of change of money wages is determined by the previous real wage, the level of and changes in unemployment, and the expected rate of inflation with a coefficient less than unity. The model therefore incorporates two of the main strands of recent research into the wage equation – the Sargan wage inflation model, and the Phillips curve. In contrast, the HMT model has adopted a reduced-form approach to the modelling of the behaviour of earnings, by substituting the determinants of demand for and supply of labour into a single equation.

The two models also follow different approaches with respect to the determination of the exchange rate. In the HMT model, the equation describing speculative capital flows is inverted to determine the exchange rate (it should be noted that these flows are influenced by changes in the exchange rate). Expectations play an important role in this mechanism, which is discussed in more detail in the following section. In the NIESR model, no attempt is made to model capital flows and the real exchange rate is determined by real interest rate differentials, the real value of the current account balance and the real value of North Sea oil reserves.

From this brief description of the NIESR and HMT models it is apparent that, whilst both models broadly follow the traditional Keynesian income/expenditure approach, money plays a more important role in the HMT model. In contrast, both the LBS and LM models are regarded as being much more monetarist. In the LBS model this is due mainly to the ubiquitous role played by money in the expenditure equations, so that changes in the money stock have a direct impact on private sector expenditure. Apart from the role of money, the real sector of the LBS model follows an approach similar to that adopted by the NIESR and HMT models. However, in comparison with both those models the monetary sector lacks detail, with a single equation determining the stock of money. Further equations describe bank lending and the private sector's holdings of deposit accounts and notes and coins. The key interest rate is the UK three-month Treasury bill rate, which is determined by the past behaviour both of itself and of the three-month Eurodollar rate. Other interest rates (including that of the building societies) follow a simple mark-up on this key rate.

Earlier versions of the LBS model adopted the internationalist monetarist approach to the determination of prices (see Ball, Burns and Warburton, 1979). The current version is, however, more cost-orientated. There exists the standard interrelationship between average earnings and price levels (both wholesale and retail); the external effect in the wage equation now comes through the influence of the term representing international competitiveness, with a movement in favour of the UK leading to an increase in average earnings.

The long-run level of the exchange rate depends on the rate of expansion of the domestic money supply relative to that in the rest of the world, the value of North Sea oil reserves and the level of balances held by OPEC countries. A decrease in the relative rate of expansion of the money supply or increases in either North Sea oil reserves or OPEC balances leads to an appreciation of the exchange rates.

The contrast between the Liverpool Model (LM) and the other models discussed is striking. A first minor difference is that the LM is an annual model, whereas the other models discussed in this section are all quarterly. Second, the underlying philosophy of the model reflects the new classical school in that markets are assumed to clear in an *ex ante* sense, and that expectations are assumed to be formed according to the rational expectations hypothesis. Third, the real stock of wealth is a major determinant of private sector expenditure. The sources of private sector nominal financial wealth are the PSBR and the balance of payments current account surplus; valuation effects due to interest rate and general price level changes convert the nominal stock into the real stock of private sector financial wealth. Total private sector real wealth follows from the addition of the stock of real assets to financial wealth as defined above.

Portfolio decision-making is segregated sequentially into three levels. First, there is the consumption decision. Second, there is the portfolio allocation between real and financial assets. Third, there is the subsidiary portfolio allocation between money and other financial assets. Determinants of the portfolio decisions include wealth and relevant rates of return on the different assets involved. It should be noted that income plays a much smaller role than in standard Keynesian-type models. As we shall see in the following section, changes in financial wealth play an important role in the transmission of monetary changes to the real sector. The quantity of money follows from the PSBR, and in the floating exchange rate version of the model the gap between the rate of growth of the money supply and the demand for real balances leads to inflation.

The supply side of the model reflects demand and supply conditions in the labour market. The equilibrium real wage depends on taxes on employment, unemployment benefits, union membership and unanticipated inflation. The equilibrium real wage rises with increases in the first three variables and falls with the other variables. The actual real wage adjusts to the equilibrium real wage with a lag.

Interest-rate determination reflects the efficient markets hypothesis discussed in chapter 4, both with regard to the relationship between nominal rates and expected inflation (the 'Fisher' hypothesis) and also exchange rate changes (interest-rate parity). We leave detailed discussion of these aspects until the examination of the role of expectations within models in the following section.

6.3 Expectations in UK models

Within the NIESR model expectations are almost exclusively represented as functions of lagged values of the variables concerned. The wage equation, for example, includes as one explanatory variable the expected rate of inflation, which is modelled as a fourth-order autoregressive process. This is of course consistent with the hypothesis that expectations are formed by extrapolating the past behaviour of the variable concerned. For the financial sector, most of the equations are estimated by the error-correction technique discussed in 4.2 above, so that any role for expectations is incorporated within the dynamic adjustment mechanism. The role of expectations within this sector is thus far from obvious. However, more explicitly, changes in the real exchange rate depend on *inter alia* the differential between the *ex post* real rates of interest on three-month UK Treasury bills and those on three-month Eurodollar deposits in London. As discussed in 4.3 above, the real rate of interest is more correctly defined as the nominal rate *less* the *expected* rate of inflation, so that this equation appears to be misspecified unless perfect foresight is assumed. Sales of government debt depend on the differential between the rates of interest on consols and certificates of deposit, and also the current and lagged values of financial assets held by the non-bank private sector. In its turn, the change in the consol rate depends on the change in the rate of interest on Treasury bills and on the acceleration of inflation. There is therefore little scope in the term structure for the role of expectations discussed in 4.3 above. Finally with regard to the NIESR model, the actual rate of inflation (lagged one period) and the short-term rate of interest (lagged four periods) appear as explanatory variables (with coefficients not constrained to be equal) in the equation representing stockbuilding in distributive trades. The justification for these two variables follows an opportunity-cost interpretation. Again, the relevant variables should be the rate of inflation *expected* to occur, rather than its actual lagged value.

Expectations play a more important role in the HMT model, especially in the sections dealing with the financial aspects and also external capital flows. Expected rates of inflation are represented by two series – consumer's expectations and a series based on the past behaviour of costs and monetary expansion. The series on consumers' expectations of inflation is modelled as being dependent on the past behaviour of prices of consumption goods. In turn, these prices are derived as a mark-up on costs with lagged adjustment representing the role of 'expectations, institutional rigidities and partial adjust-ment' (HMT 1982). This expectation series is consequently entirely backward-looking. In contrast, the second expectation series mentioned above is determined as a weighted average of the past behaviour of production costs (trend of labour and import costs) and monetary expansion adjusted for growth in productivity. As such, the second series may be interpreted as a compromise between 'backward'- and 'forward'-looking expectations, provided that past behaviour of the money supply indicates future behaviour of inflation. The expected consumer price series is used to determine the real rate of interest, which is one determinant of expenditure on consumer durables in the model. On the other hand, the real rate of interest used in the equation for manufacturers' stocks of materials and fuels is described by the current nominal rate minus the current actual rate of inflation (as measured by the wholesale price index). In the other principal investment functions, the cost of capital is represented by nominal rates of interest, or omitted altogether. The effects of expected demand in these equations is captured by current or lagged actual demand. A further example of the use of past price changes occurs with respect to wage determination. The central equation for the determination of wages and salaries is that for average earnings in the private sector; as we noted in 6.2 above, this follows a reduced-form approach, with a single equation representing demand and supply influences on the wage mechanism. One of the determinants in this equation is lagged producers' prices, which is intended to proxy inflationary expectations.

Perhaps the more interesting use of expectational variables appears in the financial and external sectors of the HMT model. Two series are of particular interest, namely the explanation of expected capital gains and the exchange rate. We noted earlier that the HMT model now contains a demand for broad money function, leaving non-bank private sector holdings of gilt-edged securities to be treated as a residual. One of the determinants of the demand for money is the rate of return on the competitive asset – gilt-edged securities. This of course includes capital gains which are specified (in a similar manner to that discussed in 5.4 above) to depend on:

1. lagged levels of the long-term rate of interest; in its turn the long-term rate of interest is determined by its own lagged value, the short-term rate of interest and the cost- and money-based expected inflation series; increases in the long-term rate of interest lead to expectations of future reductions and hence capital gains on gilts
2. (negatively) the current short-term rate of interest
3. (negatively) the cost- and money-based inflation series so that an expected increase in inflation will depress bond prices
4. (negatively) the immediate past values of the ratio of the PSBR to private sector net financial wealth; values further in the past appear with positive signs, but the net effect is negative

The exchange-rate equation is determined within the sector dealing with external capital flows. Most of these equations are based on a portfolio model which includes wealth, relevant interest rates and the expected change in the exchange rate as determinants of the asset demand functions. These equations are first differenced to generate flows. A distinction is made between structural flows and speculative flows; this latter category is treated as the residual after specifying structural capital flows, current account flows and government intervention, given that the net total of these flows is 0 via the balance of payments identity.

Absence of perfect capital mobility is assumed (or equivalently, speculators are risk-averse). This permits a two-stage explanation of the expected exchange rate. First there is the long-run sustainable exchange rate which depends on:

1. wage costs in the UK relative to those in the rest of the world (negatively)

2. domestic money supply relative to that in the rest of the world (negatively)
3. the real value of expected output of North Sea oil
4. the uncovered interest-rate differential

The expected exchange rate is modelled by an error-correction mechanism, through which the actual exchange rate adjusts to the long-run sustainable rate with a lag. The actual spot rate is obtained by inverting the speculative flow equation, so that the spot exchange rate is the dependent variable with the expected exchange rate described above being one of the determining variables.

Expectations formation in the HMT model is a form of compromise between the rational and behavioural hypotheses discussed in chapter 1. In line with the monetarist viewpoint, increased monetary expansion leads to expectations of higher rates of inflation and a depreciation of the exchange rate. Monetary expansion will similarly lead to higher rates of interest via the long-term rate of interest-equation, and also to expectations of capital losses. Nevertheless, this expectations series is also influenced by the past behaviour of costs. Furthermore, the consumer price expectations series is entirely dependent on the past behaviour of consumer prices. A method of obtaining a series of expected price variables similar to that utilised in the HMT model for the exchange rate has been adopted in the Candide model of the Canadian economy. Briefly the Candide model (2.0 version – see Rao and Lodh, 1983, for further details) is a large-scale econometric model of the Canadian economy with extensive industry detail. Within the price sector expected inflation is an important determinant of the growth of nominal wages. Expected inflation itself is a weighted average of the previous year's inflation and the rate of growth of the money supply during the two previous years. The weights are determined by regression analysis. So to the extent that past money growth indicates future inflation this price expectation series may again be regarded as a compromise between forward- and backward-looking expectations.

Within the LBS model expectations are modelled almost entirely by the past behaviour of the variables concerned. The only role for forward-looking expectations occurs with respect to the determination of the exchange rate which depends in part on the rate of monetary expansion in the UK relative to that in the rest of the world. To the extent that changes in the relative rate of monetary expansion indicate future changes in relative rates of inflation, it may be argued that the induced changes in the exchange rate reflect anticipated changes in purchasing power parity.

We now turn to discussing the LM. For a more detailed discussion the interested reader is referred to Minford, Marwaha, Matthews and Sprague (1984). As we explained in 6.1 above, the LM alone out of the models surveyed has adopted the rational expectations hypothesis. Model predictions or forecasts are consequently consistent with the expected future values of the variables incorporated within the model. The main expectations variables concern future exchange rates and rates of inflation. Dealing with nominal rates of interest first, two rates are distinguished – short and long term. The strong 'Fisher' hypothesis discussed in 4.3 above is assumed to apply at all times, so that both rates follow the general pattern of equation (4.9a), reproduced below for convenience

$$R_t = i + E_{t-1}P \tag{4.9a}$$

where i = real rate of interest
         P = rate of inflation

Two expected inflation series are consequently generated by the model to correspond to these two rates of interest. A similar procedure is adopted for the specification of the real rates of interest, which are not assumed to be constants as in the case of much of the work on efficient markets surveyed in chapter 4. Interest-rate parity is assumed to hold in real rates of interest in the UK and the USA (see 4.5 above for discussion of this concept). The relevant equations take the following general form

$$i_{UK} = i_{US} + E_t dRS \tag{6.1}$$

where dRS refers to changes in the real exchange rate

Again the model distinguishes between two time horizons for expectations formation for the future exchange rate – short and long term.

Solution of the LM is achieved through use of a computer algorithm (RATEXP, described in Matthews and Marwaha, 1981). This algorithm forces equality between the expected future values of variables entering into the model equations and the model's own prediction through use of an iterative process. In 2.2 above we discussed the problem of non-uniqueness of solution which often occurs in rational expectations models. The computer algorithm meets this problem through the imposition by the user of terminal conditions for expected values of variables at the end of a forecasting horizon specified by the user. If there are a number of stable paths, the algorithm selects the path for which the roots have the smallest absolute value. Sensitivity analysis reported in Minford and Peel (1983) suggests that the simulation results are not particularly sensitive to changes in the terminal values, provided they are set sufficiently far beyond the period which is of interest.

6.4 Conclusions on UK macroeconometric models

The methods of expectations formation in the various models surveyed in the previous sections raise several interesting questions. The first of these refers to how far (if at all) any of these models meet the Lucas critique discussed in 2.5 above. That is: To what extent do the models ignore any reaction of the private sector to changes in government policy? In principle, models are highly susceptible to the Lucas critique when expectations are modelled according to the past behaviour of the variable. A similar comment applies to models which make extensive use of the error-correction model (see 4.2 above). Of the models surveyed in this chapter, the NIESR and LBS models are particularly vulnerable to this criticism (the LM contrasts with the other models in this respect). In practice, however, 'judgemental' adjustments are likely to be made to the mechanical forecasts produced from the model. These adjustments are themselves a source of criticism in that they are subjective and reflect the modeller's prejudices. It should be remembered that the correct solution to the Lucas critique is to build a model consisting of truly *structural* equations. If there is a policy change, then this will be captured in the LM by changes in the expected values (forward-looking) of the relevant equations. On the other hand, the coefficients of the equations are assumed to remain constant, and to be invariant to policy changes. This procedure carries with it the assumption that when policy changes occur the effects on the coefficients are less important than the effects on expectations. The Lucas critique is thus only partially met. As noted earlier, expectations in the HMT model are a compromise between the rational and behavioural hypotheses, and it is consequently less vulnerable to the Lucas critique than the NIESR and LBS models, but more so than the LM. These constraints should be borne in mind when considering the result of policy prescriptions published in the news media with frequently inadequate discussion of the assumptions made.

It is also interesting to examine the properties of a macroeconomic model by looking at simulation results as well as examining individual equations. This provides additional information as to how the various equations interact when the model is shocked. In this case, the Lucas critique is less relevant since we are concerned with the properties of the model rather than policy forecasts. To illustrate the general nature of the response of the LM as compared with a more traditional model we examine the different results obtained from a change in government expenditure for both the HMT and LM models – these results are reported in HMT (1982) and Minford, Marwaha, Matthews and Sprague (1984). In practice, of course, precise comparison of results requires careful standardisation of the assumptions associated with the simulation experiment. Nevertheless since we are concerned only with general implications of the method of expectations formation, we consider the two experiments reported below adequate. The interested reader is referred to Holden, Peel and Thompson (1982) for a more detailed discussion of simulation experiments affecting these models.

For the HMT model, an increase in central government expenditure on goods and services equivalent to 0.5 per cent of nominal GDP produces a fairly rapid but moderate impact on real GDP. The initial impact on output is lost after about three years as a result of higher prices and progressively higher rates of interest necessary to meet the monetary targets. Relaxation of a target for monetary growth produces a larger increase in output. The peak multipliers are respectively in the region of 1.1 and 1.3. For the LM model only, a quite small increase in output results from an increase in government expenditure financed by increased money and bonds equivalent to £0.8 billion; in fact, the peak multiplier is well short of 1. The small impact results not only from the adoption of the rational expectations hypothesis but also from the structure of the model (and in particular the importance of wealth in private expenditure decisions). The increased rate of inflation expected due to the increased rate of monetary growth raises nominal rates of interest. Higher prices and nominal rates of interest reduce the real market value of financial wealth, thus producing a contraction of private expenditure which offsets the initial expansionary effect derived from increased public sector expenditure. It is consequently important to realise that it is not just the rational expectations hypothesis which influences the speed of adjustment of a model in response to a shock. The general structure of the model itself is also relevant, thus reinforcing the similar point made in 2.4 above that the potential role for stabilisation policy does not depend solely on the adoption in a model of the rational expectations hypothesis.

6.5 Expectations in other macroeconomic models

In this section we discuss four small-scale models of the US economy – namely the St Louis model and those developed by Sargent (1976), Barro (1978) and Laidler and Bentley (1983). These models are of interest because of the differing underlying philosophies rather than for the precise conclusions reached, since variations in the estimation period and/or data used affect the results.

The St Louis model was first presented in Anderson and Carlson (1970) and subsequently an updated version was discussed in Carlson and Hein (1983). The model consists of five equations and two identities, and a stylised version (ignoring constant terms) is shown in equations (6.2)–(6.6)

$$dY = \sum a_{1i}dM_{t-i} + \sum a_{2i}dG_{t-i} \tag{6.2}$$

$$dP = \sum b_{1i}dP^{en}_{t-i} + \sum b_{2i}d\text{Gap}_{t-i} + b_3 E_t dP \tag{6.3}$$

$$RL = \sum c_i dP_{t-i} \tag{6.4}$$

$$RS = \sum e_{1i}dP^{en}_{t-i} + \sum e_{2i}dy_{t-i} + \sum e_{3i}dP_{t-i} \tag{6.5}$$

$$U - U^f = f_1 \text{Gap}_t + f_2 \text{Gap}_{t-1} \tag{6.6}$$

where Y = nominal national income
        y = real output
        P = general price level
        P^{en} = relative price of energy
        G = full employment federal government expenditure
        Gap = gap between full employment and actual output
        RL = long-term rate of interest (rate on corporate bonds)
        RS = short-term rate of interest (four-month rate)
        U = actual unemployment
        U^f = full employment level of unemployment
        d = proportionate rate of change of the variable

The main GNP equation (6.2) describes the rate of growth of nominal GNP as being a function of current and actual lagged values of the rate of growth of the money supply and full-employment federal government expenditure. The price equation (6.3) relates the rate of inflation to current and lagged changes in demand pressure, the relative price of energy and anticipated inflation. Anticipated inflation itself is represented purely as a weighted sum of past price changes, and so is basically adaptive. Changes in real output follow automatically from an identity given the changes in nominal GNP and prices.

Three other variables are explained within the model – two rates of interest, and employment. The long-term rate of interest (equation (6.4)) is a function of past rates of inflation. In contrast, the short-term rate of interest depends on the current rate of monetary expansion and current and lagged values of changes in the relative price of energy, output and prices. Finally the deviation of unemployment from its full employment level (equation (6.6)) is determined by the gap between actual and full-employment level of output.

The St Louis model has a reputation for being strongly monetarist. This follows from two features of the model. First and foremost is the magnitude of the coefficients of money and government expenditure in the GNP equation. In the case of monetary expansion these sum to approximately unity whereas those in respect of federal government expenditure sum to 0. Second there is the role of inflation in the determination of rates of interest. Expectations are purely backward-looking so that there is no accommodation with the new classical school via the adoption of the rational expectations hypothesis.

In contrast Sargent (1976) develops a small five-equation model of the US economy embodying strong classical principles which imply that a monetary feedback rule is powerless to influence the expected values of real variables. It is estimated using quarterly data for the period 1951(1)–1973(3). The key elements of the model are:

1. a version of the natural rate hypothesis which suggests that there is no exploitable trade-off between unemployment and inflation, even in the short run
2. an expectations theory of the term structure of interest rates
3. an assumption of the rational expectations hypothesis

A simple representation of the model is shown below

$$U_t = a(p_t - E_{t-1}p_t) + \sum v_i U_{t-i} + e_1 \qquad (6.7)$$

$$n_t = b_1(p_t - E_{t-1}p_t) + b_2 U_t + \sum w_i n_{t-i} + e_2 \tag{6.8}$$

$$y_t = c_1 t + c_2(n_t - U_t + \text{pop}_t) + e_3 \tag{6.9}$$

$$R_t = R_{t-1} + d(Z_t - E_{t-1}Z_t) + e_4 \tag{6.10}$$

$$m_t = p_t + f_1 R_t + f_2 y_t + f_3(m-p)_{t-1} + e_5 \tag{6.11}$$

where U = rate of unemployment
         p = price level
         n = labour force participation rate
         y = real GNP
         pop = population
         R = nominal rate of interest
         t = time
         Z = exogenous variables in the *IS* curve
         m = money supply
         p, n, y, pop and m are logarithmic values of the variables concerned

Equation (6.7) represents the augmented Phillips curve with the rate of unemployment as the dependent variable. Equation (6.8) determines the participation ratio of the labour force and equation (6.9) is the production function. Combination of these three equations produces an aggregate supply curve in the *yp* plane with the standard positive slope. Equation (6.10) specifies the term structure of interest rates and substitution of this equation into the money demand function (equation (6.11)) produces an aggregate demand curve with the customary downward slope with respect to the price level. Clearly, therefore, the model is simultaneous in determining the current values of the endogenous variables. However, in terms of predictions the model is purely recursive. This can easily be seen by taking expectations and noting that the one-period ahead forecasts derived from the model reduce to the following simple set of equations

$$E_{t-1}U_t = \sum v_i U_{t-1} \tag{6.7a}$$

$$E_{t-1}n_t = b_2 U_t + \sum w_i n_{t-1} \tag{6.8a}$$

$$E_{t-1}y_t = c_1 t + c_2(n_t - U_t + \text{pop}_t) \tag{6.9a}$$

$$E_{t-1}R_t = R_{t-1} \tag{6.10a}$$

$$E_{t-1}(m-p)_t = f_1 R_t + f_2 y_t + f_3(m-p)_{t-1} \tag{6.11a}$$

Predictions of the model are thus all independent of the money supply, which influences only the predictions of the price level. Similarly, suppose the authorities attempt to peg the rate of interest via a feedback rule given, for example, by

$$R_t = \theta Q_{t-1} \tag{6.12}$$

where Q represents a vector of relevant endogenous variables

then equation (6.12) is inconsistent with equation (6.10), so that the interest rate is over-determined and the price level indeterminate. The model therefore incorporates classical features as far as predictive values are concerned.

For estimation purposes, the model listed in equations (6.7)–(6.11) was modified in two directions. The variable $(Z_t - E_{t-1}Z_t)$ was replaced by lagged values of R, and time-trend variables were introduced into the equations. Neither of these modifications invalidates the classical stance adopted in equations (6.7)–(6.11). A series for the unobservable estimated price variable was obtained using the instrumental variable approach discussed in 4.1 above, by regressing p_t on a set of variables dated $t-1$ or earlier; satisfactory estimates of the equations were obtained. In addition to the standard statistical tests of the goodness of fit, tests were also carried out using the Granger–Simms approach. Briefly, according to Granger (1969), Y causes X if better predictions of X are obtained using all past information including Y than if the information apart from Y had been used. Some evidence for rejecting the philosophy of the model was obtained – and in particular that the money wage rate appeared to cause (in the Granger sense) unemployment and the long-term rate of interest. Sargent argues that this is far from decisive and that in any case the tests have turned up 'little evidence requiring us to reject the key hypothesis of the model that government monetary and fiscal policy variables do not cause unemployment or the interest rate' (Sargent, 1976, p. 236). In contrast Fair (1979) has subjected the Sargent model to a comparison with other models of the US economy, and in particular a fifth-order autoregressive naive model. Fair re-estimated the model for a slightly different period and noted that 'it is an unfortunate characteristic of macroeconomic models that their coefficient estimates can change substantially as the sample period changes and this is clearly true of a number of the coefficient changes in Sargent's model' (p. 705). The conclusion of Fair's study was that Sargent's model is no more accurate than the autoregressive naive model over the sample period selected for the test.

The model of the US economy put forward by Barro (1978) was constructed to test the view that only unanticipated monetary growth will affect real output and that anticipated monetary growth will have a one-to-one effect on the price level. This view underpins the idea of the impotence of monetary policy to stabilise the economy as discussed in 2.4 above. In this connection the philosophy of the model is similar to that adopted by Sargent (1976). Basically the model consists of three equations – one equation specifying anticipated or expected monetary growth, and two reduced-form equations respectively explaining output and the price level. Anticipated monetary growth (in logarithmic terms) is estimated using the instrumental variable approach. The instruments used are lagged growth of the money supply, federal government expenditure relative to its normal level and an unemployment variable to represent cyclical features. Unanticipated monetary growth is then measured as the gap between actual monetary growth and anticipated monetary growth as predicted by the estimating equation.

The reduced form for the output equation is specified as

$$y_t = a_0 + a_1 dm_t + a_2 dm_{t-1} + a_3 dm_{t-2} + a_4 dm_{t-3}$$
$$+ a_5 \text{MIL}_t + a_6 t \tag{6.13}$$

where t = time trend to capture the secular movement of normal output
   y = logarithm of real GNP
   dm = unexpected monetary expansion
   MIL = military expenditure to capture the effects of conscription in force within the period

The estimated coefficients were well defined in statistical terms with a_1, a_2, a_3 and a_4 all being positive. Furthermore, equation (6.13) is superior to the case where total monetary expansion was substituted for unanticipated monetary expansion (dm).

The reduced-form price equation was derived from a standard money demand equation

$$m_t - p_t = b_0 + b_1 x_t - b_2 R_t + b_3 t \tag{6.14}$$

where x = measure of real expenditure
   all other variables as before

Carrying out various substitutions so that p is the dependent variable, and replacing x with the measure of GNP derived from the output equation minus government expenditure, produces

$$p_t = b_0 + m_t - b_1(a_1 dm_t + a_2 dm_{t-1} + a_3 dm_{t-2} + a_4 dm_{t-3})$$
$$- b_1 a_5 \text{MIL}_t + b_1 g + b_2 R_t - b_1(a_6 + b_3)t \qquad (6.15)$$

Again satisfactory estimates of the parameters are obtained with all coefficients being signed in accordance with *a priori* expectations and also being significantly different from 0. As before, substitution of total monetary expansion for unanticipated monetary expansion produces inferior results.

These equations are all estimated by single-equation methods, and some difficulty is obtained in reconciling the estimates with the implied cross-equation restrictions. Laidler and Bentley (1983) draw attention to the fact that it is perhaps surprising that the estimated coefficients imply that anticipated monetary expansion affects the price level with a one-to-one correspondence, whereas that monetary expansion which is known (even if originally unexpected) takes a number of years before its effects on prices are complete. Barro himself explains this phenomenon by referring to two elements. First, output responds to lagged changes in unanticipated monetary growth; second, money demand depends on lagged values of temporary income.

Using a similar methodology, Attfield, Demery and Duck (1981) examined the response of output to unanticipated monetary growth for the UK over the period 1963–78. Following Barro, anticipated monetary growth is also estimated by the instrumental variable approach using basically similar variables. The main differences are the substitution of the real value of the central government borrowing requirement for federal government expenditure, and the addition of the current account balance of payments surplus. The conclusion reached by Attfield *et al.* is that their results are generally (but not exclusively) in favour of the model that unanticipated monetary growth affects output whereas anticipated monetary growth fails to exert a significant effect on output.

Laidler and Bentley (1983) report the construction and estimation of a model of the US economy for periods 1954–78 and for 1946–76. This model starts from a basically different philosophy from that adopted by the previous two models discussed. It consists of six equations

$$y_t = a_1 (m^s - m^d)_{t-1} + a_2 t + a_3 g_t + a_4 R_{t-1} \tag{6.16}$$

$$m_t^d = b_0 + b_1 y^* + b_2 R^n + p \tag{6.17}$$

$$p = c y_{t-1} + E_{t-1} P_t \tag{6.18}$$

$$R_t^n = R_t + E_t P_t \tag{6.19}$$

$$R_t = d_0 + d_1 (m^s - m^d)_{t-1} + Z_t \tag{6.20}$$

$$E_t P_t = f p_t + (1 - f) E_{t-1} P_t \tag{6.21}$$

where y^* = real permanent income
R^n = nominal rate of interest
R = real rate of interest
Z = other influences on the real rate of interest
other variables as before

Equation (6.16) represents an output equation with the gap between the quantity of money supplied and that demanded as one important determinant of real output. Note that this term refers to *actual* money, not expected or anticipated money as in Barro's model. The demand for money function is equation (6.17) and equation (6.18) is an augmented Phillips curve. The strong Fisher hypothesis (discussed in 4.3 above) is adopted to explain the relationship between nominal and real rates of interest, with the real rate being determined by a loanable funds type of relationship specified in equation (6.20). Finally the expected rate of inflation is assumed to be determined by the adaptive expectations process (equation (6.21)). This model is of interest because it adopts what may be called a traditional monetarist approach. Money is important because it influences real output (y) on a temporary basis through the term $(m^s - m^d)$ in equation (6.16). Similarly the strong Fisher hypothesis is adopted. However, expectations are formed according to the past behaviour of prices, and there is no allowance made in this model for the distinction between anticipated and unanticipated monetary expansion.

For estimation purposes, the two equations containing non-observable dependent variables ((6.17) and (6.21)) were substituted out, and the model is estimated by full information maximum likelihood method. Laidler and Bentley contrast the explanatory power of the resulting model with Barro's model for the two basically similar output and price variables. As regards output, the evidence from the residuals suggests that the predictive power of the two models is essentially the same. For the price variable, the comparison depends on the period selected. If the period selected for comparison runs from 1946–76, there is little to choose between the two models; if the comparison starts from 1950 the performance of the Barro model is superior.

6.6 Conclusions

In this chapter, we have surveyed a range of models demonstrating how expectations series have been specified in macroeconomic models. The most widely-used methods are the adaptive expectations and error-correction models, rather than the rational expectations approach. In cases where rational expectations have been incorporated into a model, the instrumental-variables approach has been the most usual method adopted for the estimation of a rational expectations series. In some cases – as, for example, in the Treasury Model of the UK economy (HMT) and the Candide Model of the Canadian economy – a compromise between a backward-looking and a forward-looking approach has been adopted.

With regard to the relative performance of the various models and their expectations series there is only meagre evidence. One interesting study is by Vanderhoff (1983) who uses quarterly US data for the period 1950–80 to present an empirical investigation into simplified versions of three models – an income/expenditure model, a St Louis-type reduced-form model and a rational expectations model (using a Lucas-type supply equation). The starting point of the analysis is consideration of two overfitted reduced-form equations in respect of nominal income and prices

$$Y_t = a_0 + a_1 Y_t^p + a_2 M_t + a_3 G_t \tag{6.22}$$

$$P_t = b_0 + b_1 Y_t^p + b_3 M_t + b_3 G_t \tag{6.23}$$

where Y = nominal income
 Y^p = potential income
all other variables as before, but defined in terms of growth rates

Vanderhoff argues that the income/expenditure model predicts that potential income would affect both income and the price level since potential income affects aggregate supply and hence output. In contrast, the St Louis and rational expectations models postulate that potential output will affect only prices. In the former case nominal income is related to the growth rates of money supply and of government expenditure and is independent of real output; in the latter case output depends on its trend and also the variance of the rate of inflation. It is consequently possible to test the distinction between the income/expenditure model and the other two models by testing the hypothesis that

$$a_1 = b_1 = 0$$

The income/expenditure model implies rejection of this hypothesis whereas the other two models imply its acceptance. The test showed that the hypothesis that potential output does not affect the rate of inflation cannot be rejected by the data. A further discrimination between the St Louis and rational expectations model (with Lucas-type supply equation) involves checking whether the parameters in respect of the effect of money and government expenditure on income and the rate of inflation are constant. The rational expectations model implies parameter stationarity for the income equation but not for the price equation, whereas the St Louis approach implies stationary parameters in both equations. In fact, the data rejects parameter stationarity in the price equation providing support for the rational expectations model. Nevertheless as we have noted earlier, Fair (1979) both presents evidence against Sargent's new classical model and also advocates caution regarding the performance of macroeconomic models outside their estimation period. There is consequently little evidence which points conclusively to one method of expectations formulation being always superior to others.

7

Aggregate Expectations Formation

7.1   Methods of combining forecasts

In the previous chapters we outlined the various ways used in the economics literature to model agents' expectations or forecasts of the future value of variables. In fact, many other techniques – such as the Holt–Winters method, exponential smoothing, and Brown's linear exponential smoothing – which involve varying degrees of complexity are available (see Makridakis and Hibon, 1979, for further details). These have been widely used in the management science literature and are consequently candidates as expectation formation mechanisms. The typical approach in the economics literature is for a researcher to choose just one of the competing forecasting methods and use this to generate expectations. An alternative, which was originally suggested by Bates and Granger (1969), is to combine forecasts from different sources into a single composite forecast. In this chapter, we consider some of the issues raised by this suggestion.

Bates and Granger point out that when a number of different forecasts of the same event are available, each can (in general) be expected to embody useful information. This arises first because one forecast may be based on variables or information that the other forecasts ignore, and second different assumptions may be made about the form of the relationship between the variables. To illustrate the central idea of Bates and Granger, consider the two *unbiased* forecasts P_A and P_B of P, such that

$$P = P_A + \varepsilon_A \qquad (7.1)$$

$$P = P_B + \varepsilon_B \qquad (7.2)$$

where $\varepsilon_A, \varepsilon_B =$ the forecast errors which have respectively constant variances Var (A) and Var (B) and covariance Cov (AB)

The optimal combination of the two forecasts, which we call CP, is given by Bates and Granger as

$$CP = \lambda P_A + (1 - \lambda)P_B \qquad (7.3)$$

where $\lambda = \dfrac{\text{Var } (B) - \text{Cov } (AB)}{\text{Var } (A) + \text{Var } (B) - 2 \text{ Cov } (AB)}$

For the general case, see Newbold and Granger (1974). The combined forecast CP will have lower error variance than either of the individual forecasts. The reader who is familiar with the elements of portfolio theory (as in, for example, Copeland and Weston, 1979), will notice the similarity between the idea of combining different forecasts to reduce the variance of the predictor and that of combining different assets to reduce the variance of a portfolio. We also note that the optimal weight on a forecast can be negative; this would not necessarily imply that the forecast is absolutely bad, but rather that the forecasts are highly correlated. However, there are circumstances in which combining different forecasts may not be an improvement on using the individual forecasts. These can occur for a number of reasons. First, if one of the forecasts is based on the 'true' data-generating process it is therefore the rational expectation and consequently has the minimum variance of all forecasts (see chapter 2). Second, if a biased forecast is combined with an unbiased forecast then in general we would expect the combined forecast to exhibit larger errors than the unbiased forecast. Third, if non-optimal weights are chosen the combined forecast will have a poor performance. The second and third possibilities are of particular interest since *ex ante* a researcher may be uncertain about the properties of some of the forecasts available (such as, for example, different macroeconomic forecasts). Consequently the optimal weights of equation (7.3) will not be known at the commencement of combining forecasts. It follows that the value given to the weight may change as evidence is accumulated about the relative performance of the forecasters. The combined forecast for each time period t, CP_t can be written as

$$CP_t = \lambda_t P_{A,t} + (1 - \lambda_t) P_{B,t} \tag{7.4}$$

where $P_{A,t}$ = the forecast at time t for the forecaster A, and
          $P_{B,t}$ = the forecast at time t for forecaster B

Bates and Granger suggest that methods used to combine the different forecasts should have the following properties:

1. the average weight λ should approach the optimum value (defined by equation (7.3)) as the number of forecasts increases, provided that the forecast series is stationary
2. the weights should adapt quickly to new values if there is a lasting change in the performance of one of the forecasters
3. the weights should vary only a little about the optimum value
4. the methods should be moderately simple in order that they can be of use to businessmen

Property 3 is necessary since 1 is not sufficient on its own. If the optimum value of λ is 0.4, for instance, a poor combined forecast may be obtained if λ takes only two values, being 0 on 60 per cent of occasions and 1.0 on the remainder. In a world of relatively cheap computing facilities 4 has less force than at the time the Bates and Granger paper was written. Nevertheless, the methods they go on to propose are not readily improved upon. They suggest five ways of determining the weights which embody (to a lesser or greater degree) the properties outlined above. These are

1. $\lambda_t = \dfrac{E_{2t}}{E_{1t} + E_{2t}}$ (7.5)

where $E_{1t} = \sum\limits_{i=1}^{t-1} e_{Ai}^2$, $E_{2t} = \sum\limits_{t=1}^{t-1} e_{Bi}^2$

and $e_{A1}, e_{A2}, \ldots e_{At-1}$ and $e_{B1}, e_{B2}, \ldots e_{Bt-1}$ are the known past errors respectively from the forecasting methods A and B. The weights are thus determined from known past errors. If no past history of the forecasting agents exists then the initial weights must be chosen arbitrarily.

2. $\lambda_t = x\lambda_{t-1} + (1 - x)\dfrac{E_{2t}}{E_{1t} + E_{2t}}$ (7.6)

where x = a constant between 0 and 1

3. $\lambda_t = \dfrac{\delta_{2t}^2}{\delta_{1t}^2 + \delta_{2t}^2}$ (7.7)

where $\quad \delta_{1t}^2 = \sum\limits_{i=1}^{t-1} w^i e_{Ai}^2, \qquad \delta_{2t}^2 = \sum\limits_{i=1}^{t-1} w^i e_{Bi}^2, \qquad$ and

$w =$ a weight which for $w > 1$ gives more weight to recent errors than to distant ones

4. $\qquad \lambda_t = \dfrac{\delta_{2t}^2 - C_t}{\delta_{1t}^2 + \delta_{2t}^2 - 2C_t} \qquad\qquad\qquad (7.8)$

where the weighted covariance, C, is defined by

$$C_t = \sum_{i=1}^{t-1} w^i e_{Ai} e_{Bi}$$

5. $\qquad \lambda_t = x\lambda_{t-1} + \dfrac{(1-x)|e_{Bt-1}|}{|e_{At-1}| + |e_{Bt-1}|} \qquad\qquad (7.9)$

The properties of the combined forecasts will depend upon λ and the choice of the parameters x and w. Bates and Granger note that method 5 is the only one which fails to satisfy criteria 1. They consider forecasts of airline passenger data, and combine Box–Jenkins and Brown forecasts using the methods outlined above. Their result is that combined forecasts with changing weights are sometimes superior to forecasts using a constant weight determined from past individual forecast errors.

7.2 Empirical evidence

Since Bates and Granger's paper there have been a large number of investigations of ways of combining different forecasts. In general, these forecasts have been based on current and past values of the series being forecast (see, for example, Makridakis and Hibon, 1979; and Newbold and Granger, 1974). Some researchers report results which encourage the view that combinations of forecasts using variable weights give superior results to the individual forecast series. For instance Newbold and Granger find that Box–Jenkins forecasts are improved when combined with other forecasting methods (such as step-wise autoregression and Holt–Winters).

However, Jenkins (1974) and others have pointed out that there are reasons for being somewhat sceptical of these results. First, the different methods used to generate forecasts based on the current and past history of a variable are usually special cases of the Box–Jenkins approach. It follows that a linear combination of these methods with the Box–Jenkins method must correspond to a more general ARIMA process than that employed in the study. Consequently if the combined model gives a better forecast than the original ARIMA model, then the original model was inappropriate and should not have been selected. There thus appears to be no obvious rationale for combining different ARIMA forecasts.

Second, the weights in the combined forecast are often chosen empirically *ex post* and are derived from the series of outcomes. For a combined forecast to be preferred, what is necessary is that the weights obtained from, say, the first half of a data set should lead to a superior forecasting performance when applied to the second half.

The recent study by Figlewski and Urich (1983) meets both of the above criticisms. It also illustrates that if the different forecasts are highly correlated and there is some instability in the variance–covariance matrix between them then a simple average of forecasts is likely to outperform more complicated schemes in which allowance is made for additive biases, differences in individual accuracy, and the correlation between forecasts (see also Dickinson, 1973). Figlewski and Urich had access to time series of the forecasts of money supply of twenty of the fifty–sixty forecasters who respond to the Money Market Services Inc. weekly survey of US government security dealer firms. Previously, Urich and Wachtel (1981) found that the median forecast from this survey was clearly superior to the predictions from an ARIMA model based on all the sample data. Furthermore, the survey mean appears to be a good measure of the market's expectation of the change in the money supply as incorporated in short-term interest rates. Numerous studies find that monetary surprises (as measured by the difference between the actual change and the mean expectation from the survey), are significant determinants of the change in Treasury bill yields immediately after the money supply announcement. Moreover, the mean expectation itself had no explanatory power, which of course supports market efficiency.

Figlewski and Urich had data for 118 weeks. Beginning in week 59, the optimal forecast weights were estimated from all current and earlier data and a forecast for week 60 was determined. The actual value for week 60 was then added to the data set, the optimal forecast weights were re-estimated, and a prediction for week 61 was obtained. This process was repeated, period by period, to the end of the data. These 'optimal' forecasts were then compared with the simple average of the forecasts. The result was that the average did as well as the more complicated 'optimal' forecast. This contrasted with earlier work by Figlewski (1983) on the respondents to the Livingston inflation expectations survey, where the 'optimal' weighted combination outperformed the simple mean. Figlewski offers an explanation for this finding – the 'optimal' combination of different forecasts is likely to be better than the simple average when a heterogeneous group of forecasters is being considered. The Money Market Services respondents are unlike the Livingston respondents in that they are an exceptionally homogeneous group. Consequently, this limits the possibility of exploiting differences within the forecaster population. Moreover, if one agent's forecasts are correlated with another agent's errors the optimal weight for the former will be negative, and if the correlation is high, the weight could be large. Small changes over time in these correlations could produce large changes in the weights, and hence poor forecasts.

7.3 Combined forecasts as expectations

Despite the empirical results on combinations of forecasts, there appear to be two good *a priori* reasons for suggesting that taking account of different public forecasts may be a fruitful method of forecasting, and hence of modelling expectations.

First, we know that if there is a change in policy regime (say, fixed to floating exchange rates, or perhaps a change in government) an ARIMA forecasting method can produce biased and inefficient forecasts (see Appendix 6, 2.13 above). On the other hand, forecasts from econometric models or surveys may be expected, through judgemental adjustments or by formally modelling the structural change, to provide better forecasts at such times.

Second, we have suggested in chapter 2 that, from a consideration of the marginal costs and benefits of information, publicised forecasts are likely to condition the expectations of agents. The differing incentives for agents to obtain accurate forecasts imply that the resources used will also vary. While some agents may take simple averages of the various forecasts available to them, other agents may thus investigate more complicated weighting schemes.

In this regard the following evidence is of interest:

1. A simple average or consensus of public forecasts is now produced in the UK, and is frequently quoted in newspaper discussion. Thus,

for example, Jenkins (1983) wrote in the *Guardian*: 'The Chancellor's forecasts of 3 per cent growth next year with inflation down to 4.5 per cent are generally regarded as over-optimistic. However, the consensus of the forecasters (as worked out by the *Financial Times*) is for growth at about 2.5 per cent, with inflation creeping up to 5.75 per cent'.

2. Koten (1981) in the *Wall Street Journal* reports that major corporations in the USA use consensus forecasts because, according to D. Hilty, Chrysler's corporate economist, 'it helps keep you from going too far out on a limb in your forecasts'.

3. Surveys of the forecasting methods used by companies, as reported in Wheelwright and Makridakis (1980), suggest that econometric models are important sources of forecasts.

4. Some unions use consensus forecasts in formulating their measure of expected inflation. Kaufman and Woglom (1983) cite evidence that the United Autoworkers union in the USA, which negotiates over 2 000 contracts, subscribes to a collection of forecasts (blue chip indicators) and derives from them measures of expected inflation for use in the wage bargaining process.

5. Some provisional evidence that public forecasts may be given a weight by agents in financial markets is provided by Peel, Pope and Walters (1983). They examine the behaviour of the UK stock market on the day of the announcement of the National Institute's forecasts. In an efficient market, the stock market price should respond only to the new information or innovation in the forecast – that is, the difference between the forecast and the market expectation of it. There is obviously a difficulty in applying the concept of an innovation here. Using data for 1969–82 (fifty-one observations) Peel, Pope and Walters estimate

$$\Delta S = \alpha_0 + \alpha_1 F + \alpha_2 X + u \tag{7.10}$$

where ΔS = the percentage change in the *Financial Times* 500 index from close of trading on the day prior to release of the public forecast to close of trading on the day of forecast

F = the one year-ahead National Institute forecast of inflation

X = a vector of controls for the market expectation and includes the previous National Institute one year-ahead forecast of inflation and the rate of inflation in the year, quarter and six-month period up to the announcement of the National Institute Forecast

Equation (7.10) will be recognised as an unrestricted estimate of the equation

$$\Delta S = \alpha_0 + \alpha_1 (F - F^e) + \alpha_2 F^e + u \qquad (7.11)$$

where $\alpha_2 X =$ a proxy for $(\alpha_2 - \alpha_1)F^e$
$F^e =$ the market expectation of the forecast
$F - F^e =$ the innovation

Peel, Pope and Walters obtain estimates of α_1 which are significantly negative – that is, when the National Institute one year-ahead inflation forecast is higher than anticipated the stock market falls; this seems plausible.

Whilst the above empirical evidence is tentative and provisional, it does offer support, when taken with the other evidence, for the view that public forecasts are likely to condition agents' expectations in an economy.

7.4   Aggregation of forecasts in asset markets

Whatever the 'optimal' *ex post* weights which a statistician or economist would wish to give diverse forecasts, Figlewski (1978) has shown that the weights that an asset market will give may differ. He considers the aggregation within an asset market of heterogenous forecasts of a company's future prospects. He takes the case of a market made up of equal numbers of two types of traders. Members of these two groups may differ in price expectations, risk-aversion, predictive ability and wealth; Figlewski shows that the current market price (or expectation) will be a weighted average of the traders' forecasts where the weights are functions of the traders' wealth and degrees of risk-aversion. In this model, wealth redistribution amongst traders occurs as a consequence of traders' forecast errors. However, an important result is that better forecasters do not drive inferior forecasters out of the market. This is because an inferior forecaster tends to lose money only as long as his independent information is overvalued in the market price; since the market weights expectations by wealth, as a trader loses wealth it becomes more likely that he will make money on his next trade. Consequently, Figlewski's work suggests that because the asset market weights traders' information not by its quality but by 'dollar' votes neither in the short nor long run is the market likely to be efficient in the sense that the market forecast is the optimal statistical combination of traders' information. It follows that the market forecast is not the rational expectation (minimum variance) predictor.

The recent work of Bilson (1983) is perhaps explicable in terms of the Figlewski model. Bilson finds that, *ex post*, the forward rate as a predictor of the future spot rate can be supplemented by information on the current spot rate and from the Predex forecasting agency. This implies that non-optimal (dollar) weights are given by trading agents to the spot rate and Predex agency forecasts in determining their expectations.

7.5 Implications of weighted public forecasts

Consideration of the points raised above leads us to suggest that expectations variables which enter behavioural equations of economic models may best be thought of as aggregates of the individual expectations of agents within the economy. The individual expectations themselves will be conditioned by the information set available to each agent. The appropriate weight to give to each agent's expectation in the aggregate should be related to their importance (by some measure of size) in the economy. In general, these expectations (and hence the aggregate expectation) are unobservable. However, if public forecasts are important inputs into the economy then they will affect the aggregate expectation. The weights a statistician might give to the different inputs into an aggregate expectations measure may not be those which arise from agents' behavioural decisions. However, when the statistician's index is published it will presumably become an input into agents' individual expectations, leading to an aggregate expectation outcome which is closer to the statistician's measure. We believe that the publication of experts' forecasts with their resulting availability to less-informed agents at a low marginal cost is an important mechanism by which aggregate expectations formation can be improved. The information set utilised is much richer than that generally envisaged in, for instance, adaptive expectations. Consequently, we would argue that it is difficult to see how adaptive expectations (or some other mechanistic lag structure) can be justified as a method of modelling expectations in the behavioural equations of a model. Rather, we would argue that in macroeconomic analysis weighted averages of public forecasts are appropriate candidates for this role.

If this point is accepted then a number of implications follow. These have been considered in Holden, Peel and Thompson (1982) chapter 6, and we note some of the salient features here. First, it is unlikely that anticipated changes in monetary policy will in general be neutral to changes in real economic activity. Second, if public forecasts are produced from a model in which expectations in the behavioural equations are modelled adaptively (see chapter 6) then the model builder is implicitly assuming that agents give 0 weight to his public forecast. Conversely, if public forecasts are produced using rational expectations in the behavioural equations (as in the LM) it is as if the model builder assumes that agents give a unit weight to his forecasts. This latter possibility is unlikely to be true in practice, except in the case where a model is regarded by agents as being the true model of the economy (since in this case agents would ignore other public forecasts). If the model was indeed the 'true model' of the economy then the public forecast is the rational expectation. One suggestion is that public forecasters should produce a range of forecasts which are based on different assumptions as to the weight given to them in aggregate expectations. A consistent public forecast as in the LM, even though it may not be the 'true' aggregate expectation, would at least seem to avoid the worst problems associated with the Lucas critique of policy simulations (see 2.5 above).

7.6 Conclusions

Bates and Granger (1969) showed that if a number of different forecasts of the same event exist then an *ex ante* combination of the forecasts may be superior to any individual forecast. From a consideration of both statistical and economic factors we suggest that *a priori* the combination of different public forecasts of experts may be a useful method of modelling expectations in an economy. Clearly, empirical work that investigates expectations modelled in this way in behavioural equations would be of some interest.

The major implication of the view that aggregate expectations are conditioned by competing public forecasts is that modellers should produce public forecasts in which explicit attention is given to the weight that agents are assumed to give to the public forecast in their aggregate expectations. Some of the differences which this can make to the public forecasts is shown in Peel and Marwaha (1981), where the LM is solved when agents are assumed to form expectations as (various) weighted averages of the Liverpool and Cambridge public forecasts.

8

Conclusions

This book has been concerned with ways of representing agents' expectations within the behavioural equations of economic models. We now draw together some of the points which emerge from earlier chapters and outline what appear to be the implications for future analysis. Perhaps the single most important hypothesis to have been 'discovered' in macroeconomics in the past few decades is that of rational expectations. No longer is a researcher able to model expectations formation in some mechanistic manner without some explanation or defence of the chosen information structure available to agents. The great strength of the rational expectations hypothesis is that it forces us to give explicit attention to the information set which agents are assumed to face. As a modelling technique it can make explicit the variety of cross-equation restrictions in a model. We consequently anticipate that there will be an increased flow of research which investigates these implied restrictions in different behavioural models (see Hansen and Sargent, 1980; Sargent, 1981).

However, *a priori* consideration of the marginal costs and benefits of information facing agents in a typical advanced economy leads us to suppose that the rational expectations hypothesis cannot be taken as literally true. Currently, we do not have agreement between economists as to what is the correct model of the economy. A variety of radically different macroeconomic models exist, and are used to produce forecasts (see chapter 6). It is consequently difficult to see the mechanisms by which *ex ante* aggregate expectations can meet the *ex post* requirements of the rational expectations hypothesis. Further analytic weight to this is provided by the work by Figlewski on how asset markets aggregate diverse forecasts (see 7.4 above). This raised the question of how far aggregate expectations will depart from the 'as if' assumption of rational expectations, and whether any other plausible alternative method of modelling expectations exists.

In chapter 3 we considered the empirical results on direct surveys of agents' expectations. The majority of these surveys were found not to meet the *ex post* requirements of the rational expectations hypothesis. This could of course be because the survey method is inappropriate as a way of measuring aggregate expectations; in particular, there are only weak incentives for agents to give truthful answers to survey questions. However, the empirical evidence on the behaviour of observed or modelled aggregate expectations in asset markets (chapter 4) and other behavioural equations (chapter 5) is sufficiently mixed for us to suppose that there is a case for modelling expectations in a way that does not necessarily meet the *ex post* requirements of the rational expectation hypothesis. In chapter 7 we suggested that public forecasts have been neglected as a source of information to agents; it appears to us that a weighted combination of public forecasts may be a plausible method of obtaining economically rational expectations for use in behavioural equations. Future research is required to test the efficacy of this suggestion against the more usual alternatives. If the suggestion is correct, it implies that public forecasters have an important role in the evolution of an economy. Consequently, at least where public funds are involved, it is necessary that their techniques and assumptions be constantly monitored to ensure 'best practice'. In this regard the sentiments expressed by Friedman (1983) are of interest. He writes: 'In the absence of a well-chosen incentive structure, the experts may indulge in game playing which distorts their stated probability distributions. For instance, casual observation of economic forecasters suggests that experts who feel they have a reputation to protect will tend to produce a forecast near the consensus, and experts who feel they have a reputation to build will tend to overstate the probabilities of events they feel are understated in consensus'. In the management science literature, much research deals with the issue of how to elicit the 'true' opinions of experts, and make their stated probabilities correspond with their judgement. This literature is concerned with scoring rules which involve the computation of a score based on the forecasters' statement of probabilities and the event which actually occurs. Insofar as the expert understands how he is to be evaluated and attempts to maximise his expected score, a scoring rule addresses the elicitation problem (see Friedman, 1983; Matheson and Winkler, 1976; Winkler, 1969; and Savage, 1971). To the extent that public forecasts are prone to the problems raised by Friedman it would help agents who base their decisions on these public forecasts to have them purged of such influences. We consequently suggest that the issues raised by the 'scoring rules' literature might have some future applicability by those agencies responsible for the provision of public funds to public forecasters. One simple suggestion might be that public forecasters be encouraged to assign probabilities to different outcomes, rather than simply producing point estimates. This might help to make judgemental factors more explicit, and would provide more information for the *ex post* evaluation of different forecasts.

References

Agenor, P. R. (1982) 'Le traitement des anticipations en econometric', doctoral thesis (University de Paris I, Pantheon-Sorbonne).

Almon, S. (1965) 'The distributed lag between capital appropriations and expenditures', *Econometrica*, vol. 33, pp. 178–96.

Anderson, L. C. and K. M. Carlson (1970) 'A monetarist model for economic stabilisation', *Federal Reserve Bank of St Louis Review*, vol. 52, April, pp. 7–25.

Ando, A. and F. Modigliani (1963) 'The life cycle hypothesis of saving: aggregate implications and tests', *American Economic Review*, vol. 53, pp. 55–84.

Attfield, C. L. F., D. Demery and N. W. Duck (1981) 'A quarterly model of unanticipated monetary growth, output and the price level in the U.K. 1963–1978', *Journal of Monetary Economics*, vol. 8, pp. 331–50.

Baillie, R. T., R. E. Lippens and P. C. McMahon (1983) 'Testing rational expectations and efficiency in the foreign exchange market', *Econometrica*, vol. 51, pp. 553–64.

Ball, R. J., T. Burns and P. J. Warburton (1979) 'The London Business School model of the UK economy: an exercise in international monetarism', in Ormerod (1979).

Barro, R. J. (1974) 'Are government bonds net wealth?', *Journal of Political Economy*, vol. 82, pp. 1095–1117.

Barro, R. J. (1978) 'Unanticipated money, output and the price level in the United States', *Journal of Political Economy*, vol. 86, pp. 549–80.

Barro, R. J. (1980) 'A capital market in an equilibrium business cycle model', *Econometrica*, vol. 48, pp. 1393–1417.

Batchelor, R. A. (1982) 'Expectations, output and inflation', *European Economic Review*, vol. 17, pp. 1–25.

Batchelor, R. A. and T. D. Sheriff (1980) 'Unemployment and unanticipated inflation in post-war Britain', *Economica*, vol. 47, pp. 179–92.

177

Bates, J. M. and C. W. J. Granger (1969) 'The combination of forecasts', *Operations Research Quarterly*, vol. 20, pp. 451–68.

Baumol, W. J. (1970) *Economic Dynamics*, Macmillan, New York.

Begg, D. K. H. (1982) *The Rational Expectations Revolution in Macroeconomics*, Philip Allan Publishers Ltd, Oxford.

Bierwag, G. O. and M. A. Grove (1971) 'A model of the structure of prices of marketable US Treasury securities', *Journal of Money Credit and Banking*, vol. 3, pp. 605–29.

Bilson, J. F. O. (1979) Comment on paper by R. L. Levich, pp. 267–70, in Dornbusch and Frenkel (1979) *International Economic Policy*.

Bilson, J. F. O. (1980) 'The rational expectations approach to the consumption function: a multi-country study', *European Economic Review*, vol. 15, pp. 273–90.

Bilson, J. F. O. (1983) 'The evaluation and use of foreign exchange rate forecasting services', in R. J. Herring (ed.), *Managing Foreign Exchange Risk*, Cambridge University Press, Cambridge.

Black, J. (1975) 'A dynamic model of the quantity theory', in M. Parkin and A. R. Nobay (eds), *Current Economic Problems*, Cambridge University Press, Cambridge.

Blume, L. E., M. M. Bray and D. Easley (1982) 'Introduction to the stability of rational expectations equilibrium', *Journal of Economic Theory*, vol. 26, pp. 313–17.

Bomhoff, E. J. (1980) *Inflation, The Quantity Theory and Rational Expectations*, North-Holland, Amsterdam.

Box, G. E. P. and G. M. Jenkins (1970) *Time-Series Analysis: Forecasting and Control*, Holden-Day, San Francisco.

Brasse, V. (1983) 'The inaccuracy of exchange rate forecasting services in the United Kingdom', *City University Business School Economic Review*, vol. 1, no. 1, pp. 35–44.

Brown, B. W. and S. Maital (1981) 'What do economists know? An empirical study of experts' expectations', *Econometrica*, vol. 49, pp. 491–504.

Burmeister, E. (1980) 'On some conceptual issues in rational expectations modelling', *Journal of Money and Banking*, vol. 12, pp. 800–16.

Burmeister, E. and A. R. Dobell (1970) *Mathematical Theories of Economic Growth*, Macmillan, London.

Cagan, P. (1956) 'The monetary dynamics of hyperinflation', in M. Friedman (ed.), *Studies in the Quantity Theory of Money*, University of Chicago Press, Chicago.

Calvo, G. A. and D. A. Peel (1983) 'Growth and inflationary finance: variations on a Mundellian theme', *Journal of Political Economy*, vol. 91, pp. 880–7.

Carlson, J. A. (1977a) 'A study of price forecasts', *Annals of Economic and Social Measurement*, vol. 6, pp. 27–56.

Carlson, J. A. (1977b) 'Short-term interest rates as predictors of inflation: comment', *American Economic Review*, vol. 67, pp. 469–75.

Carlson, J. A. (1979) 'Expected inflation and interest rates', *Economic Inquiry*, vol. 17, pp. 597–608.

Carlson, J. A. and J. M. Parkin (1975) 'Inflation expectations', *Economica*, vol. 42, pp. 123–38.

Carlson, K. M. and S. E. Hein (1983) 'Four econometric models and monetary policy: the longer run view', *Federal Reserve Bank of St Louis Review*, vol. 65, January, pp. 13–24.

Chow, G. C. (1960) 'Tests of equality between sets of coefficients in two linear regressions', *Econometrica*, vol. 28, pp. 591–605.

Chow, G. C. (1975) *Analysis and Control of Dynamic Economic Systems*, John Wiley and Sons, New York.

Copeland, T. E. and J. F. Weston (1979) *Financial Theory and Corporate Planning*, Addison-Wesley, Reading.

Cornell, B. (1977) 'Spot rates, forward rates and exchange market efficiency', *Journal of Financial Economics*, vol. 5, pp. 55–65.

Coutts, K., R. Tarling and F. Wilkinson (1976) 'Wage bargaining and the inflation process', *Cambridge Economic Policy Review*, no. 2, pp. 20–7.

Cyert, R. M. and M. H. De Groot (1974) 'Rational expectations and Bayesian analysis', *Journal of Political Economy*, vol. 82, pp. 521–36.

Danes, M. (1975) 'The measurement and explanation of inflationary expectations in Australia', *Australian Economic Papers*, vol. 14, pp. 75–87.

Darby, M. R. (1975) 'The financial and tax effects of monetary policy on interest rates', *Economic Inquiry*, vol. 13, pp. 266–76.

Davidson, J. E. H. and D. F. Hendry (1981) 'Interpreting econometric evidence: the behaviour of consumers' expenditure in the UK', *European Economic Review*, vol. 16, pp. 177–92.

Davidson, J. E. H., D. F. Hendry, F. Srba and S. Yeo (1978) 'Econometric modeling of the aggregate time series relationship between consumers' expenditure and income in the United Kingdom', *Economic Journal*, vol. 88, pp. 661–92.

Deaton, A. (1977) 'Involuntary saving through unanticipated inflation', *American Economic Review*, vol. 67, pp. 899–910.

De Canio, S. (1979) 'Rational expectations and learning from experience', *Quarterly Journal of Economics*, vol. 93, pp. 47–57.

Defris, L. V. and R. A. Williams (1979a) 'The formation of consumer inflationary expectations in Australia', *Economic Record*, vol. 55, pp. 136–48.

Defris, L. V. and R. A. Williams (1979b) 'Quantitative versus qualitative measures of price expectations', *Economics Letters*, vol. 2, pp. 169–73.

De Leeuw, F. and M. J. McKelvey (1981) 'Price expectations of business firms', *Brookings Papers on Economic Activity*, no. 1, pp. 299–313.

De Menil, G. and S. S. Bhalla (1975) 'Direct measurement of popular price expectations', *American Economic Review*, vol. 65, pp. 169–80.

Demery, D. and N. W. Duck (1978) 'The behaviour of nominal interest rates in the United Kingdom, 1961–1973', *Economica*, vol. 45, pp. 23–37.

Dhrymes, P. J. (1971) *Distributed Lags: Problems of Estimation and Formulation*, Holden–Day, San Francisco.

Dickinson, J. P. (1973) 'Some statistical results in the combination of forecasts', *Operations Research Quarterly*, vol. 24, pp. 253–60.

Dooley, M. P. and J. R. Shafer (1976) 'Analysis of short-run exchange rate behaviour: March 1973 to September 1975', International Finance Discussion Papers, no. 76, Federal Reserve System, Washington DC.

Dornbusch, R. (1976) 'Expectations and exchange rate dynamics', *Journal of Political Economy*, vol. 84, pp. 1161–76.

Fair, R. C. (1979) 'An analysis of the accuracy of four macroeconometric models', *Journal of Political Economy*, vol. 87, pp. 701–18.

Fama, E. F. (1970) 'Efficient capital markets: a review of theory and empirical evidence', *Journal of Finance*, vol. 25, pp. 383–417.

Fama, E. F. (1975) 'Short-term interest rates as predictors of inflation', *American Economic Review*, vol. 65, pp. 269–82.

Fama, E. F. (1977) 'Interest rates and inflation: the message of the entrails', *American Economic Review*, vol. 67, pp. 487–96.

Feige, E. L. and D. K. Pearce (1976) 'Economically rational expectations: are innovations in the rate of inflation independent of innovations in measures of monetary and fiscal policy?', *Journal of Political Economy*, vol. 84, pp. 499–522.

Feldstein, M. (1976) 'Inflation, income taxes and the rate of interest: a theoretical analysis', *American Economic Review*, vol. 66, pp. 809–20.

Figlewski, S. (1978) 'Market "efficiency" in a market with heterogeneous information', *Journal of Political Economy*, vol. 86, pp. 581–97.

Figlewski, S. (1983) 'Optimal price forecasting using survey data', *Review of Economics and Statistics*, vol. lxv, pp. 13–21.

Figlewski, S. and T. Urich (1983) 'Optimal aggregation of money supply forecasts: accuracy, profitability and market efficiency', *Journal of Finance*, vol. xxviii, pp. 695–710.

Figlewski, S. and P. Wachtel (1981) 'The formation of inflationary expectations', *Review of Economics and Statistics*, vol. lxiii, pp. 1–10.

Firth, M. (1977) *Valuation of Shares and the Efficient Markets Theory*, Macmillan, New York.

Fischer, S. (1977) 'Long-term contracts, rational expectations and the optimal money supply rule', *Journal of Political Economy*, vol. 85, pp. 191–205.

Flemming, J. S. (1976) *Inflation*, Oxford University Press, Oxford.

Foster, J. and M. Gregory (1977) 'Inflation expectations: the use of qualitative survey data', *Applied Economics*, vol. 9, pp. 319–29.

Frenkel, J. A. (1975) 'Inflation and the formation of expectations', *Journal of Monetary Economics*, vol. 1, pp. 403–21.

Frenkel, J. A. (1977) 'The forward exchange rate, expectations and the demand for money: the German hyperinflation', *American Economic Review*, vol. 67, pp. 653–70.

Frenkel, J. A. (1981) 'Flexible exchange rates, prices and the role of "news": lessons from the 1970s', *Journal of Political Economy*, vol. 89, pp. 665–705.

Frenkel, J. A. and R. M. Levich (1975) 'Covered interest arbitrage: unexploited profits?', *Journal of Political Economy*, vol. 83, pp. 325–38.

Frenkel, J. A. and R. M. Levich (1977) 'Transaction costs and interest arbitrage: tranquil versus turbulent periods', *Journal of Political Economy*, vol. 85, pp. 1209–24.

Friedman, B. M. (1980) 'Survey evidence on the "rationality" of interest rate expectations', *Journal of Monetary Economics*, vol. 6, pp. 453–65.

Friedman, D. (1983) 'Effective scoring rules for probabilistic forecasts', *Management Science*, vol. 29, pp. 447–54.

Friedman, M. (1957) *A Theory of the Consumption Function*, Princeton University Press, Princeton.

Friedman, M. (1968) 'The role of monetary policy', *American Economic Review*, vol. 58, pp. 1–17.

Friedman, M. (1969) *The Optimum Quantity of Money*, Macmillan, London.

Gibson, W. E. (1972) 'Interest rates and inflationary expectations: new evidence', *American Economic Review*, vol. 62, pp. 854–65.

Giddy, I. H. and G. Dufey (1975) 'The random behaviour of flexible exchange rates', *Journal of International Business Studies*, vol. 6, pp. 1–32.

Gordon, R. J. (1976) 'Recent developments in the theory of inflation and unemployment', *Journal of Monetary Economics*, vol. 2, pp. 185–219.

Gramlich, E. M. (1983) 'Models of inflation expectations formation', *Journal of Money Credit and Banking*, vol. 15, pp. 155–73.

Granger, C. W. J. (1969) 'Investigating causal relations by econometric models and cross spectral methods', *Econometrica*, vol. 37, pp. 424–38.

Granger, C. W. J. and P. Newbold (1977) *Forecasting Economic Time Series*, Academic Press, New York.

Granger, C. W. J. and H. J. B. Rees (1968) 'Spectral analysis of the term structure of interest rates', *Review of Economic Studies*, vol. 35, pp. 67–76.

Grant, J. A. G. (1964) 'Meiselman on the structure of interest rates: a British test', *Economica*, vol. 31, pp. 51–71.

Graybill, F. A. (1961) *An Introduction to Linear Stochastic Models*, vol. 1, McGraw-Hill, New York.

Grice, J. and A. Bennett (1981) 'The demand for sterling M3 and aggregates in the United Kingdom', Government Economic Service working paper, no. 45, HMSO, London.

Grossman, S. J. (1981) 'The "rationality" of money supply expectations and the short-run response of interest rates to monetary surprises', *Journal of Money, Credit and Banking*, vol. 13, pp. 409–24.

Grossman, S. J. and J. E. Stiglitz (1976) 'Information and competitive price systems', *American Economic Review*, vol. 66, pp. 246–53.

Grubel, H. G. (1968) *Forward Exchange, Speculation and the International Flow of Capital*, Stanford University Press, Stanford.

Hall, R. E. (1978) 'Stochastic implications of the life cycle–permanent income hypothesis: theory and evidence', *Journal of Political Economy*, vol. 86, pp. 971–87.

Hall, V. B. and M. L. King (1976) 'Inflationary expectations in New Zealand: a preliminary study', *New Zealand Economic Papers*, vol. 10, pp. 118–51.

Hansen, L. P. and R. J. Hodrick (1980) 'Forward exchange rates as optimal predictors of future spot rates', *Journal of Political Economy*, vol. 88, pp. 829–53.

Hansen, L. P. and T. J. Sargent (1980) 'Formulating and estimating dynamic linear rational expectations models', *Journal of Economic Dynamics and Control*, vol. 2, pp. 7–46.

Harvey, A. C. (1981) *Time Series Models*, Philip Allan, Oxford.

Hellwig, M. F. (1982) 'Rational expectations equilibrium with conditioning in past prices', *Journal of Economic Theory*, vol. 26, pp. 279–312.

Hendry, D. F. (1979) 'Predictive failure and econometric modelling in macroeconomics: the transactions demand for money', in Ormerod (1979).

Hess, P. J. and J. L. Bicksler (1975) 'Capital asset prices versus time series models as predictors of inflation: the expected real rate of interest and market efficiency', *Journal of Financial Economics*, vol. 2, pp. 341–60.

Hickman, W. B. (1943) *The Interest Rate Structure and War Financing*, National Bureau of Economic Research, New York.

Hicks, J. R. (1939) *Value and Capital*, Clarendon Press, Oxford.

HMT (1982) *Macroeconomic Model Technical Manual*, HM Treasury, London.

Holden, K. and D. A. Peel (1977) 'An empirical investigation of inflationary expectations', *Oxford Bulletin of Economics and Statistics*, vol. 39, pp. 291–9.

Holden, K. and D. A. Peel (1983) 'Forecasts and expectations: some evidence for the UK', *Journal of Forecasting*, vol. 2, pp. 51–8.

Holden, K. and D. A. Peel (1984) 'An evaluation of quarterly National Institute Forecasts', mimeo, University of Liverpool, Liverpool.

Holden, K., D. A. Peel and J. L. Thompson (1982) *Modelling the UK Economy: An Introduction*, Martin Robertson, Oxford.

Horne, J. (1981) 'Rational expectations and the Defris–Williams inflationary expectations series', *Economic Record*, vol. 57, pp. 261–68.

Hudson, J. (1978) 'Expectations of wage inflation and their formation', *Applied Economics*, vol. 10, pp. 195–201.

Jenkins, G. M. (1974) 'Discussion of Newbold and Granger', *Journal of the Royal Statistical Society*, series A, vol. 137, pp. 148–50.

Jenkins, P. (1983) *Guardian*, 21 December 1983.

Johnston, J. (1972) *Econometric Methods*, 2nd edn, McGraw-Hill, New York.

Joines, D. (1977) 'Short-term interest rates as predictors of inflation: comment', *American Economic Review*, vol. 67, pp. 476–77.

Judge, G. C., W. E. Griffiths, R. Carter-Hill and T. C. Lee (1980) *The Theory and Practice of Econometrics*, Wiley, New York.

Kalman, R. E. (1960) 'A new approach to linear filtering and prediction problems', trans ASME, *Journal of Basic Engineering*, series D, vol. 82, pp. 35–45.

Kane, E. J. and B. G. Malkiel (1976) 'Autoregressive and non-autoregressive elements in cross-section forecasts of inflation', *Econometrica*, vol. 44, pp. 1–16.

Kaufman, R. T. and G. Woglom (1983) 'Estimating models with rational expectations', *Journal of Money Credit and Banking*, vol. 3, pp. 275–85.

Kessel, R. A. (1963) *The Cyclical Behaviour of Interest Rates*, National Bureau of Economic Research, New York.

Keynes, J. M. (1923) *A Tract on Monetary Reform (Collected Writings of J. M. Keynes)*, vol. iv, Macmillan, New York (1977).

Khan, M. S. (1983) 'Estimating models of expectations', *Economics Letters*, vol. 12, pp. 175–80.

Knöbl, A. (1974) 'Price expectations and actual price behaviour in Germany', *International Monetary Fund Staff Papers*, vol. 21, pp. 83–100.

Koten, J. (1981) 'They say no two economists ever agree...', *Wall Street Journal*.

Laffer, A. B. and R. Zecher (1975) 'Some evidence on the formation, efficiency and accuracy of anticipations of nominal yields', *Journal of Monetary Economics*, vol. 1, pp. 329–42.

Laidler, D. and B. Bentley (1983) 'A small macro-model of the post-war United States', *The Manchester School*, vol. 51, pp. 317–40.

Laumer, H. and M. Ziegler (1982) (eds) *International Research on Business Cycle Surveys*, Gower Publishing Co. Ltd, Aldershot.

Leonard, J. S. (1982) 'Wage expectations in the labor market: survey evidence on rationality', *Review of Economics and Statistics*, vol. lxiv, pp. 157–61.

Levich, R. M. (1979) 'On the efficiency of markets for foreign exchange', in Dornbusch and Frenkel (1979) *International Economic Policy*.

Ljung, G. M. and G. E. P. Box (1978) 'On a measure of lack of fit in time series models', *Biometrika*, vol. 66, pp. 67–72.

Logue, D. E. and R. J. Sweeney (1977) 'White noise in imperfect markets: the case of the franc/dollar exchange rate', *Journal of Finance*, vol. 32, pp. 761–8.

Lucas, R. E. (1972) 'Econometric testing of the natural rate hypothesis', in O. Eckstein (ed.) *Econometrics of Price Determination Conference*, Board of Governors, Federal Reserve System, Washington DC.

Lucas, R. E. (1973) 'Some international evidence on output-inflation trade-offs', *American Economic Review*, vol. 68, pp. 326–34.

Lucas, R. E. (1976) 'Econometric Policy Evaluation: a critique' in *The Phillips Curve and Labour Markets* (K. Brunner and A. H. Meltzer (eds)), vol. 1, pp. 19–46, Carnegie–Rochester Conferences on Public Policy, supplement to *Journal of Monetary Economics*, North-Holland, Amsterdam.

Lucas, R. E. and T. J. Sargent (eds) (1981) *Rational Expectations and Econometric Practice*, University of Minnesota Press, Minnesota.

McCallum, B. T. (1975) 'Rational expectations and the natural rate hypothesis: some evidence for the United Kingdom', *The Manchester School*, vol. 43, pp. 56–67.

McCallum, B. T. (1976a) 'Rational expectations and the natural rate hypothesis', *Econometrica*, vol. 44, pp. 43–52.

McCallum, B. T. (1976b) 'Rational expectations and the estimation of econometric models', *International Economic Review*, vol. 17, pp. 484–90.

McCallum, B. T. (1983a) 'The liquidity trap and the Pigou effect: a dynamic analysis with rational expectations', *Economica*, vol. 50, pp. 395–406.

McCallum, B. T. (1983b) 'On non-uniqueness in rational expectations models: an attempt at perspective', *Journal of Monetary Economics*, vol. 11, pp. 139–68.

McCallum, B. T. and J. K. Whittaker (1979) 'The effectiveness of fiscal feedback rules and automatic stabilizers under rational expectations', *Journal of Monetary Economics*, vol. 5, pp. 171–86.

McDonald, J. and J. Darroch (1983) 'Consistent estimation of equations with composite moving average disturbance terms', *Journal of Econometrics*, vol. 23, pp. 253–67.

McNees, S. K. (1978) 'The rationality of economics forecasts', *American Economic Review*, vol. 68, pp. 301–5.

Makridakis, S. and M. Hibon (1979) 'Accuracy of forecasting: an empirical investigation', *Journal of the Royal Statistical Society*, series A, vol. 142, pp. 97–145.

Matheson, J. E. and R. L. Winkler (1976) 'Scoring rules for continuous probability distributions', *Management Science*, vol. 22, pp. 1087–96.

Matthews, K. G. P. and S. Marwaha (1981) 'RATEXP mk 2', mimeo, University of Liverpool, Liverpool.

Meiselman, D. (1962) *The Term Structure of Interest Rates*, Prentice-Hall, Englewood Cliffs.

Minford, A. P. L. and M. Brech (1981) 'The wage equation and rational expectations', in D. Currie, R. Nobay and D. Peel (eds), *Macroeconomic Analysis*, Croom-Helm, London.

Minford, A. P. L., S. Marwaha, K. G. P. Matthews and A. Sprague (1984) 'The Liverpool macroeconomic model of the U.K.', *Economic Modelling*, vol. 1, no. 1, pp. 24–62.

Minford, A. P. L., K. G. P. Matthews and S. Marwaha (1979) 'Terminal conditions as a means of ensuring unique solutions for rational expectations models with forward expectations', *Economics Letters*, vol. 4, pp. 117–20.

Minford, A. P. L. and D. A. Peel (1983) *Rational Expectations and the New Macroeconomics*, Martin Robertson, Oxford.

Mishkin, F. S. (1980) 'Is the preferred-habitat model inconsistent with market efficiency?', *Journal of Political Economy*, vol. 88, pp. 406–11.

Mishkin, F. S. (1981) 'The real rate of interest: an empirical investigation', National Bureau of Economic Research working paper, no. 622.

Modigliani, F. and R. J. Shiller (1973) 'Inflation, rational expectations and the term structure of interest rates', *Economica*, vol. 40, pp. 12–43.

Modigliani, F. and R. C. Sutch (1966) 'Innovations in interest rate policy', *American Economic Review*, vol. 56, pp. 178–97.

Muellbauer, J. (1983) 'Surprises in the consumption function', in *Conference Papers: A Supplement to the Economic Journal*, pp. 34–50.

Mullineaux, D. J. (1978) 'On testing for rationality: another look at the Livingston price expectations data', *Journal of Political Economy*, vol. 86, pp. 329–36.

Muth, J. F. (1961) 'Rational expectations and the theory of price movements', *Econometrica*, vol. 29, pp. 315–35.

Nelson, C. R. and G. W. Schwert (1977) 'Short-term interest rates as predictors of inflation: on testing the hypothesis that the real rate of interest is constant', *American Economic Review*, vol. 67, pp. 478–86.

Nerlove, M. (1983) 'Expectations, plans and realisation in theory and practice', *Econometrica*, vol. 51, pp. 1251–79.

Newbold, P. and C. W. J. Granger (1974) 'Experience with forecasting univariate time series and the combination of forecasts', *Journal of the*

Royal Statistical Society, series A, vol. 137, pp. 131–46.

Officer, L. H. and T. D. Willett (1970) 'The covered-arbitrage schedule: a critical survey of recent developments', *Journal of Money, Credit and Banking*, vol. 2, pp. 247–57.

Ormerod, P. (ed.) (1979) *Economic Modelling*, Heineman Education Books, London.

Ormerod, P. (1982) 'Rational and non-rational explanations of inflation in wage equations for the United Kingdom', *Economica*, vol. 49, pp. 375–87.

Papadia, F. (1983) 'Rationality of inflationary expectations in European Economic Communities Countries', *Empirical Economics*, vol. 8, pp. 187–202.

Parkin, M., M. Sumner and R. Ward (1976) 'The effects of excess demand, generalised expectations and wage–price controls on wage inflation in the U.K. 1956–1971', *Journal of Monetary Economics*, vol. 2, supplement, pp. 193–21.

Pearce, D. K. (1979) 'Comparing survey and rational measures of expected inflation', *Journal of Money Credit and Banking*, vol. 11, pp. 447–56.

Peel, D. A. (1977) 'On the properties of alternative monetary rules in an extension of Black's model', *European Economic Review*, vol. 9, pp. 195–208.

Peel, D. A. and S. Marwaha (1981) 'Solution of the Liverpool model embodying Cambridge inflation forecasts', *Quarterly Economic Bulletin*, Liverpool Research Group in Microeconomics, University of Liverpool, Liverpool.

Peel, D. A. and J. S. Metcalfe (1979) 'Divergent expectations and the dynamic stability of some simple macroeconomic models', *Economic Journal*, vol. 89, pp. 789–98.

Peel, D. A., P. F. Pope and K. Walters (1983) 'On macroeconomic model building, public forecasts and expectation formation', mimeo, University of Liverpool, Liverpool.

Pesando, J. E. (1975) 'A note on the rationality of the Livingston price expectations', *Journal of Political Economy*, vol. 83, pp. 849–58.

Pesando, J. E. (1978) 'On the efficiency of the bond market: some Canadian evidence', *Journal of Political Economy*, vol. 86, pp. 1057–76.

Pesaran, M. H. (1984) 'Expectations formation and macroeconomic modelling', in P. Malgrange and P. A. Muet (eds), *Contemporary Macroeconomic Modelling*, Basil Blackwell, Oxford.

Phelps, E. S. and J. B. Taylor (1977) 'The stabilizing powers of monetary policy under rational expectations', *Journal of Political Economy*, vol. 85, pp. 163–90.

Pindyck, R. S. and D. L. Rubinfeld (1981) *Econometric Models and Economic Forecasts*, 2nd edn, McGraw-Hill, New York.

Poole, W. (1967) 'Speculative prices on random walks: an analysis of ten time series of flexible exchange rates', *Southern Economic Journal*, vol. 33, pp. 468–78.

Prell, M. J. (1973) 'How well do the experts forecast interest rates', *Reserve Bank of Kansas City Monthly Review*, Sept.–Oct., pp. 3–13.

Rao, P. S. and B. K. Lodh (1983) 'Anatomy of Canadian inflation: an analysis with Candide model 2.0', *Empirical Economics*, vol. 8, pp. 13–45.

Roley, V. V. (1983) 'The response of short-term interest rates to weekly money announcements', *Journal of Money, Credit and Banking*, vol. xv, pp. 344–54.

Roll, E. (1972) 'Interest rates on monetary assets and commodity price index changes', *Journal of Finance*, vol. 27, pp. 251–77.

Saidi, N. H. (1980) 'Fluctuating exchange rates and the international transmission of economic disturbances', *Journal of Money, Credit and Banking*, vol. 12, pp. 575–91.

Santomero, A. M. and J. J. Seater (1978) 'The inflation–unemployment trade-off: a critique of the literature', *Journal of Economic Literature*, vol. xvi, pp. 499–544.

Sargent, T. J. (1976) 'A classical macroeconomic model for the United States', *Journal of Political Economy*, vol. 84, pp. 207–37.

Sargent, T. J. (1979a) *Macroeconomic Theory*, Academic Press, New York.

Sargent, T. J. (1979b) 'A note on the maximum likelihood estimation of the rational expectations model of the term structure', *Journal of Monetary Economics*, vol. 5, pp. 133–43.

Sargent, T. J. (1981) 'Interpreting economics time series', *Journal of Political Economy*, vol. 89, pp. 213–48.

Sargent, T. J. and N. Wallace (1975) 'Rational expectations, the optimal monetary instrument and the optimal money supply rule', *Journal of Political Economy*, vol. 83, pp. 241–54.

Saunders, P. (1980) 'Price and cost expectations in Australian manufacturing firms', *Australian Economic Papers*, vol. 19, pp. 46–67.

Saunders, P. (1981) 'The formation of producers' price expectations in Australia', *The Economic Record*, vol. 57, pp. 368–78.

Saunders, P. (1983) 'A disaggregate study of the rationality of Australian producers' price expectations', *The Manchester School*, vol. 51, pp. 380–98.

Savage, L. J. (1971) 'Elicitation of personal probabilities and expectations', *Journal of the American Statistical Association*, vol. 66, pp. 783–801.

Sheffrin, S. M. (1983) *Rational Expectations*, Cambridge University Press, Cambridge.

Shiller, R. J. (1978) 'Rational expectations and the dynamic structure of macroeconomic models: a critical review', *Journal of Monetary Economics*, vol. 4, pp. 1–44.

Shiller, R. J. (1979) 'The volatility of long-term interest rates and expectations models of the term structure', *Journal of Political Economy*, vol. 87, pp. 1190–219.

Smith, G. W. (1978) 'Producers' price and cost expectations', in M. Parkin and M. T. Sumner (eds), *Inflation in the United Kingdom*, Manchester University Press, Manchester.

Smith, R. G. and C. A. E. Goodhart (1983) 'The relationship between exchange rate movements and monetary surprises: results for the United Kingdom and the United States compared and contrasted', mimeo, Bank of England, October 1983.

Spencer, P. (1981) 'A model of the demand for British Government stocks by non-bank residents 1967–1977', *Economic Journal*, vol. 91, pp. 938–60.

Strigel, W. H. (ed.) (1980) *Business Cycle Analysis*, Gower Publishing Co. Ltd, Farnborough.

Summers, L. H. (1983) 'The non-adjustment of nominal interest rates: a study of the Fisher effect', in J. Tobin (ed.), *Macroeconomics, Prices and Quantities*, Basil Blackwell, Oxford.

Symons, J. S. V. (1983) 'Money and the real rate of interest', *The Manchester School*, vol. 51, pp. 250–65.

Taylor, J. B. (1975) 'Monetary policy during a transition to rational expectations', *Journal of Political Economy*, vol. 83, pp. 1009–22.

Taylor, J. B. (1977) 'Conditions for unique solutions in stochastic macroeconomic models with rational expectations', *Econometrica*, vol. 45, pp. 1377–86.

Theil, H. (1965) *Economic Forecasts and Policy*, 2nd edn, North-Holland, Amsterdam.

Turnovsky, S. J. (1969) 'A Bayesian approach to the theory of expectations', *Journal of Economic Theory*, vol. 1, pp. 220–7.

Turnovsky, S. J. (1972) 'The expectations hypothesis and the aggregate wage equation: some empirical evidence for Canada', *Economica*, vol. 39, pp. 1–17.

Turnovsky, S. J. (1980) 'The choice of monetary instruments under alternative forms of price expectations', *The Manchester School*, vol. 48, pp. 39–63.

Urich, T. and P. Wachtel (1981) 'Market response to the weekly money supply announcements in the 1970s', *Journal of Finance*, vol. 36, pp. 1063–72.

Vanderhoff, J. (1983) 'Support for rational expectations models with US data', *Journal of Monetary Economics*, vol. 12, pp. 297–308.

Vanderkamp, J. (1972) 'Wage adjustment, productivity and price change expectations', *Review of Economic Studies*, vol. 39, pp. 61–72.

Visco, I. (1979) 'The measurement and analysis of inflation expectations: the case of Italy', *Bank of Italy Economic Papers*, pp. 149–242.

Wachtel, P. (1977) 'Survey methods of expected inflation and their potential usefulness', pp. 361–95, in J. Popkin (ed.), *Analysis of Inflation 1965–1974*, Ballinger, Cambridge, Massachusetts.

Walters, A. A. (1971) 'Consistent expectations distributed lags and the quantity theory', *Economic Journal*, vol. 81, pp. 273–81.

Ward, A. V. and J. F. Pickering (1981) 'Preliminary testing of the explanatory power of the EEC consumer attitudes survey in the UK', *Applied Economics*, vol. 13, pp. 19–34.

Weiss, L. (1980) 'The role for active monetary policy in a rational expectations model', *Journal of Political Economy*, vol. 88, pp. 221–33.

Wheelwright, S. C. and S. Makridakis (1980) *Forecasting Methods for Management*, 3rd edn, Wiley, New York.

Whittle, P. (1963) *Prediction and Regulation by Linear Least Squares Methods*, English Universities Press Ltd, London.

Wickens, M. R. and H. Molana (1984) 'Stochastic life cycle theory with varying interest rates and prices', in Conference Papers, supplement to *Economic Journal*, vol. 94, pp. 133–47.

Winkler, R. L. (1969) 'Scoring rules and the evaluation of probability assessors', *Journal of the American Statistical Association*, vol. 64, pp. 1073–8.

Wold, H. (1954) *A Study in the Analysis of Stationary Time Series*, 2nd edn, Almquist and Wiksell, Stockholm.

Wold, H. (1963) 'Forecasting by the chain principle', in M. Rosenblatt (ed.), *Proceedings of the Symposium on Time Series Analysis*, Brown University 11–14 June 1962, Wiley, New York.

Zarnowitz, V. (1969) 'The new ASA–NBER survey of forecasting by economic statisticians', *American Statistician*, vol. 23, pp. 12–16.

Zarnowitz, V. (1984) 'The accuracy of individual and group forecasts from business outlook surveys', *Journal of Forecasting*, vol. 3, pp. 11–26.

Zellner, A. (1962) 'An efficient method of estimating seemingly unrelated regressions and tests for aggregation bias', *Journal of the American Statistical Association*, vol. 57, pp. 348–68.

Author index

189

Subject Index